LUCY WEST ✤ ANTONIA CAMERON

Agents of Change

How Content Coaching
Transforms Teaching & Learning

HEINEMANN
Portsmouth, NH

Heinemann
361 Hanover Street
Portsmouth, NH 03801–3912
www.heinemann.com

Offices and agents throughout the world

The online video referenced throughout this book was developed solely for educational purposes and is not an item for independent sale. The creators of the online video will not profit from its distribution.

The authors and publisher wish to thank those who have generously given permission to reprint borrowed material:

Excerpts from "Principles of Learning for Effort-Based Education" by Lauren Resnick and Megan Hall (2000). www.instruction.aurorak12.org/ar/files/2011/06/Resnick-Principles-of-Learning-for-Effort.pdf. Reprinted by permission of Aurora Public Schools, Aurora, CO.

"Framework for Lesson Design and Analysis" from *Content-Focused Coaching: Transforming Mathematics Lessons* by Lucy West and Fritz C. Staub. Copyright © 2003 by Lucy West and Fritz C. Staub. Published by Heinemann, Portsmouth, NH. All rights reserved.

Credit lines continue on page vi.

Library of Congress Cataloging-in-Publication Data
West, Lucy.
  Agents of change : how content coaching transforms teaching and learning / Lucy West and Antonia Cameron.
      pages cm
  Includes bibliographical references.
  ISBN-13: 978-0-325-01383-1
  1. Mentoring in education.   2. Teachers—In-service training.   I. Title.
LB1731.4.W43 2013
371.102—dc23   2013016080

Editor: Katherine Bryant
Production: Victoria Merecki
Typesetter: Publishers' Design and Production Services, Inc.
Cover and interior designs: Monica Ann Crigler
Cover photos: Marble © Jules Frazier | Photodisc | Getty Images | HIP; Butterfly (front) © Photodisc | Getty Images | HIP; Butterflies (back) © Getty Images | HIP
Video production: Melissa Cooperman
Manufacturing: Steve Bernier

Printed in the United States of America on acid-free paper

22 21 20 19 18 VP 5 6 7 8 9

Contents

Foreword

In the past two decades, coaching has become one of the most talked-about methods for improving student learning. School leaders around the world have recognized that traditional forms of professional development have insufficient impact on teaching and learning, that something more powerful is needed.

Coaching has the potential to be this something more. It moves professional development away from talking about practice (declarative knowledge) to improving practice (procedural knowledge). Every time a coach helps a teacher implement a new teaching or learning strategy, that coach is also helping every student that teacher will teach. One step forward for a teacher is one step forward for hundreds of children. In a very real sense, coaches help schools create better futures for our children.

Educators and researchers take different paths to the same destination. My colleagues and I at the Kansas Coaching Project, for example, have dedicated fifteen years to developing, refining, and validating instructional coaching. Our research suggests that instructional coaches can have a significant, positive impact on teaching and learning if they (a) begin by getting a clear picture of what is happening in a teacher's classroom (often by video recording lessons), (b) collaborate with teachers to set meaningful goals, (c) identify teaching strategies to meet these goals, (d) provide support that helps teachers implement these practices effectively (clear explanations, a chance to see the practice in action, collaborative modifications), and (e) collaborate with teachers until the goal is achieved (which sometimes requires trying more than one new teaching practice).

Other approaches to coaching emphasize other methods. Lucy West and Toni Cameron's *Agents of Change* describes content coaching, an approach that emphasizes the importance of planning and co-teaching. The book's detailed description of how to be a content coach will benefit anyone interested in coaching.

First, West and Cameron explain that coaching should not be top-down. Rather, coaches should approach a teacher as a dialogic partner in "robust, academic discourse" about the environment of and activities in the teacher's classroom. Perhaps most important, West and Cameron describe what coaches should *not* do—the things that keep them from making a difference in teachers' and students' lives.

The authors also expand the focus of coaching beyond a one-to-one relationship. Coaches are agents of change, catalysts for cultural transformation in schools and districts, and should therefore attend to both individual teachers and their students and the broader culture and structure of the school. In conjunction with principals, coaches should create "an environment of questioning" in which teacher conversation focuses on improving practice to improve learning.

West and Cameron also make several suggestions for setting up a successful coaching program. They explain the importance of developing a shared vision of what coaches do and what they are intended to accomplish, distinguishing the coach's and the principal's role, establishing lines of supervision, and enlisting the support of district administrators. They also point out that coaches need to receive ongoing, targeted, professional learning to improve the art and skill of their own practice.

Above all, West and Cameron explain that coaching should not be implemented carelessly, without carefully thinking about and planning what coaches do, how they are developed, how they are supported, and how they challenge a district to move forward. They stress that coaching is not a program to be implemented the way a reading program might be: rather, it is a way to transform schools into organizations focused on student learning. This book can help anyone interested in achieving that goal.

Jim Knight
Instructional Coaching Group
www.instructionalcoaching.com

Acknowledgments

We thank and acknowledge the educators who have influenced the evolution of our thinking and our work over these many years. We have been fortunate to have many inspirational mentors along the way.

It is interesting that we both came to mathematics education in unexpected ways. For Lucy, the journey began at Bank Street College of Education under the tutelage of Hal Melnick, whose support and encouragement helped her re-experience mathematics in ways that sparked enthusiasm and passion for ensuring her students learned the subject better and more joyfully than she had as a child.

For Toni it began when she was selected in 1995 to be part of an NSF-funded project at Math in the City at City College of the City University of New York. It was here that Toni, under the guidance of four remarkable educators (Catherine Twomey Fosnot, Sherrin Hersch, Maarten Dolk, and Willem Uittenbogaard), experienced for the first time in her life the beauty and wonder of mathematics. This experience transformed Toni's thinking and changed the course of her professional life. In 2000, Toni became a member of the Math in the City staff, and later, co-directed the project with Cathy Fosnot. It was as a member of this incredible team of educators that Toni learned about the art of lesson design and the power of co-teaching. Her Dutch colleagues were instrumental in helping her understand the role of context, mathematical models, and how to think about designing units of study based on learning trajectories. This knowledge was essential to writing the fifteen Facilitator Guides that accompany the *Young Mathematicians at Work* video library, which Toni co-wrote with Sherrin and Cathy.

As part of their experiences at Bank Street and Math in the City, both Toni and Lucy were given the opportunity to teach mathematics to teachers. Lucy did this for several years with her co-teacher Linda Metnetsky and it was this experience that planted the seed that blossomed into her vision for coaching as a powerful process for educators. Marilyn Burns later welcomed Lucy into her national consultant team where she spent several years teaching the Math Solutions courses and learning from Marilyn and so many of the amazing educators she had the privilege to work with. Lucy learned about persistence, collaboration, continual refinement of lessons, and even about designing professional development, which later informed her work as Director of Mathematics for Community School District 2 and her business, Metamorphosis Teaching Learning Communities.

As part of Math in the City, Toni was also given the freedom to design inservice professional development and experimented with structures that led to on-site collaborations with schools. This work led to the development of teacher leaders whose classrooms became lab sites for professional learning communities focused on the instructional core. In this experimental phase,

Toni also had the good fortune to collaborate with Carol Mosesson Teig, the Director of Mathematics in District 15. It was in this collaboration that Toni was able to explore the essence of effective coaching. The NYC Coach Collaborative emerged from this work and is still instrumental in supporting coaches today. In fact, it is the current coaches in this collaborative who continue to challenge and inspire her to refine her ideas about coaching!

Lucy's most influential colleagues were those she worked with in Community School District 2 under the remarkable, courageous, and visionary leadership of Anthony Alvarado. As the Superintendent, Tony supported Lucy in myriad ways as she worked to cultivate supportive relationships with principals, the skill set of math coaches, the role of teacher leaders, and a common understanding of the characteristics of effective mathematics instruction across the district. One piece of advice Tony offered to Lucy when she later became Deputy Superintendent of Region 9 and was struggling to stay focused on improving instruction and learning, "People get fired at this level all the time. Get fired for the right reasons," gave her the courage and fortitude to do "the right thing" even when the right thing wasn't obvious and went against what policymakers were advocating.

In District 2, Lucy had several other key experiences that influenced her thinking as an educator. First was her work with Anna Switzer, who brought Lucy to District 2. As the principal of a very successful elementary school, Anna had a keen eye for discerning potentially excellent teachers—she also had a way of developing teachers into leaders. Working with Anna helped Lucy develop a repertoire for developing and nurturing potential leaders. Second was the team of coaches Lucy cultivated when she spearheaded the District 2 math initiative and who played a key role in developing our model of content coaching. Third was her collaboration with Fritz Staub, Lucy's coauthor on her previous book, *Content-Focused Coaching: Transforming Mathematics Lessons*. This partnership developed when District 2 collaborated with the Learning Research and Development Center at the University of Pittsburgh to develop the Institute for Learning.

The work, friendship, and assistance of Margaret Wheatley was another profound influence. Her seminal book, *Leadership and the New Science*, was transformative. Margaret coached Lucy when she was Deputy Superintendent of Region 9 and helped her refine her thinking about how to lead change in ways that tapped rather than drained the energy of educators.

We would also like to thank a number of other people who supported us in our journey to complete this book. In terms of the actual writing, we'd like to thank Katherine Bryant, our very patient and persistent editor, who kindly nudged us along as we faced one obstacle after another. A big thank you to our support staff, David and Abbey, whose excellent organizational skills and attention to the details of running the business kept us free to focus on writing. Abbey even assisted us with our writing. Sherrin Hersch also read our chapters and gave us invaluable feedback. Our wonderful coaching team read parts of the book and gave us very useful feedback as well. Thank you! Thanks to Jim Knight for agreeing to write the Foreword on very short notice and for doing this with enthusiasm. Finally, we would like to thank our families. Toni would like to thank her husband, James, and her son, Seamus, who put up with her ongoing mental absence for the past several years. She would also like to thank her mother, Millie, who has always been an inspiration and a source of encouragement. Lucy would like to thank her friends, Charles, Deborah, Hollis, and Susan, for their support and encouragement and her family for being understanding when she missed so many family functions in order to complete the project.

There are others too numerous to mention who have influenced our thinking along the way and we are truly grateful for all of the thought-provoking, risk-taking, tell-it-like-it-is mavericks, scholars, and educators who have generously shared their work and ideas with us along the journey. You have truly made a difference in our lives!

Introduction

A GOOD QUESTION

We are often asked, "How do you do it? How do you get robust coaching conversations to happen on a regular ongoing basis in schools where time and tradition seem to be obstacles and external bureaucratic pressure the driving force?" We have spent the last decade pondering these questions as we work with coaches, administrators, and teachers across the United States and in Canada. We have worked with teachers at every grade level, in every possible setting— urban, suburban, rural—from pre-K through high school, in struggling and successful schools, and in some cases in content areas in addition to mathematics such as literacy, science, and technology. This book is written in response to the challenges we have witnessed and contains many surprising discoveries we have made and solutions we have tried.

A DECADE OF PRACTICE

Since the publication of *Content-Focused Coaching: Transforming Mathematics Lessons* (by Lucy along with Fritz Staub) in 2003, educators from across the USA and Canada have acknowledged that content coaching is a powerful and effective approach to improving teacher practice in the service of student learning. Coaches in many disciplines, along with principals and district supervisors, have used the book as a resource and guide. Many readers have told us that the book is a dog-eared companion providing practical advice. Coaches, teacher leaders, and principals who participate with us in our coaching collaboratives, coaching sessions, or teaching learning communities have been energized, able to incorporate new practices that perceptibly improve school culture, teacher capacity, and student ability to think and engage in discourse and learn at deeper levels.

District administrators, principals, and coaches are often impressed by how willing and able teachers are to improve their instructional practices when they engage in content coaching sessions. They have told us that our work provides images of what they are aiming for in coaching sessions—robust, rigorous, and reflective conversations that focus on the instructional core and result in skillful and artful teaching of a broad range of students.

We have spent the last decade utilizing, mutating, refining, and exploring the techniques laid out in that initial book. This new book is designed to share what we have learned over the past decade and how our experience has informed our practice.

The Goals of This Book

This book revisits the underlying theories (knowledge-based constructivism; incremental intelligence and principles of effort-based learning) explained in *Content-Focused Coaching* and expands their application to content areas beyond mathematics. It explores the material on a larger scale (e.g., building a learning community within and across schools; systems thinking, change theory), and revisits the small scale (specific techniques and tools for coaches and teacher leaders) while adding new tools and techniques. The new video case study provides an example of Toni coaching a teacher, and Chapters 7–9 unpack the nuances of the sophisticated practice now known more simply as *content coaching*.

Our primary audience is K–8 coaches and teacher leaders. However, this book will also be useful for administrators in the process of designing a coaching initiative and for principals trying to understand the value of coaching and how to support the development of a coaching community in their schools. Our ultimate vision is the cultivation of a coaching community in which every adult in every school is coaching and being coached by colleagues or specialists concerned with developing informed, innovative, and powerful instructional practices that meet the diverse needs of students, including special needs and second language learners.

The goals of the book are twofold:

1. To give educators (coaches, teacher leaders, and administrators) a big-picture understanding of the transformative potential of content coaching and its use as a strategy to improve student learning and achievement systemwide. This goal includes developing a school-wide, sustainable, and vibrant coaching culture.

2. To give coaches and teacher leaders specific techniques, tools, and strategies (drawing on the content coaching methods from *Content-Focused Coaching* and the authors' continued work in the field) for working with individual or small groups of teachers. These techniques focus on the instructional core of planning, implementing, and debriefing lessons, and looking for evidence of student learning. The book also addresses the importance of reflection and refinement in the coach's practice as well as the teacher's.

The content coaching approach laid out in this book differs from other coaching methods in two key ways:

1. Content coaching emphasizes knowing and understanding the particulars of the content in order to teach it well. We focus on both the conceptual and skill aspects of content and discuss using tools such as curriculum materials, standards, and assessments to inform teacher choices. We emphasize mindful versus mechanical teaching. Like other coaching models, we do pay a great deal of attention to pedagogy and incorporate proven pedagogical practices in our work. However, we also pay attention to content specific pedagogy, particularly in areas like mathematics.

2. Unlike many other coaching approaches, in this approach the coach does not merely observe, model, or debrief lessons; the coach and teacher work together to *plan* the lesson and to *co-teach* it, as well as to discuss and debrief afterward. Coaches take responsibility alongside the teacher for the success of the lesson as measured in student learning. Our experience has shown that it is during the planning sessions that teachers internalize habits of planning that lead to more sophisticated ways of designing lessons. Co-teaching, a rather controversial aspect of our model (see Chapter 1), allows the coach to highlight in real time when to enact the specific changes in pedagogy the teacher is aiming for. Finally, the postconference provides time to reflect on specific classroom interactions in ways that keep the teacher focused on evidence of student learning and inspire her to remain on the journey toward improved practice.

COACHING IS STILL A ROCKY ROAD

Yet, a decade after the publication of *Content-Focused Coaching* and many books on coaching, educators confide that the coaching sessions they participate in or facilitate at their schools and districts seem to fall far short of their aspired goals. In fact, coaches often find that they face a myriad of obstacles that seem to prevent them from coaching in any meaningful way.

Very few districts have found a way to fully support coach development and training to the degree necessary to impact teaching practice systemwide. To confound the situation further, coaches, and the people who supervise them, often do not have a clear understanding of their role and how to best leverage time to improve instruction and learning across a school. Coaches across the country complain of becoming the "catch all" person in the school, assigned to do anything such as covering classes when substitutes are not available, lunch duty, administering tests, ordering and distributing materials, paperwork, or working with struggling students. None of these (mis)uses of a coach's time will help to *cultivate an adult learning culture that will upgrade teaching capacity systemwide to the degree that student learning will substantially improve,* which is the primary function of coaching in educational settings.

In many cases, what frustrates coaches is the snail's pace of change. They are disheartened by the ever-present excuses that permeate a school culture defending the status quo. Their most pervasive lament is how the pressing demands on teachers' time sabotage coaches' ability to get time to talk, plan, and work with teachers. When, finally, time *is* provided to teachers in the form of common planning time or grade-level meetings, the time can be as short as half an hour once or twice a month—far from adequate to accomplish any substantive goal. In addition, there are often competing demands for this time.

In some cases coaches have difficulty gaining access to teachers at all. In just about every school there seem to be teachers who resist working with coaches or will not allow coaches into their classrooms or choose not to participate in collaborative sessions in constructive ways. In other schools coaches are spread too thin because principals insist that they work with every teacher on staff every week! These issues point to the centrality of the principal/coach relationship which, we will argue, works best as a partnership rather than a supervisory one.

Our big-picture, long-term vision is to transform factory-model schools into multigenerational learning centers. We believe that coaches can play a pivotal role in this transformative process when they, and those who supervise them, understand their potential and their role. The time is now for us to innovate, upgrade, and reinvent education in ways that empower educators and students, and to cultivate learning cultures that engender creative and healthy engagement in today's complex, multifaceted, fast-paced, and demanding times. The time has come for educators to stop behaving in ways that limit their own learning and to stop allowing outside forces to dictate practices and policies that keep us focused on testable minutiae instead of big ideas, essential questions, and the habit of learning to learn.

We see coaches as influencers who are conscious of their leadership potential and use it to change the parts of the system that do not promote equity, student achievement, and professional growth. Coaches can join forces with other leaders and infuse the system with fresh energy by inviting educators at all levels to revisit their motives and values and to remember their calling to teach and the difference they want to make. Coaches can be the voices in the system who ask the hard, provocative questions that awaken educators from their policy-imposed slumber and rejuvenate their passion and courage to do whatever it takes to educate the young people who depend on them to learn, to reason, and to act consciously, compassionately, and creatively in a world that needs all the gifts they have to offer.

HOW TO USE THIS BOOK

This book can be read cover to cover or in sections. Section I consists of the theory of content coaching, the big-picture work of creating coaching initiatives, and defining the roles of all the players. Section II dives into the general skill set all coaches need in order to coach well in any content area. In this section, we also provide activities designed to help coaches incorporate new "coaching moves" or skills. Section III (Chapters 7 through 9) is accompanied by a video example of a coaching session and examines a particular coaching session through preconference, lesson, and postconference and unpacks the specific moves a content coach makes to ensure teacher development and growth.

HOW TO ACCESS THE VIDEO CASE STUDY

Step 1: Go to www.heinemann.com
Step 2: Click on "Login" to open or create your account. Enter your email address and password or click "Register" to set up an account.
Step 3: Enter keycode **AOC2013-01383** and click "Register."

In Chapter 1, we lay out the purpose, foundational premises, and practices of content coaching, building on West's and Staub's earlier work. This chapter is a refresher for those who have read the earlier book and provides new insights from our experience since its publication, including a brief discussion on the application of systems theory as it relates to content coaching.

In Chapter 2, we examine the present state of coaching in our schools and make suggestions for a more thoughtful, systematic way to design and implement coaching initiatives. This chapter is especially useful for administrators charged with creating, supporting, and maintaining a coaching initiative. Coaches will also find this an interesting chapter in that it may spur ideas in how to advocate for role clarity, support from administrators, and training in areas that most teachers who transition to the coaching role do not bring with them. The chapter also provides useful practices and tools that assist in building a reflective coaching culture that transcends titles and tradition.

Chapter 3 homes in on the role of each player in the system—the coach, the teacher leader, the teacher, the principal, and district supervisors—to ensure that coaching is well received in schools and results in upgrading the instructional practices of all.

The second section of the book is aimed at cultivating the capacity of coaches as self-aware leaders (Chapter 4, "Know Thyself") and skillful communicators (Chapter 5, "Communication Is Key").

In Chapter 6 we turn our attention to how to tune in to the needs and aspirations of the teachers with whom we work. In this chapter we discuss how to know where to begin the coaching relationship and what to focus on at varying times during the coaching cycle.

Chapters 7, 8, and 9 take the reader through an annotated case study, with tools to assist coaches to name and practice specific coaching moves that we have found to be very effective in helping educators improve their practice. We highly recommend that you watch the corresponding online video *before* reading each of the three case study segments.

The summary chapter is a call to action designed to inspire the reader to remain optimistic and to take small, effective steps toward very large, transformative goals.

We have written this book for educators who are intent on making a difference in ways that improve the lives of all our children and who want to upgrade the teaching profession to a place among the most honored and respected of professions. We trust that you will find our book informative, provocative, and useful.

What Is Content Coaching?

I n this chapter we will explain the hypotheses underlying our work, explain the theories that inform that work, and describe the three-part-cycle of actual coaching sessions. We have come to understand that, like great teachers, effective coaches need to understand the big picture in which the coaching is situated as well as attend to the details of the day-to-day work. It is this back and forth view that enables creative solutions to solve challenging issues.

Content coaching is an organic, eclectic, and responsive model of coaching. It is inquiry-based and continually evolving. Since the publication of *Content-Focused Coaching: Transforming Mathematics Lessons*, we have played with content coaching in every kind of school setting, across content areas, and at all grade levels. We continue to learn from our practice and refine our thinking through experience.

FOUR HYPOTHESES

Our experience has led us to four hypotheses that underlie our practice of coaching:

> ➤ *In order to prepare students for life in the twenty-first century, the focus of education needs to be on learning to learn, create, innovate, communicate, and discern.*

> ➤ *In order for teachers to facilitate robust learning habits in their students they need to practice these learning habits themselves.*

> ➤ *To upgrade instruction we need to focus on the underpinning concepts in a domain as well as attend to the development of skill within that domain. Therefore, teachers need to have deep and flexible knowledge about the content they teach and about how people learn that content.*

> ▸ *To ensure a consistent level of effective instruction across a school or district, we need to think systemically and take actions that ensure that all the adults in the system are interacting in productive ways.* (We will address systems thinking later in this chapter.)

Learning to Learn

We see how rapidly the world is changing, and how important it is to be focused, flexible, and resilient. Let's face reality: students do not need to go to school to get information; they have Google, and this search engine is much better at providing information than any individual. Educators who think their primary goal is to provide information have already had—whether they know it or not—their jobs outsourced to the Internet! For this reason alone, today's classrooms cannot just be about covering the curriculum or providing information to students.

Is there a role for schools and educators in this new paradigm? Absolutely. Computers and the Internet can never teach students to be discriminating consumers, nor can they develop their capacity to reason. This, then, is the job of educators. And to do this job well, we need to rethink and redefine our purpose.

Educators who do not discern, question, engage, and grow, personally and professionally, cannot possibly teach these skills to students. We, the authors, have taken this challenge on as educators and as human beings. It is one we sometimes struggle with, as we, like so many, would often prefer to do what we know how to do well, rather than stretch into new learning. Like so many others, we often find ourselves teaching what we are trying to learn and practice ourselves. In our view, it is the coach's job to help teachers develop critical learning behaviors and learn how to utilize those behaviors to think deeply about what it means to teach well. Our bottom line definition of "teach well" means that we can identify evidence on a daily basis showing that students are learning content, learning to articulate their ideas orally and in writing, and managing their own learning. Coaches can model learning to learn by their commitment to their own learning and by engaging in a professional community in which we use creativity and inquiry to find solutions to pressing problems.

Teachers Need to Practice Learning Habits

When was the last time adults in your school engaged in an in-depth conversation about a topic they teach, and did this so robustly that they learned new ways of thinking, new strategies for approaching the topic, and new ideas to meet the needs of all students? How often do such conversations happen at grade-level or departmental meetings, whole-staff meetings, or even workshops?

If teachers are not engaging in academic dialogue centered on the content they teach and how people learn, then it is highly unlikely that they are engaging their students in these practices either. We are not referring to "data driven" meetings in which teachers look at student test scores and acknowledge the fact that students are struggling with specific subject matter, or meetings in which administrators admonish teachers to work on this or that and essentially nothing changes. We have learned that admonishing people to do better often stems from a belief that people are unmotivated to do better rather than an understanding that teachers are generally teaching to the best of their present ability, knowledge, and skill and will need to learn something they don't know in order to teach better. In other words, we confuse motivation with skill and use pressure instead of coaching to make improvements.

Instead, we are talking about meetings of a very different nature, meetings in which teachers are challenged (and willing) to *learn* publicly—alongside their colleagues and in each other's classrooms—new skills and practices that will improve student learning. We are talking about ongoing and regular forums that help teachers continually question and refine their practice.

Content coaching is a process that is designed to cultivate rigorous, collaborative, professional learning habits among adults. We have found that when we challenge ourselves to learn—to question, to reflect, to refine our thinking—these habits are mirrored in classrooms. Our expectations for ourselves become our expectations for our students. Interactions among adults—how they talk with one another, what they talk about, to what depth they examine and question the content and curriculum they teach, how often they consider the pedagogy they use, how often and to what degree they collaborate—in turn is reflected in how well students do these things.

This insight is not just our idea; Vygotsky's sociocultural theory contends that children grow into the intellectual community that surrounds them. We are simply saying that when teachers engage in rich academic conversations that inquire deeply into content and pedagogy they have a better shot at cultivating student capacity to engage in rich academic discourse. Through discourse we find out what others are thinking and can learn to stay open and become more willing to consider various perspectives. If we can stay in dialogue we can develop richer understanding of the content under discussion. This is most important when we experience tensions in the field due to conflicting policy messages such as teach to the test, using a mechanistic pacing calendar while at the same time differentiating to meet the needs of individual kids, and using sophisticated techniques to master a concept, strategy, or skill.

The Importance of Content Knowledge

Our hypotheses are based on the idea that teaching is a complex, "unnatural" act (Ball and Forzani 2009). Teaching well requires a complex set of skills, which includes having a large body of knowledge at one's fingertips and being able to use this knowledge in ways that give a wide range of learners access to it. Because knowledge in any given field is not stagnant, teachers need many opportunities to expand what they know throughout the course of their careers. This type of learning can happen in workshops or in university courses. However, classroom teachers also need opportunities to see how children experience the content in order to design effective lessons. They need many opportunities to experiment with different pedagogical techniques that support learning. Knowing what to teach is one thing; knowing how to teach it is something entirely different. Content coaching addresses both the *what* and the *how* of teaching.

Teachers may need to shore up their content knowledge or may have rich understanding of the content they teach. But having to think about how to implement a lesson, what questions to use, how to differentiate to meet the needs of a range of learners, moves one quickly beyond content knowledge and into the realm of pedagogy. Teachers need to understand how content comes to life in the minds of learners. Thinking about how children develop big ideas or grapple with essential questions, what strategies they will use and what struggles they will have, helps teachers predict what might happen in the classroom and plan how they can respond in ways that facilitate learning.

Content coaches focus coaching conversations on the content that will be taught and the evidence that will inform us to what degree students articulate their understanding of the content. Using this lens, we have an opportunity to cultivate instructional coherence from classroom to classroom and simultaneously support innovation and individual style in instruction. Note that coherence is different from uniformity. We are not aiming for all teachers to teach the same material on the same day in the same way as if they were robots and children were factory-produced widgets. Coherence means that all teachers are mindfully considering ways to teach the same curriculum to students in ways that meet their needs while simultaneously meeting the demands of the standards for the grade and honoring the unique style of the teacher. Achieving coherence is more likely when principals and coaches work as partners to tease out the differences between policies that promote mechanistic approaches from practices that promote mindful and informed teaching.

THEORETICAL UNDERPINNINGS

Content coaching is based on a few theories that inform our practice:

- ▸ The incremental theory of intelligence and the effort-based principles of learning derived from this theory.
- ▸ Knowledge-based constructivism which adds to the Piagetian and Vygotskyan views of constructivism.

▸   Systems theory which states we must consider the whole system and how the parts in the system interact with one another, not just focus on the parts in the system that may need to improve.

An Incremental Theory of Intelligence

Underpinning our work as content coaches is an underlying theory of intelligence known as the incremental theory of intelligence. This theory suggests that intelligence is situational and learnable. In other words, we can all become smarter if we decide to put in the effort and surround ourselves with people who can encourage us.

The incremental theory of intelligence stands in contrast to the entity theory of intelligence. The entity theory of intelligence is the theory upon which most of our educational policies have been based for over a century.

> For nearly a century, the American education system has been using IQ scores and similar normed measures to compare children to each other on a statistical bell curve, to predict who would and would not profit from a rigorous academic education. We have institutionalized the belief that the most reliable predictor of achievement is the kind of innate mental ability we call 'intelligence'. . . .
>
> For most of this century, American education has operated on the premise that inherited ability is paramount, that there are innate limits to what people can learn, and that the job of the schools is to provide each student with an education that befits his or her naturally-occurring position on the statistical bell curve.
>
> Many people now also believe that greater effort by and for students who don't learn easily can compensate for limitations in students' native ability. This idea lies behind programs of "compensatory education" such as Head Start and Title I. But the compensatory idea still features aptitude: Only the not-so-smart have to put in much effort. (Resnick and Hall 2000, 1–2)

Which theory of intelligence—aptitude or incremental—we tend toward impacts motivation, self-esteem, and goals. If we think having to practice and struggle is a sign of low intelligence, we are likely to avoid tasks that require us to do so. We are also likely to believe that standardized and intelligence tests accurately measure our capability. This stance is known in the research as "performance oriented" (Dweck and Elliott 1983). Adults and children who tend to give up easily and avoid challenges generally have internalized an entity theory of intelligence. When you hear teachers, administrators, or anyone else say things like, "these kids can't," or refer to "my higher level kids" they are operating from an entity theory of intelligence, whether or not they are aware of it. US education policy is performance based as evidenced by its emphasis on testing coupled with punitive sanctions. There is mounting evidence that policies like No Child Left Behind and Race to the Top raise anxiety and ultimately hinder learning by focusing on performance rather than learning (Ravitch 2010).

If, on the other hand, we think that effort is part of learning and that we can learn to be more intelligent, we operate from an incremental theory of intelligence. In this frame of thinking, mistakes and failure are a necessary part of the learning process. It follows then that hard tasks present interesting challenges and people who think like this are more likely to be learning oriented.

> People with learning-oriented goals, by contrast, have an *incremental* theory of intelligence. They believe intelligence develops over time by solving hard problems, working on them, "massaging" them, "walking around" them, and viewing them from another angle. This goes with the belief that high problem-solving effort actually makes you smarter. In general, these individuals display continued high levels of task-related effort in response to difficulty. They love challenge and will often ask for a harder problem or a more difficult book. (Resnick and Hall 2000, 4)

Content coaches encourage a learning orientation, and listen for beliefs about intelligence during their discussions with teachers. When beliefs surface, coaches highlight them for teachers and help them inquire into the expressed beliefs. What would educational systems look, feel, and sound like if we truly believed that all people can learn anything they put their minds to with the right kind of effort and with the help of knowledgeable others?

Content coaches invite educators to rethink our instructional approaches by learning to notice, question, and inquire into our beliefs about intelligence. Learning to learn is tantamount to becoming successful in our rapidly changing world.

Constructivism

We believe that people learn by constructing meaning for themselves. We can't simply transfer knowledge from one person to another. Each person must actively construct meaning. Piaget is known as the father of constructivism, a learning theory that essentially says that we construct meaning in our own minds as we actively engage in learning.

Vygotsky, a *social* constructivist, went on to point out that learning takes place in social settings (Vygotsky and Cole 1978). We learn from others and with others, through conversation and observation of the cultural norms, habits of discourse, and ways others interact in a given setting. Resnick and her colleagues coined the term "socializing intelligence" and named it as a principle of learning through which they essentially apply Vygotsky's theory to educational settings (see principles of learning below).

Resnick added a new term, *knowledge-based* constructivism, to the mix. She contends that it is not possible to teach people to think without giving them rich, relevant things to think about.

> There is no such thing as a thinking skill without good, solid stuff to think about. In fact, what you know is the biggest determinant of how well you will understand the next thing you read on a topic or how crisply you will be able to make and defend your arguments. Reading comprehension, reasoning skill, writing skill, problem solving—all of these thinking skills depend on what you know. The only way to develop thinking skills is around a knowledge core. Endorsing the constructivist argument that kids have to be active learners in order for learning to take hold does not free us of the obligation to offer a very solid, academically rigorous curriculum with important facts and ideas in it that kids have to know. (Resnick and Hall 2000, 4)

One of the main reasons content coaches focus on content is to make sure that students have something important to wrap their minds around as they learn to think, reason, and engage in productive discourse.

From Theories to Principles of Learning

Lauren Resnick and others have translated the learning and intelligence theories above into principles of learning. Content coaches use these principles as the basis for lesson design. You can find the complete list of principles at http://ifl.lrdc.pitt.edu/ifl/index .php/resources, but the principles we focus on in particular are: organizing for effort, accountable talk, socializing intelligence, academic rigor in a thinking curriculum, and self-management of learning.

- ▶ **Organizing for effort** means building a school and a classroom around the idea that students' success depends on continued, directed effort, not innate ability.

- ▶ **Accountable talk** requires everyone involved in a discussion to use accurate, appropriate evidence and reasoning, pay attention to and respond to what others say, and take responsibility for their contributions.

- ▶ **Socializing intelligence** refers to the belief that intelligence is more than being able to think quickly; it is "a set of problem-solving and reasoning ca-pabilities along with the habits of mind that lead one to use those capabilities regularly. Intelligence is equally a set of beliefs about one's right and obligation to understand and make sense of the world, and one's capacity to figure things out over time" (http://ifl.lrdc.pitt.edu/ifl/index.php/resources).

Teachers can teach these skills and habits of mind by expecting students to use them, and holding them accountable.

> ▸ **Academic rigor in a thinking curriculum** emphasizes lessons and units of study centering on major concepts and pedagogy that cultivates active reasoning and engaged, deep thinking.

> ▸ **Self-management of learning** focuses on key metacognitive skills of self-monitoring, questioning, evaluating feedback, time management, using background knowledge, and monitoring one's progress toward a learning goal.

THE IMPORTANCE OF SYSTEMS THINKING

Content coaching requires systems thinking: thinking about a whole organism or organization and the interactions within that organization when we try to influence the organization to improve in some way. Dr. Russ Ackoff explains a system this way:

> A whole . . . that consists of parts each of which can affect its behavior or its properties. . . . Each part of the system when it affects the system is dependent for its effect on some other part. In other words the parts are interdependent, no parts of the system or collection of the parts of the system has an independent effect on it. . . . The parts are all interconnected. Therefore, the system is a whole that cannot be divided into independent parts. (Ackoff 1994)

Somewhat like ecosystems in nature, schools and districts are considered living systems. They are made up of people—living systems—who have different jobs within the system and work more or less together to accomplish the work of the system. When we identify mutual purpose (e.g., improved student learning) and consider the variables that impact student learning (e.g., instruction, curriculum, learning environments, teacher skill and knowledge base, external policy pressures, student characteristics, habits and prior knowledge, etc.) and how those variables interact with one another (e.g., relationships), we can influence a system and nudge it toward improvement.

Living systems are ever changing, interdependent, and self-organizing. They continually try to maintain equilibrium (e.g., the status quo). We often try to regulate parts of the system only to find out we rarely get the results we are aiming for through this approach. For example, we try to improve instruction by imposing standardized tests that supposedly "raise the bar" and find that teachers end up teaching to tests in ways that actually lower the bar by narrowing the curriculum. We add sanctions when test scores don't increase in hopes that this will motivate teachers to do a better job, only to find out that the sanctions raise anxiety, not performance, because the issue is not motivation but skill. Teachers may not have the content knowledge and pedagogical repertoire to meet the higher demands, and the testing initiative has not taken into account how to improve teacher content and pedagogical skill.

The point is that when we want to infuse something new into the system, we need to think about all the variables at play and consider how the new addition might impact the entire system. We need to think about unintended impact as well as the improvement we are trying to accomplish.

Schools as Systems

Systems are designed to get the results they presently get. In order to get different results we have to redesign the system. For example, our company had issues getting paid on time from some school districts we worked with and on a couple of occasions we never got paid for work we provided. In order to resolve this issue we had to look at our entire system from the time we accepted a job to the time we actually got paid. Not surprisingly, our findings showed that everyone—the leaders, the assistants, the book-keepers, the consultants, and the clients—had a role to play in both creating and resolving the problem. Once we traced all the components of the system and noticed where the breakdowns in communication and process were occurring, we created a system from first contact with a potential client to payment for services rendered that now has our accounts receivable up to date almost all the time. We looked at both the details and the interactions in the overall system. The solution was in the details, once we understood how the whole system interacted.

How does this apply to school systems? When we consider how schools are organized, we realize that many schools and districts are organized as if the parts are independent from one another. Teachers tend to work independently in individual classrooms and principals rarely meet with principals from other schools to learn from one another. Districts are organized into separate departments. For example, people who are in charge of assessment may be in a different department than those who supervise instruction, who in turn are in a different part of the organization than those who select curriculum materials, who are separate from those in charge of special education. In most instances these players from across the organization rarely come together to collaboratively make decisions with the whole system in mind. Often they are using different funding streams and have different goals in mind. This fragmentation in the design of the organization causes people to search for solutions for the part of the organization they work in rather than to get the various parts of the organization to work together.

Fixing Parts Instead of Wholes

Another way to think about this is that people attempt to fix things in one part of the system and rarely understand that their attempts to do so are extremely unlikely to succeed because they have not been based on systems thinking (Ackoff 1994). Consider a district that buys a new program in an attempt to upgrade instruction in a particular content area. In order to succeed, the district would also have to ensure that teachers have the knowledge and skills to implement the new materials well, principals are able to identify and provide feedback to ensure that implementation of lessons from the new program are effective, appropriate assessment tools are shared and used to identify degrees of student learning, and practitioners have permission to modify the program based on useful data resulting from the shared assessments. In addition, the district office would have to ensure that all initiatives are transparently and explicitly aligned, make sense to the people expected to implement them, and do not overload people with too many new skills simultaneously. This means that a whole lot of players from all different departments need to plan and work together on an ongoing basis. Buying materials without attending to the variables described above is a classic fix-the-part approach rather than a systemic approach, which generally does not result in the desired outcome, namely more sophisticated instruction and more robust student learning.

Systems thinkers understand that healthy systems require the various parts of the system to work together. Content coaches in their role as agents of change attempt to understand the interactions in the whole system and use their circles of influence to get the different departments talking to one another in the service of improving student learning across the board.

Hierarchies

In addition, school systems are generally hierarchal in structure. Policy is generated at the top of the pyramid and imposed on those at the lower levels of the pyramid (e.g., classroom teachers) with little or no input from the people who are expected to carry out the policy. Often the very people expected to carry out the new policy do not understand the policy and the reasoning behind it or do not have the skill set to implement it well. In our travels, when we suggest to teachers that they can use their power of influence to talk up the hierarchy, they are often hesitant to do so and fear reprisal. This is a sign of an unhealthy, hierarchical system. Systems thinkers understand that communication must flow in all directions and getting the various players in a system to talk with one another is a very important strategy for improving results. Content coaches understand that as agents of change they are the conduits who mediate between different parts of the system—they connect principals with faculty, principals with district-level supervisors, and teachers with other teachers within and across schools.

Fighting Fragmentation

The present design of school systems causes fragmentation and territoriality, wastes vast amounts of resources, causes burnout, and engenders resistance, compliance, and cynicism. These systems rarely manifest the levels of coherence and collaboration that would produce higher student achievement throughout the system. Attempts to improve the system generally involve tinkering within the present design (such as providing time for people to talk with one another in forums such as grade-level meetings or staff meetings). Often the allotted time set for meetings is inadequate and causes frustration because it is difficult to accomplish any real work in under an hour once a week or month. School systems are not presently designed for adult learning. Content coaches are aware of this tension and work with principals and district-level supervisors to mitigate the obstacles to adult learning. Removing obstacles is an important part of being an agent of change.

OVERVIEW OF CONTENT COACHING

From our perspective, anyone with expertise in something can coach someone with less expertise. Teachers can coach other teachers, students, or athletic teams. Students can coach each other (e.g., peer coaching) or adults (e.g., in using technology). Principals, when they employ coaching techniques rather than evaluating, can coach too. A coach is **anyone** *whose job description or informal interactions (e.g., collaborative planning with colleagues) involves assisting teachers and/or principals in improving teacher performance, either part-time or full-time, in the service of improving student learning.*

Content coaching requires expertise that goes beyond generic forms of coaching. Similar to other models of coaching, content coaches work on instructional strategies, cultivate relationships, and build trust among faculty members. However, content coaching takes coaching in educational settings further than other forms of coaching. Content coaches center coaching conversations on application of conceptual content knowledge in ways that give all students access to it.

Content coaches know that if students are to learn important and relevant content well, teachers need to focus their lessons on the big ideas, structures, and/or essential questions relevant to the domain under study. Teachers need to deeply understand those ideas and structures and learn to make them accessible to students. Therefore, content coaches have expertise in *at least* two areas: the content they are helping others teach and how children learn that content. Coaches need this expertise to assess levels of teacher and student understanding and ensure teachers have the expertise needed to give all students access to the concepts embedded in the lesson as well as to customize the work with each teacher.

Even though content coaches tend to have expertise in one content area, because we focus on essential components of the instructional core and base our work on research-based learning and intelligence theories, we are able to help teachers rethink and refine their practice in ways that are transferrable from one subject to another.

The Three-Part Cycle

Content coaching is a very specific process that focuses on the instructional core: planning, teaching, reflecting on, and refining lessons. This process includes creating environments conducive to both adult and student learning. Content coaches work one-on-one or in small groups. With small groups of educators, focused around a set of core issues (see Appendix A: Guide to Core Issues), content coaching can have a positive impact on the quality and content of the instructional practices and on the culture in an entire school or district. When it is interwoven with professional learning communities and/or aspects of lesson study it can improve the benefits of both of those professional development practices.

Content coaching uses a three-part cycle—plan, teach, and debrief.

The Preconference: Lesson Planning

As a rule of thumb, content coaches will not work in classrooms without a preconference. We believe it is not only respectful to meet with teachers prior to engaging with them in their classrooms, but essential to find out what they are working on, how their students are doing, and how we can best serve *them*. (The preconference is described in detail through the case study in Chapter 7.)

We emphasize lesson planning because we have found that habits of planning have a significant impact on the successful implementation of the lesson. In our experience, many teachers need to strengthen their capacity to design or adapt lessons to meet the needs of diverse learners and to center lessons on the big ideas or essential questions in the content to be taught. Often the problems that arise in the implementation of a lesson can be traced back to the lesson design. Our ultimate goal is teaching students to think deeply, critically, and creatively when in the process of learning. In order to do so, teachers must think deeply, critically, and creatively when designing lessons.

Content coaches co-plan lessons with teachers rather than come into the session with a fully developed lesson. Co-planning honors the principle that people learn best by doing in the

CURRICULUM MATERIALS

Sometimes coaches see their job as helping teachers deliver the next lesson in the book, especially when the district or school adopts a new set of materials. In contrast, content coaches see the teaching of important content, big ideas, and essential questions as their job. We take a questioning stance in relation to the curriculum materials and make informed decisions about how to best use these tools in the service of ensuring all students have access to the content under study. Rather than enforcing a mechanical "fidelity to the curriculum" approach, we believe we should have "fidelity to student learning important and relevant content" and that curriculum materials are tools to be used mindfully.

company of knowledgeable others. One of the critical factors in the success of a lesson is the teacher's depth of understanding of what it is she is trying to teach and why she is implementing the lesson in a particular way. When teachers are unsure or don't "own the design," they tend to have difficulty implementing the lesson as intended. This is true whether they are following a set of curriculum materials or a lesson plan given to them from a colleague or coach. Our goal is for teachers to internalize lesson-planning habits of mind and plan future lessons with more depth and know-how.

Focus on Big Ideas and Essential Questions Content coaching focuses on the big ideas and essential questions to be taught—the what, why, how, and who questions to be explored in lesson design. The diagram below was introduced in *Content-Focused Coaching: Transforming Mathematics Lessons* (West and Staub 2003), and is designed to show how all of these questions interact in relation to the various resources, tools, and philosophies at play in any given lesson.

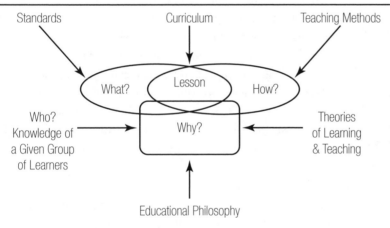

Planning Segments of the Lesson Content coaches tend to take teachers on a deep dive into content and focus on specific segments of the lesson. For instance, we might plan the launch in great detail during the preconference and then enact it side-by-side with the teacher during the lesson. We decide on what segment of the lesson to plan (e.g., launch, conferring, summary, minilesson) based on observations of the teacher or on our discussions during which the teacher asks for assistance with a specific part of the lesson. By working on chunks of the lesson, we can build the capacity to implement the whole lesson well over time. The launch is often a good starting place because it requires less skill than the summary conversation, for example. Also, if a lesson gets off to a good start, the students tend to be more engaged, and the teacher can see immediate positive impact and is generally more willing to then roll up her sleeves to work on the more difficult segments of lesson implementation.

Keeping autonomy in mind, the coach may model the launch for the teacher the first time they work together, but the next time, the coach would encourage the teacher to execute the launch with the coach standing by to guide the process in real time. In this way the coach encourages the teacher to be a learner in the same manner she wants the teacher to encourage students to be learners.

Co-Teaching

Guiding instruction during class is also unique to content coaching. We are not aware of any other coaching models that advocate the coach actively coach during a lesson. In fact, there are some who disagree with this aspect of our practice. Most coaching models generally have the coach take notes during a lesson and then provide feedback. While this is easier for the coach, and may be easier on the teacher, it often does not result in observable changes in teacher practice. By judiciously interjecting at pivotal moments during lessons, content coaches resemble athletic coaches. They are instructing the play during the game in order for the teacher to note and internalize cues for certain teaching moves. The coach also has the opportunity to model specific moves so the teacher can see what that move looks and sounds like in real time with her students.

In our experience, working side-by-side with the teacher during the lesson is a very effective way to encourage the teacher to try new practices at pivotal times during the lesson and allows the coach to provide immediate, actionable feedback. Timely, specific feedback is one of the most effective ways to ensure learning at any age (Hattie and Timperley 2007). The teacher can often act on the feedback and give the practice another try during the same lesson.

For example, teachers often listen *for* what they want students to say rather than listen *to* what students are actually saying. Slowing down the conversation, listening actively, and checking for understanding are all nameable moves that can be identified and worked on during a lesson. When the coach notices that the teacher misheard or skipped over something relevant said by a student, she might say something like, "What Tanisha said is really interesting. I'm wondering if we can have her restate it and see what other students think about her idea." She can then hand the reins back to the teacher, who can work on asking the student to explain her idea and get other students to listen and paraphrase the ideas of a classmate. The teacher can learn to use these critical discourse moves in all content areas. Later, during the postconference, the coach and teacher can explore why the coach made that move in order to highlight the practice of listening to students.

This implies that the coach is in close proximity to the teacher during the lesson. They are working side-by-side. Sometimes coaches model a piece of the lesson or a specific instructional move and then hand the lesson back to the teacher. Sometimes they interject a question into the conversation at hand and sometimes they might play scribe, writing down students' ideas or demonstrate other ways of representing student thinking. The coach is *not* an extra pair of hands working with a small group of students while the teacher works with other students. Teacher and coach work together to learn from and with each other.

There are pitfalls to taking an active role during the lesson. The main pitfall is the tendency on the part of the coach to take over the class. Another potential pitfall is intervening too often or in ways that disrupt the flow of the lesson or change the course of the planned lesson. It is extremely important that the coach and teacher discuss the practice of actively coaching during the lesson and determine to what degree the teacher is open to this practice and what signals and agreements need to be made in order to ensure its success.

We will discuss co-teaching further in Chapter 8.

The Postconference

When the lesson is over, the coach and teacher(s) sit together and think through the lesson in great detail. They examine student work, and think about its implications for tomorrow's lesson. In some cases, where coaching is happening in small groups, an observing teacher may agree to teach the lesson to another group of students incorporating the refinements suggested during this debrief. When teachers teach one subject to multiple classes (e.g., science in middle school) they can retry the lesson in a second class with new insights and refinements brought out during the postconference.

Like all effective coaching models, we view the postconference as an important opportunity to build reflective habits of mind. We also take this opportunity to prioritize a couple of specific things for the teacher to work on until the next coaching session. Usually we provide one process goal (e.g., begin to use turn and talk more often in your lessons) and one content goal (e.g., identify and name the network of related big ideas in this unit and select one or two to highlight in the lesson as part of your plan). Setting one or two doable goals where the new behaviors are observable helps the coach, the teacher, and the principal acknowledge and build on progress.

Our aim in the postconference is to focus on one or two important aspects of teaching that are generalizable and resonate. By this we mean that the strategies are essential and can be applied beyond the one lesson worked on in depth in any given session. Learning to listen well to what students are saying, for example, is a habit worth cultivating across the board.

We look at the postconference in detail in Chapter 9.

Comparing Content Coaching with Other Coaching Models

Content coaching is a powerful form of coaching that has one main purpose: improving instruction to improve student learning. Other coaching models such as instructional coaching, cognitive coaching, and so forth also aim to improve instruction. The underlying values, and some premises, of these three models of coaching (instructional, cognitive, and content) are similar:

> ‣ It is important to build respectful relationships based on trust and willingness to inquire into beliefs and hypotheses;

> ‣ Commitment to professional learning matters and is more likely to occur when we find mutual purpose and co-construct goals.

> ‣ Asking questions rather than providing answers tends to generate more learning.

> ‣ Focusing the coaching conversation at the level of the lesson.

> ‣ We learn by doing the work together.

While all three models aim at improving teacher practice as a means to improve student learning, the difference is in the focus and the processes. Instructional coaches tend to emphasize certain instructional tools and/or processes that have proven to be of benefit to students (e.g., graphic organizers). Cognitive coaches use questioning techniques to help a teacher identify and think through how to accomplish their goals. Content coaches focus on naming and exploring the content to be taught and identify to what degree each student understands it.

Content coaches keep their attention on the instructional core—lesson planning, implementation (co-teaching), and reflection on and refinement of a lesson based on evidence of student learning. We might offer instructional tools similar to instructional coaches and ask questions to ascertain goals or ideas similar to cognitive coaches; however, we believe that we must explicitly name the content to be taught first and foremost in order to ensure an effective lesson. Naming the content to be taught may seem obvious, but in fact, the lack of clarity about what is to be taught is often at the heart of what goes awry in lessons. Often the content identified by the teacher is too narrow, too skills based, and does not center on important concepts, hypotheses, or essential questions.

Content coaching is a proactive model of coaching and content coaches often offer suggestions as well as ask questions. While we totally agree that inquiry is the main practice of coaching, and that learning happens best when people come to their own understanding, we have found that sometimes offering suggestions is necessary. For example, when teachers don't know their content deeply, or have a very limited repertoire of instructional practices, or are unaware that their present beliefs are actually inhibiting student learning, it is often more productive to offer suggestions than to continue to question. Because we do offer suggestions and help craft a lesson, content coaches take fifty percent responsibility for the success of the lesson they collaboratively plan and co-teach with teachers. We share the decision-making process and the accountability.[1]

Many coaching models use a two-part cycle: observe/debrief or model/debrief. We are aware that some coaching models do include a three-part cycle—talk/model/debrief, but through our conversations with coaches around the country, particularly literacy coaches, the actual process employed in the three-part cycle differs from the process used in content coaching. In some coaching practices, for example, coaches do not engage in lesson planning with the teacher, but share a lesson that has been fully planned by the coach and will be modeled in the classroom. In contrast, content coaches co-create the lesson plan with the teacher.

Modeling lessons is another aspect of the work that differs in content coaching. We may occasionally model a complete lesson for a teacher or group of teachers, but we do so judiciously and encourage teachers to co-teach with us as soon as possible. We want to develop the teacher's skill set as quickly as possible and avoid creating any dependency on the coach. Also, we find that there is so much happening while modeling an entire lesson that it is difficult to focus on important aspects that will inform and improve practice. Teachers need to be able to "name the teaching moves" the coach is making and decipher the cues for using those particular moves in order to then practice using the same moves whether or not the coach is present. We have found that modeling is best done in small doses with specific moves in mind.

SUMMARY

Coaching is a vehicle for developing rigorous planning habits and effective instructional practices across a system. It is not, in and of itself, a panacea. It is a part of the whole. Content coaching in particular attempts to use a systemic approach to upgrading professional practices that result in *evidence of student learning* on a daily basis in any given lesson.

---

[1] In talking with Bena Kallick, her colleague Art Costa (a developer of cognitive coaching), and Jim Knight (author of *Instructional Coaching*), we have found that our ideas about coaching are quite similar. However, we have found that people who have studied these coaching models (or even content coaching) often have internalized ideas about those models that were not intended by the authors, such as "Cognitive coaches can never offer a suggestion" or "Content coaches do not work on instructional strategies, management, or culture, just on content." This phenomenon happens in all human attempts to learn from one another and is a natural part of the learning process.

We focus on the instructional core and co-create and assess lessons with our colleagues. Content coaching does not favor one instructional strategy, lesson format, or set of curriculum materials over another. We work at gathering evidence of what works with which students. We focus on building learning communities in which people question the status quo and imagine a learning environment that is compelling and inspiring for adults and children alike. We then partner with our colleagues—administrators and teachers—to create that environment.

In Chapter 2 we turn to creating a powerful coaching initiative designed to get systemic, sustainable, and measurable results.

Designing and Refining Coaching Initiatives

Coaching initiatives impact players at every level of the system—supervisors, coaches, teachers, students, and the board. The design must take into account the potential cost, responses, needs, and disruption coaching might have on everyone concerned. Coaching has the potential to transform schooling as we presently know it. To come anywhere close to fulfilling its transformative potential, we need to proceed thoughtfully, deliberately, patiently, and wisely as we deploy coaches into the present bureaucratic and fragmented systems operating in most school districts. The emerging research suggests that we need to pay particular attention to principals in our design as they are key players and their support is necessary for the success of a coaching initiative (Johnson and Donaldson 2007; Steiner and Kowal 2007; Taylor et al. 2007; Noyce Foundation 2007; Wren and Vallejo 2009).

Content coaches have two main functions: 1) to transform schools, in partnership with principals, into multi-generational learning communities (the leadership aspect of coaching), and 2) to improve instruction—planning, enacting, assessing, and reflecting on lessons/units of study—as a means to improve student learning. The dual function of the coach means that coaching is woven into both the leadership and classroom practice aspects of education. Both of these aspects need to be considered in the deployment of coaches.

The success of a coaching initiative in any school is largely dependent on the support of the principal, the skill set of the coach, the school culture, the clarity of vision, commitment to an agreed upon purpose, supporting structures, and definition of roles. Rarely are all these ducks in a row at the onset of coaching initiatives. With all of these variables impacting coaching, we have found that coaching initiatives generally take three to five years to gain sustainable momentum and show measurable results. This requires substantial funding for coaching prior to seeing significant improvements.

Other variables that impact coaching include: the stability and effectiveness of the leadership team at the district level, the relationship between principals and the district office, the relationships between principals and coaches, clarity of vision and purpose, how well the initiative was and continues to be communicated to all constituents, whether people view their present actions as successful or in need of improvement, how carefully coaches are selected, trained, and deployed, who coaches report to, and how many other initiatives are being implemented simultaneously. With so many variables at play, it often takes years and the willingness to revisit the coaching initiative on a regular basis to get the most from coaching.

PLANNING AN INITIATIVE: WHO DOES IT AND HOW LONG DOES IT TAKE?

A coaching initiative can begin at the school level or at the district level. Sometimes an initiative starts when a principal at a particular school hires an outside consultant as a coach or assigns a lead teacher as a peer coach to assist teachers who are new or need to learn more effective instructional strategies and enrich their content knowledge and/ or assessment techniques. Generally the motivation behind the initiative is to improve student learning by implementing a new program or incorporating "best practices." Coaching often starts in one academic area, usually literacy, and often at the elementary level. If a principal for an individual school starts the initiative and it is successful (e.g., scores go up), then colleagues or the district leaders might decide to hire coaches to support other schools.

Though many initiatives start as described, others begin at the district level. In these instances, funding is usually provided for each school to hire a coach in a given content area or as a generalist. While the district may be footing the bill, the principal in each building is usually given the freedom to select the coach (often from the existing faculty), define the work of the coach, and supervise the coaches that work in her school. This approach often has mixed results depending on the choices each individual principal makes, their understanding of the role of the coach, and their capacity to ensure that teachers engage with coaches in productive ways.

If a district began a coaching initiative in the manner described above, district leaders will assess the coaching once results start coming in. Often it is at this point that coaching initiatives are centralized, with someone at the district level selecting and supervising coaches (sometimes in conjunction with principals, sometimes not). This closer look may be prompted by indicators of improvement (e.g., test scores) not improving in some of the schools that had coaches. The board may be looking for places to cut the budget at the same time the principals may want more coaching support. The district leaders need to assess the benefits of coaching in terms of costs and may have difficulty because there has not been a consistent approach or clear benchmarks for success.

Evolution of a Coaching Initiative

The process of using coaching as a theory of action for improving instruction generally evolves over several years. Coaches need ongoing training—with quite a bit of that training coming in the first two years—to develop the skill set of coaching, understand how to influence change, and build relationships with colleagues, principals, and supervisors. This means that coaches may be less effective in years one and two than in later years. Many choices made by coaches in the first year or two in relation to time management, who they work with and how often, what else is on their plates, and so forth, prove to be problematic and require new choices. We've worked in districts that have had coaches for four or five years and people are still trying to figure out how coaches should spend their time, who they should work with, what the benchmarks of progress are, and so forth.

In addition, principals need to learn to productively manage a coaching initiative at their schools in ways that spread promising planning habits and instructional innovations and inhibit the use of planning and instructional strategies that are less effective. Most principals initially want coaches to work with the most struggling teachers, thereby not gaining momentum for whole-school change and perpetuating the fallacy that coaching is for the inept. Other principals insist that the coach work with every teacher on staff. This approach generally results in spreading coaches too thin and maintaining the status quo. These and other principal and/or district choices, such as not providing the needed professional learning opportunities for coaches and principals up front, tend to result in the coaching initiative evolving slowly over a period of years as people learn what does and doesn't work in their setting.

Benefits of Centralized Models

We think that a centralized model of coaching is generally better than one that is designed anew at each school. This is not to say that what happens at each school has to be uniform, because one size does not fit all when it comes to coaching. However, agreed upon framework, formats, goals, purpose, roles, etc. should underpin the work across the district. Co-creating a design that everyone in the district can commit to is easier to accomplish when you have the authority to get all the main players in the same room and allow them to help shape the work. A district has access to all the principals and can use regular meeting times to involve principals in crafting the initiative, determining their responsibilities, shaping the role of the coach, getting clear about expectations of teacher selection for work with the coaches, and so forth. Even better, the district can involve lead teachers, potential coaches, and maybe even members of the board or community to help shape the design. The coaching model should be flexible enough so that it can be customized for the needs and culture of a given school yet recognizable from school to school as the district model. Involving principals and other key players in the design of a centralized initiative, rather than asking them to unilaterally invent a coaching model for their school, will result in a more coherent view and practice of coaching.

When coaches report to a district-level supervisor, the feedback loops created can allow the district to troubleshoot in schools where the coaching model may be floundering. In a centralized model coaches become conduits between schools and districts and between school administrators and teachers. The feedback they provide allows for adjustments when unintended consequences of initiatives or policies surface. Perhaps most important, coach feedback can alert the district to innovative practices that are emerging in specific schools and the district can partner with coaches to invent a coordinated approach to help spread these practices. This last point is an important one because it exemplifies the shift from a deficit model of thinking about change and teacher development to a model that focuses on what's working and one that strives to strengthen and build those practices across the system.

Through a centralized model the district is more likely to be able to pinpoint and support the collective needs of coaches and principals to ensure the success of the coaching initiative. A centralized model is more likely to be better funded and have a more coherent agenda because the district generally has more resources and can leverage them to train all of the coaches collectively rather than each one individually at the school level.

Time Frame

As mentioned earlier, we think of coaching as a process that takes three to five years to take root in a system. In year one, new hires are often people with little or limited coaching experience or are people from outside the district who have experience but are not knowledgeable about the culture and do not yet have a network of relationships within the district. Year one is often a time when people are finding their way; trying to define their role, initiate and develop relationships, and establish schedules that work. The more thoughtfully the initiative has been conceived and communicated and the more receptive the culture at the school level, the less time it takes to plant the seeds of success. If the initiative has been imposed upon the schools and communication has been top down, it is more likely that the launch of the initiative will be bumpy at best.

In our experience, year two is when coaches seem to gain confidence and have enough experience to know what questions to ask in relation to their own development and about the design and challenges of the initiative. They may realize that they need more support and training in certain areas (e.g., communication skills; leadership, content, curriculum materials) and begin to advocate for it. They may have ideas about what schedules and structures (e.g., common planning times) might produce better results. They may have developed a few collegial relationships with teachers and/or administrators to see some success in individual classrooms or on particular grade levels.

If the district and school administrators have been communicating with coaches, and coaches have been allowed to coach much of the time, by year three there should be acceptance by the faculty that coaching is a helpful resource for their own learning. It should be evident by improved practice in the classrooms and grade levels in which the coach has focused her energy and improved student achievement in those classrooms and grade levels. The caveat being that the coach has had the opportunity to work with relatively successful teachers, as well as new or struggling teachers, and that she has worked both individually and in small groups with teachers on a regular basis around the instructional core. It takes at least another year or two to spread the work across the entire staff depending on the culture of the school/district in which the coaching is taking place and the support of the principal at the school.

START WITH THE END IN MIND

In order to get the most from coaching, leaders need to design coaching initiatives with the end in mind. We need to consider purpose and goals, provide the necessary training of coaches and principals, define the roles of each player, determine the trade-offs, and commit to the time and resources over the long haul (not the norm in public education today where we tend to plan year to year rather than long-term). In other words, we need to become intentional and deliberate in the training, funding, and deployment of coaches across the system if we intend to get measurable, sustainable results and we need to define what those results look like along the journey.

Less Successful Approaches

Leaders often underestimate what it takes to design a coaching initiative that results in better instruction, greater student achievement, and a more collaborative professional culture. For example, people often think that they can tap excellent classroom teachers, department chairs, or assistant principals to become coaches. Frequently this leads to the realization that the skill set coaches need is different from the skill set of the people selected, and the district is unprepared to provide the training to develop the necessary skill set. Selection criteria are often too general, the hiring process a simple application and interview process rather than a simulation or actual coaching session. Role definitions are like laundry lists, assigning coaches responsibilities not aligned with their core mission, minimizing their impact on improved instruction and student learning.

Sometimes coaches are hired to assist with the implementation of a new program. When this happens the coaching initiative is about *fidelity to a program* as if the program is the answer to the problem of lack of teacher content or pedagogical knowledge. It would be more beneficial to see coaching as an investment in teacher's content, pedagogical, and professional knowledge and have them focus on *fidelity to teaching well as evidenced in improved student learning*. With this longer-term focus, it is more likely that teachers can implement whatever program comes along mindfully and in the best interest of their students. In cases where coaches are told to focus on implementing the new program, they are often given insufficient training in the new program and may or may not have ever used the program in their own classes. In these scenarios, teachers tend to view coaches as the curriculum police and often resist working with them.

Backward Design for Successful Coaching Initiatives

In the classroom, where there is a much greater chance that the students will learn from a well-designed lesson than a poorly planned one, a well-designed coaching initiative has a much better chance of having a significant and transformative impact. When planning effective lessons, we often employ a "backward design" approach. We start with a unit of study and ask ourselves, "What are the essential questions we want students to grapple with in this unit of study?" and then plan our instruction with those questions in mind. We can employ this backward design approach to a coaching initiative.

If we employ the basic principles of backward design to the design of a coaching initiative, we might start with a question like: What will be different after one, two, three, or more years as a result of a coaching initiative? What complex issues do we want coaching to grapple with? On what aspects of teaching and learning can coaching have the greatest positive impact? How can coaches mediate between segments of the system that have often been at odds with each other (e.g., teachers and administration)? In order to answer these questions we would have to consider several sub-questions and identify our desired outcomes. In doing so, it is likely that we could design a coaching initiative that would have a powerful impact on school culture and on teaching and learning at all levels of the system. Some of these sub-questions and possible desired outcomes might be:

1. **What would schools and classrooms look, feel, and sound like if our coaching efforts were successful?**
   - Adults would be talking about improving their practice with one another in the hallways, the teachers' lounge, and would be discussing instruction in each other's classrooms after observing lessons.

◆ Students would be engaged in meaningful tasks and/or projects, talking to each other about the content under discussion using the reasoning related to the given domain (e.g., argumentation in mathematics), and listening well to the voices of their classmates, working to understand and build on one another's ideas.

2. How would adult meetings such as grade-level, department, or staff meetings be used as effective forums for coaching?

◆ Meetings would be facilitated by coaches and focused on the instructional core. Perhaps a meeting would be used to collaboratively plan one lesson deeply, and everyone in the meeting would teach that lesson under the guidance of a coach or the observation of a peer. The next meeting would involve studying the student work from the collaboratively designed lesson that would then be used to design a new lesson based on what was gleaned about student understanding of the topic at hand.

3. How might we ensure that all players in the system have similar images of success?

◆ We might go out in small, cross-role groups and observe classes that someone in the group has identified as effective. The group might then work to distill the essential features of effective instruction using evidence of student learning as criteria.

4. What would adults have to learn in order to accomplish the shared vision?

◆ How to collaborate with one another around the instructional core.

◆ How to engage in and engender robust academic discourse.

◆ How to select, adapt, or design rich tasks that fully engage students in their own learning.

5. What formats, time frames, and investments would support adult learning in our present structure, and what changes to the structure might be needed?

◆ Extended days for adults that do not include more teaching time.

◆ Mini-courses in content areas in which adults have less confidence and students are not doing well.

◆ Common preparation periods that are used to plan a lesson in depth.

6. What would coaches, teachers, principals, and district level supervisors need to do differently and in relation to each other to ensure success?

◆ Blur the lines of authority in order to learn from one another across roles.

◆ Encourage the questioning of policies and practices across roles, schools, and classrooms based on evidence of student learning rather than on compliance with mandates.

    ✦ Learn to give and receive feedback non-defensively to and from supervisors, subordinates, and colleagues.

7. **What benchmarks along the way, in addition to high-test scores, could we identify and value that would indicate we were making progress?**

    ✦ Changes in pedagogy resulting in more student discourse and/or writing.

    ✦ Increased student participation.

    ✦ Use of more cognitively demanding tasks.

8. **What do the coaches need to know and be able to do to take a pivotal role in accomplishing the vision?**

    ✦ Learn to speak up skillfully in ways that challenge the existing norms and/or practices.

    ✦ Willingly take the risks they are asking others to take by planning, teaching, and reflecting on their own work in front of colleagues and supervisors.

    ✦ Ask those they work with how they, the coaches, can improve.

9. **Where and when will the coaches learn the skills necessary to have the desired impact?**

    ✦ Regular meetings provided by the district, facilitated by a knowledgeable supervisor, outside consultant, or effective coach.

    ✦ Coaching institutes outside the district.

10. **How will we get commitment from all of the people this initiative will impact?**

    ✦ Have multiple meetings over an extended period of time.

    ✦ Ask for input and continually refine the initiative and role definitions as the initiative unfolds.

Starting with this "backward design" approach provides clarity and purpose to the work. It can also lead to the development of useful informal and formal assessment indicators of the success of the coaching initiative. Questions like those listed above can be used to inform the design of the coaching initiative and should be raised periodically throughout the initiative to tweak the design as needed.

Goals and Challenges to Consider

The main goal of a coaching initiative is to improve student learning. However, it is difficult to determine exactly what specific actions result in more student learning. It is also difficult to determine what impact coaching had on student learning because coaches are once-removed from students. Coaches work to improve student learning by assisting teachers to learn more about teaching, student learning, and content through the practice of planning, teaching, and reflecting on lessons. Teachers in turn assist students to learn about their learning and about the content under study.

Deciding What Is Essential

Teachers need to know their curriculum deeply and flexibly enough to make it accessible to all their students. They need a large repertoire of instructional strategies that go beyond the one way they may have learned the content or presently know how to teach it. Coaches need to not only know the content and have a large pedagogical repertoire, but also need the wherewithal to give teachers permission to think deeply, experiment intelligently, and analyze their results systematically to make the necessary adjustments to ensure student success. Principals need to be able to recognize effective instruction when they see it and encourage more of it. As important, principals need to understand what teacher learning looks like and support that learning so as not to inadvertently sabotage the very improvements they are trying to cultivate.

In order to accomplish this, educators at all levels need to tease out the essential from the superficial to ensure we have common images and understanding of what really matters when we observe or teach a class. For example, when it comes to instruction, is the format we use for a lesson superficial or essential? The workshop model is presently in vogue. It is one instructional model, but it is not the only effective instructional model. Leaders in the district may be advocating that everyone use this "best practice" and principals may be holding teachers accountable to use it. We see this as a mechanistic approach that essentially keeps us all focused on superficial aspects of teaching and learning. Teachers can comply by using the workshop model, but what happens when they find that it is not effective for some of their students or in all content areas or for rich projects? What then?

Similar points can be made about the effective use of mandated curriculum materials. Curriculum materials are useful, yet they are not the curriculum and they do not replace robust teacher content knowledge and pedagogical know how. A teacher can use curriculum materials "with fidelity" and the lesson can still fail to

CURRICULUM MATERIALS

Please understand that we are not advocating that individual teachers should be given carte blanche to select or invent whatever materials they want, but rather that curriculum materials are tools, not panaceas. The true focus of any coaching initiative needs to be on improving instruction and learning, not on fidelity to any given set of materials. Teaching is a complex craft and success requires a great deal more than a particular set of tools.

We have come to believe that while well-designed curriculum materials are definitely better than poorly designed ones, in and of themselves they have limited impact on improving instruction and learning. We acknowledge that this is a controversial stance and invite the reader to examine her own beliefs about curriculum materials. Our point is that curriculum materials are tools and one aspect of the coach's job is to assist teachers in learning to use these and other tools well. The coach may also have to attend to the teacher's content knowledge, pedagogical repertoire, and beliefs about teaching, learning, and intelligence in order to guarantee that the teacher has the capacity to assist every student in her class using a given set of tools. If a teacher does not know her content and/or how to design effective lessons, it may not matter what curriculum materials she is given. The reverse is true as well. If a teacher is steeped in content, and the developmental landscape for how students learn that content, she can use just about any materials to assist her.

reach some learners. What then? Is it the role of coaches to enforce the use of the new program? Is the goal of coaching to ensure fidelity to the curriculum materials? Is fidelity to the curriculum materials superficial or essential? When the curriculum materials change again in a year or two, are we now to have fidelity to those materials?

To us, the role of the coach is to keep raising questions that challenge our present way of doing business. Are we willing to allow for the possibility that a well-designed coaching initiative means giving everyone permission to question the latest mandate and to inquire into the impact it is having on student learning? How might the coach and principal have to relate in order for the principal to consider allowing teachers to deviate from the mandate?

These examples begin to highlight the complexity of coaching in our bureaucratic public system. The system has been experiencing increasing pressures from policymakers to comply with conflicting demands which means coaches, leaders, and teachers must carefully unravel these demands, sort and prioritize them, and then act courageously to do what's best for students. And the truth is, though we don't always know what's best, we do tend to know what isn't working!

Cultivating an Adult Learning Culture

While navigating the complexity we have been discussing, a coach needs to focus simultaneously on cultivating an adult learning culture in the school. This usually involves changing some entrenched norms and challenging present schedules, use of time, ways of relating, and habits of mind—the leadership side of coaching.

Both the instructional and the leadership complexities should be considered in designing a coaching initiative. For coaching initiatives to have a transformative impact on the profession and student learning, we need to acknowledge the complexity of teaching, the fragmentation in our present system, the tendency toward mechanical fixes, and the unrealistic demand for immediate results. In designing a coaching initiative with a long-term vision, we have the opportunity to upgrade the teaching profession as a whole and bring it squarely into the twenty-first century. Our approach to designing such an initiative implies a profound trust that educators can solve the challenges education faces if we do so collaboratively. It also implies the willingness to invest in educators and the profession itself over the long haul.

DESIGNING COACHING INITIATIVES THAT HAVE TRANSFORMATIVE POTENTIAL

Here are some ideas for designing coaching initiatives that have the power to have a positive and lasting impact on both the professional culture in schools and instruction and learning. As a coach, you have the power to influence the design of an initiative, your role in it, and, over time, advocate for a more profound vision of coaching.

1. Include all players in the design process.

As we attempt to create an initiative that has the potential to transform school culture and systemically improve instruction, we will inevitably bump into cultural challenges and traditions that push back at our attempts to make change. One way to circumvent resistance to change is to bring together those players who will be impacted by the initiative, namely district administrators, principals, coaches, union leaders, and teachers, when designing a coaching initiative. Giving *voice* to those who will be expected to engage in the initiative is vital to its success. Principals, teacher leaders, and district-level staff should be brought together in various forums and invited to engage in dialogue over a sustained period of time (it usually takes at least a year) to consider the need for, purpose, and goals of coaching. As a team, they should engage with and be able to answer the question: *Three years from now, what is going to be different because of the coaching work we engage in?* The group should identify the benefits to be gained from coaching, the systems needed to enable coaching, and the trade-offs in time and resources (e.g., time out of classrooms for teachers or larger class sizes to pay for the new resource) required for coaching to have a positive impact on classroom practice and adult learning.

2. Examine Models of Coaching and Customize.

Defining what we mean by a specific term as concretely as possible is crucial because it ensures that we are all focused on accomplishing the same vision. Presently, "coaching" can mean many different things and coaches often perform a laundry list of tasks that are not particularly relevant to improving instruction and transforming culture (e.g., lunch duty, covering for teachers who are absent, distributing test prep materials, or data input). This generally results in coaching initiatives being less successful than anticipated and can sometimes result in coaches being cut when budgets are tight.

There are many models of coaching and many ideas about how coaches should spend their time. Choosing a coaching model that best serves a given school or district is important. Different models work better at different times in a change process. Although time constraints make examining different models of coaching difficult, we believe that doing so can have a big payoff in the long run.

A committee could be formed to investigate various models of coaching (e.g., peer coaching, instructional coaching, cognitive coaching, content coaching) and assess the present culture to determine what model of coaching would best serve present need. For example, peer coaching is often a good starting place. How often and formally are teachers now meeting to collaboratively plan a lesson? How often do teachers watch one another teach? If not very often, perhaps doing these things could precede a full-fledged content coaching approach or even an instructional coaching approach. The latter models require an outside consultant or designated coach to work with teachers on their practice before, during, and after lessons. Peer coaching—sometimes called "critical friends"—is a stepping stone to building the culture necessary for giving and receiving feedback focused on issues of practice. This model is often less threatening at first.

In contrast, content coaching is better implemented when teachers are already engaged in inquiry about their teaching and its impact on student learning. They are not only willing to look deeply at their practice but also at the content they teach. This does not mean that a content coach cannot be the one to build a coaching culture, but when she is doing so she will be employing tools from cognitive or peer coaching models to ready the field for a rigorous content focus. Cognitive and peer coaching models pay a lot of attention to the building of relationships, which is critical to any coaching model.

3. Define roles.

A coaching initiative is not just about coaches, it is also about cultivating a coaching culture. We want all players to understand that they have a role to play in ensuring that the work of the coach results in improved instruction in every classroom. For example, the initiative might be designed so that coaches initially focus on potential lead teachers. Those lead teachers will then assist in spreading effective instructional practices and pedagogical content knowledge among the faculty in succeeding years. Or a theory of action might be to focus on a particular subject or particular grade levels in year one and then expand from there in years two and three.

The design team would need to flesh out who the relevant players are and what is expected of each player. What will teachers need to do differently once the coaching initiative is underway (e.g., use preparation periods to plan one lesson deeply with a coach; allow others into their classrooms while teaching and be open to receive feedback from peers)? What would principals need to do to ensure that the coaching work in their building gets results (e.g., set aside funds to hire subs to cover teachers who are engaged in a coaching cycle; meet with coaches to create schedules that include planning lessons and debriefing lessons with teachers)? (We discuss roles further in Chapter 3.)

4. Cultivate a common image and understanding of effective instruction and how to support its development.

Principals and coaches should find ways to spend a period or two a week, especially at the beginning of their work together, visiting classes and discussing their impressions of the teaching and evidence of learning they observed. They engage in this informal process to cultivate a common image of effective instruction. From these visits they can set appropriate goals for the staff as a whole. Principals and coaches also can use this time to identify potential teacher leaders, discuss the needs of individual teachers, determine which grade levels the coach will focus on, and name the practices they want to spread across the school.

5. Hire wisely.

Create clear criteria for the selection of coaches based on a lean and focused definition of the work of the coach. Develop a hiring process that includes, but is not limited to, coaches demonstrating their coaching abilities using role plays, videos of coaching sessions, or an actual coaching session with a teacher from the district. Ask coaches to self-assess in terms of the knowledge domains identified for successful coaching and identify in which domains they would benefit most from training (e.g., leadership skills, change process, content knowledge, instructional strategies, analysis of teacher needs, analysis of school culture, etc.). If coaches are unwilling to admit areas for their own growth and learning, they are probably not ready to lead others in doing so.

6. Provide ongoing training for coaches.

It is important to set aside time for coaches to receive ongoing training in a collaborative coaching community. During this training time, they work on identified knowledge domains of coaching. Principals are informed when coaches will meet every week, and therefore do not schedule coaching time in their schools during those periods.

What might high-quality training look like? In Virginia, one NSF-funded project required math specialists (i.e., coaches) to take five content courses and training in leadership as part of their jobs (Campbell and Malkus 2011). In Community School District 2, where one of the authors was Director of Mathematics and spearheaded a highly-successful coaching initiative, teacher leaders and coaches not only took several content and pedagogical content courses, they also had seminars focused on leadership, change theory, communication skills, and negotiation skills.

In our experience, it is the rare district that adequately prepares coaches for the challenges of their roles—especially the leadership aspects. We encourage coaches to avail themselves of opportunities outside of their districts, such as institutes and seminars on various models and approaches to coaching, leadership skills, content and pedagogical content knowledge, assessment, and so on. In other words, coaches are self-motivated learners. They self-assess the areas in which they need to grow and pursue opportunities to assist their growth. They can advocate for themselves by asking that their districts provide financial support and/or time to take advantage of useful offerings outside of the district.

7. Set clear lines of supervision.

Determine who will supervise and evaluate coaches and the criteria used for doing so. It is often best to centralize the coaching effort: coaches report to someone at the *district* level who is knowledgeable about instruction and experienced in leading a change initiative (ideally someone who has also been a coach or professional developer at one time). Centralizing supervision is more likely to result in a coherent approach to coaching and eliminates some of the idiosyncratic practices that can emerge in districts where coaches report directly to principals. Principals who have never worked with or supervised coaches are often unclear about how to get the most leverage from them. Sometimes principals inadvertently require coaches to engage in activities that will not necessarily improve instruction or transform culture (e.g., bus duty, substituting for absent teachers). We advocate a partnership between principals and coaches, which also makes a supervisory role for principals problematic. Coaches need to be free to challenge a principal's perspective, policies, or requests.

Principals can be included in the supervision process by being asked about their perceptions of and experience working with the coach assigned to their building. Together the principal and district supervisor can determine if the coach is a good match for the school. If benchmarks of progress are laid out, input from principals can be very useful in determining the effectiveness of the coaches working in their schools.

8. Create a long-term plan.

A strategic, long-term action plan (e.g., 3–5 years) for introducing and scaling up the coaching initiative that includes the development of teacher leadership is essential. This plan needs to have a clear vision of the end result of the coaching initiative (e.g., *Three years from now, what is going to be different because of the coaching work we do?*). One possible vision is that at some point every adult will be coaching and being coached because the goal is to develop a culture in which adults coach one another as a matter of course. Anyone who wants to make a difference is a leader, no matter their title. In this case, leader and coach might be considered synonymous. What would coaches have to do in years one and two to ensure that in year three a full-blown coaching culture is thriving?

9. Determine short-term action steps for beginning the process.

It is critical that short-term actions align with the long-term goal. For example, if coaches work exclusively with new and/or struggling teachers in year one, the message sent is clear: Coaches are for those who don't know or can't do. This is exactly the opposite message we would want to send. We want people to realize that coaching is an investment in their development as professionals, and that the entire profession benefits from that development. We want to invest in people who have the potential to succeed and are willing to do whatever it takes to upgrade instruction and learning. So instead of focusing on new or struggling teachers, we might first choose teachers whose practice we can leverage to assist all teachers to improve by eventually hosting collaboration site classrooms. This first round of teachers will, at the end of a year of sustained coaching, open their doors to their colleagues and their classrooms will become laboratories for further refining practice in the service of improved learning (e.g., study lessons).

Our point is that the teachers with whom the coach initially works should be selected based on criteria designed to meet the initiative's long-term goals. Start with teachers who are willing to learn and whose practice other teachers respect and you generate momentum. Coaching will be seen as an investment in those with potential, not a sanction against those who can't or don't know how.

Coaches might also work in year one with teams of teachers at grade-level meetings and thereby introduce everyone to the practice of collaboratively learning from and with each other. This paves the way for use of collaboration-site classrooms in year two and exposes everyone to new habits of planning.

Some of a coach's time can also be spent with new teachers or struggling teachers in year one, but focusing *solely* on these categories of teachers is highly unlikely to get the momentum needed to transform a culture. Sometimes, new or struggling teachers can be invited to sit in on coaching sessions with identified lead teachers and thus receive some of the benefits of coaching without jeopardizing the image of the coaching initiative. But don't try to focus on too many teachers at the beginning; you'll spread the work too thin and nothing substantive will be accomplished.

10. Set clear, focused, and specific goals at each school site.

Principals, the school leadership team (if there is one), coaches, and lead teachers will determine a short list of essential school-wide goals that align with district goals for improvement in a given content area or goals related to more widespread use of pedagogical strategies (e.g., widespread use of ELL techniques that benefit all learners or development of robust academic classroom discourse in all content areas). Once the leadership team has identified specific strategies they want to develop, you can focus the school-wide coaching work on these identified high-leverage goals. Having one, two, or at most three over-arching goals keeps the work focused and builds coherence among the staff. Find ways to make connections among initiatives and help teachers see that coaching is not another initiative so much as a process that can be used to integrate the initiatives already at play.

11. Differentiate professional learning opportunities based on the expressed and identified needs of each teacher.

Coaching is not a panacea. It is a tool that better serves some needs than others. For example, teachers who have fragile content knowledge in a given domain may initially benefit from taking a course rather than from working with a coach. Perhaps in conjunction with the course or after the course is completed, coaching could help them assimilate pedagogical content knowledge into new understanding of the content they have been studying and have to teach.

Coaches and principals work together with teachers to determine how to differentiate professional learning opportunities to meet the stated goals of the school. Coaching would be one option in a small menu of options offered (e.g., workshops, courses, inquiry groups, book studies, study lessons) to meet the needs of new or less skillful teachers and to develop lead teachers. What is non-negotiable is that *all* teachers are expected to participate in professional learning opportunities every year and, as a result, to show marked improvement in their craft.

12. Create consistent schedules and stick with them.

Creating effective schedules and sticking to them is a challenge for many coaches. The more consistent the schedule, the more likely the results, especially when the work revolves around the instructional core—planning, teaching, and debriefing lessons. For this reason, we believe that coaches should schedule at least eighty percent of their time around these activities. The rest of their time can be used for their own learning and for planning, documentation, and data analysis.

Create and test different formats, structures, and schedules to see which ones yield the best results in terms of improved instructional practices and improved student achievement. For example, use of grade-level meetings for collaborative lesson design facilitated by the coach can be combined with one-on-one planning, co-teaching, and debriefing sessions with designated teachers. This might mean that the coach works with the designated grade levels twice a month every month, meets with the same teachers at the same time every week for a given coaching cycle, and meets with the principal one period a week at the same time all year long.

13. Create sensible coaching cycles.

A coaching cycle is the duration of time a coach works with a given teacher or set of teachers. Coaching cycles must be defined and can vary depending on the goals. A cycle can mean meeting once per week all year to plan, teach, and debrief with potential teacher leaders (3 periods per week per teacher). Or a cycle can mean implementing one unit of study using the plan, teach, and debrief cycle with a grade level for the duration of the unit. What rarely works, however, are sporadic, ad hoc coaching sessions upon request from a teacher. There can be some flexibility in a coach's schedule for occasional time spent upon request from teachers that have not been selected to work with the coach on a regular basis. However, our experience has shown that strategically and consistently working with specific teachers or groups of teachers over time with a clear purpose and goal is by far the more effective way to schedule coaching time.

CONFIDENTIALITY

The confidentiality issue is often raised in relation to coaching. We take the stand that coaching is not therapy. It is a powerful process designed to improve professional capacity. When all players are involved in setting the parameters, formats, goals, and purpose of the work, then all players should also be kept in the loop of how things are progressing. Teachers should be invited to think alongside coaches and principals about how to improve both their teaching practice and the coaching process to ensure their students' success.

14. Set clear expectations and benchmarks of progress.

As part of setting clear expectations and establishing and assessing benchmarks of progress, principals should meet with coaches on a regular basis (e.g., weekly). This time can be used to select and invite teachers into the coaching process, to set benchmarks and determine progress, address issues, and establish goals and allocate time and resources to ensure success.

As part of this process, coaches, principals, and teachers working with the coach should meet together at the beginning, middle, and end of a coaching cycle to establish goals, determine benchmarks of progress for that specific teacher, address issues, and adjust strategies as needed. The backward design process you engaged in earlier will help you focus on the most critical issues. This three-way meeting lessens concerns about confidentiality and makes learning public. You can create protocols for addressing issues and concerns or use tuning protocols or other protocols such as those provided by the National School Reform Faculty at www.nsrfharmony.org. Before you begin, all the players involved should discuss how the work will be documented and what criteria will be used to determine success.

ASSESSING YOUR SITUATION

If the ideas laid out above were not part of the design process and/or are not presently common practices in your district or school, fear not. Most districts often employ coaches before they have thought through all aspects of the coaching initiative. Initiatives are a process, and refining and honing them is part of the process. Most initiatives raise issues and have unintended consequences that were not foreseen at the outset of the initiative. This too is just part of a change process. Coaches can play important roles in the change process by respectfully utilizing their circle of influence to inform administrators about how the initiative is working in the field.

Because of their unique position, coaches have the opportunity to make known to the powers that be what is and is not working in the schools. Coaches can advocate for improvements that would assist everyone in reaching the ultimate goal of improving the learning experiences of students. By sharing stories of success, obstacles, and dilemmas that people are facing in the schools coaches can make administrators aware of the consequences of their policies. By following those stories with potential solutions, useful suggestions, and creative ideas for addressing the dilemmas coaches can influence the process of change in healthy and productive ways.

Roles in a Coaching Initiative

I n this chapter we will briefly situate coaching in the big picture of education in the twenty-first century and spend the bulk of the chapter on the role of the coach and the supporting roles of principals, teachers, and the district in a successful coaching initiative.

SITUATING COACHING IN THE BIG PICTURE

Innovation in one place can become grist for the learning of the larger collective if word of these innovations is deliberately spread through professional conversation rather than through an authoritative mandate. Coaches have the potential to make sure that innovative practices inform the collective because they usually have conversations with many teachers and administrators in more than one school. In many districts coaches network with one another and when they do so, their conversations can seed promising innovations across the district.

Professionalizing Teaching

Coaching has the potential to professionalize teaching by helping to identify and spread skilled pedagogical practices informed by recent research in fields like cognitive science, brain research, social psychology, and so forth. By helping to name and cultivate the practices that are at the heart of great teaching, coaching can help lift teaching to a more respected place among professions in the US. Harvard professor Richard Elmore, whose specialty is school reform, notes:

> What educators don't have are explicitly shared practices which is what
> distinguishes educators from other professionals ... practice ... a set of

protocols and processes for observing, analyzing, discussing, and understanding instruction that can be used to improve student learning at scale . . . Practice . . . creates a common discipline and focus among practitioners with a common purpose and set of problems. (City et al. 2009, 4)

Skillful teaching doesn't come in a box and it cannot be mandated. It must be cultivated. Who better than coaches, the Johnny Appleseeds of education, to begin the process of codifying and spreading shared practices across the profession? Coaches, when they work in classrooms, stay informed of the research, stay focused on the instructional core, and interact with teachers and administrators across schools, have a better probability of spreading effective instructional practices than any other role in our present system. When coaches work side-by-side with teachers, they can influence real-time teaching practice. This is the hardest thing to influence through policy or programs.

Uplifting our status as a profession is a tall order, but we believe coaching is a process that can be used at every level of the system in a strategic and systematic way to substantively improve the culture and practices in education. This implies that the practice of coaching must also be professionalized, employing agreed-upon methods, principles, and theories in practice. The most important thing is to stay focused on what does matter—learning. "Learning is the work!" as Michael Fullan has concluded (2011).

How Should Coaches Support New Teachers?

Many teachers have insufficient training. Too many US elementary teachers do not feel confident in their understanding of mathematics or science or even social studies. How could they when many preservice teachers are required to take *only* one course in each subject to get their elementary teaching license? Many middle school teachers work under elementary licenses. Even though they may be assigned to teach a particular subject, they may not have expertise in that academic domain. Is this degree of training sufficient for teachers to meet the expectations of the Common Core State Standards or to teach in ways that motivate and engage a diverse student population? Where will they get the training they need to meet the changing demands of education?

Many incoming teachers do not have experience managing a class of thirty children, especially if they came through alternative programs like Teach For America. Even if they attended a university teacher education program, they may have had minimal student teaching experience during which they were required to manage a class for an extended period of time or teach more than one subject or more than a small group of students. Talking about pedagogy in a university course and actually practicing effective instructional strategies in a classroom are two very different things. How will they expand their limited pedagogical repertoire once they have their own class, when it is still rare for teachers to observe one another during the act of teaching?

When teachers enter the profession ill equipped to handle the complex demands of the classroom, districts are faced with having to provide additional training. This is not an easy task or one most districts are well equipped to handle. One way to begin providing this training is through the strategic use of coaches. While this may seem like a contradiction to what we said earlier, the emphasis is on *strategic*. If coaches focus *first* on refining the skills of knowledgeable teachers who can quickly (within one year) become teacher leaders, then using a combination coaching/teacher leader model will have the greatest potential to address the needs of new teachers (assuming the district does not have a separate mentoring or apprenticeship program for incoming teachers). In addition, coaches can work with small groups of teachers to increase teacher skill and decrease teacher anxiety by using the lead teacher's classroom as a collaboration site. With the support of the principal, who can provide coverage for say three or four teachers a few times a year, coaches can assist these teachers to plan, implement, and reflect on lessons in real time, offer suggestions, model techniques, and also assist with deciphering what supports specific children may need. Using this small group format, which can be launched during a grade-level meeting, coaches can introduce the entire staff to the coaching process and occasionally immerse them in the process depending on how creative the principal and coach can be in terms of carving out time for coverage. Once the participating teachers have observed or participated in a co-planning, teaching, and debriefing cycle they can then teach the collaboratively planned lesson in their own classes with or without observation from the lead teacher, coach, or a peer. This process begins to cultivate a coaching culture and provides some support for all teachers while focusing the coach's efforts on potential lead teachers. In year two, lead teachers can facilitate grade-level meetings in which teachers collaboratively plan a lesson together.

When coaching is designed well coaches can help semi-skilled teachers as well as skilled educators refine their practice on the job in all essential areas—pedagogy, management, assessment, and content—and help to ensure that every student is working with a highly-qualified, caring teacher. By designing, implementing, and reflecting on lessons at grade-level meetings coaches can build a collaborative culture and robust habits of lesson planning. These are the typical definitions of what coaches do. They work on-site, side-by-side with teachers.

Coaches can also help deepen teachers' content understanding through study groups, institutes, and seminars. While these activities are not actual coaching sessions, we believe that knowledgeable coaches provide these services as part of their role. They are well positioned to determine what content teachers may need to learn more deeply and bring that need to the attention of the district. The coach can then design and implement content workshops or other formats that best serve the professional community or recommend a consultant who can meet the needs of the district.

Self-Monitoring

Coaches can contribute to the development of the teaching profession as a full-fledged profession by helping to establish ways for educators to self-monitor their work from within the profession. Self-monitoring is a feature of other highly respected professions that is lacking in our profession (Tell 2001). The American Medical Association monitors the work of doctors and the American Bar Association monitors the work of lawyers. Each profession has quality standards that permeate the entire profession. In education today, most teachers still work in isolation, conducting their classes according to their personal preferences, independently planning lessons and idiosyncratically grading student work according to their own values and biases. While we believe teachers should have latitude in classroom management, lesson design, and pedagogical strategies, we know from experience that teaching is both an art and a science and often the science is relegated to second fiddle. Perhaps we need to perfect the science in order to exercise the art with skill. Like all great artists, skill precedes style. Coaches are poised to bring the science of teaching to the fore by focusing on the instructional core and by working collaboratively with groups of teachers within schools.

As teachers, with the help of knowledgeable coaches, begin to establish agreed upon norms and polish and spread effective practices across schools and districts they can begin to forge new relationships with administration. In today's climate of top-down evaluation, teachers need to become more articulate and skillful in engaging with administrators and focus on developing a shared lens for understanding the characteristics of effective lessons in action as evidenced by student learning. The coach can be instrumental in forging these new relationships.

THE DAY-TO-DAY ROLE OF THE COACH

The coach's role is to ensure that there is a skilled and effective teacher in every classroom by cultivating a coherent set of instructional practices among the faculty. The coach, in partnership with teachers and administrators, can craft and implement professional learning opportunities that revolve around the instructional core, including deepening content knowledge and keeping everyone focused on learning. The coach, using a variety of formats, can seed and cultivate adult learning in schools and districts. In so doing, coaches must also use their power of influence to invite administrators into the learning process and act as their partners. They can assist administrators to develop the capacity to assess the content and pedagogical content knowledge at play in a lesson, encourage administrators to invite teachers into this process, identify which teachers are reflective and skillful in ways that can assist colleagues to improve, and engender lines of communication between principal and faculty that keep everyone focused on learning. Here the coach is wearing the hat of agent of change focused on transforming culture.

This work takes many forms and can happen in different formats and forums. The key is to be crystal clear about what a coach does and does not do.

What a Coach Does

Below we describe the specific activities we believe a coach should engage in.

> ▸ **Assess and analyze the needs of the staff as a whole; assess and analyze the individual needs and strengths of each teacher.** This assessment is best done in collaboration with principals and can be done by providing teachers with a short self-survey focused on professional learning. The critical question is: What do you want to learn this year to improve your practice? The survey might list individual content areas such as math, science, social studies, etc. and ask questions about confidence in teaching in each content area. To determine what informal professional relationships are at play, the survey might include questions such as: Whom do you enjoy working with on staff? Which teachers do you plan with outside of grade-level meetings? The survey might also offer a short list of high-leverage goals teachers can select from (see Appendix D for more on goal setting). The goals focus on essential areas of growth, such as: learning to plan lessons that center on big ideas or essential questions in a given content area, learning to orchestrate robust academic discourse among students, improving student capacity to articulate their ideas verbally and in writing, and learning to provide specific, actionable, and timely feedback using an iterative cycle.
>
> Using information from the survey, classroom observations, and conversations with individual teachers, the coach and principal can create a long-term plan to address the goals and needs of each teacher on staff. The plan should capitalize on existing relationships and individual teacher strengths. It should also align with the major goals of the school/district.
>
> ▸ **Strategically select teachers for support and development in collaboration with the principal.** There are essentially three categories of teachers we might work with: new teachers, experienced teachers willing to learn and share, and teachers whose practice is cause for concern. As we described in Chapter 2, we take a counterintuitive approach and start with willing experienced learners. This is because we want to keep the bigger picture in mind—upgrading the profession by ensuring that all teachers are highly skilled. Teachers with five to fifteen years of experience are in the prime of their careers. If they are learners,

they can impact the work of many colleagues during their remaining years in education. Thus we start with them and develop their capacity to influence others.

Coaches may also work with new teachers in year one as described above, but the larger idea is that the cadre of lead teachers focused on in year one will take newer teachers under their wing in year two. Often a peer coach can have a greater impact on new teachers than the designated coach because the peer coach has just one or two colleagues to work with and can devote more time and energy to an individual colleague or two, as opposed to the coach who works with many teachers and does not have a class of her own to use as a laboratory with fledgling teachers. Peer coaching frees the coach to focus on the next cadre of potential teacher leaders.

What about veteran teachers who need to improve or are reluctant to try new teaching strategies? We believe they should not be denied the opportunity to be coached. However, they should not take up the bulk of a coach's time. Even though coaching ineffective or reluctant teachers may be helpful to teachers in need of improvement, insisting a coach spend a lot of time with them one-on-one can be counterproductive to the long-term coaching initiative. Ineffective teachers are not likely to improve quickly enough to support others, thus limiting the impact of the coaching initiative. Working *only* with teachers in need of improvement perpetuates the notion that coaching is only for unskilled teachers. Teachers in need of improvement are often the most guarded and defensive, and can be energy drainers to coaches— sustaining and building energy and momentum is critical for the success of a coaching initiative.

One way to support ineffective or reluctant teachers is to include them in small-group professional learning sessions (e.g., study lessons, grade-level meetings). This is often a better beginning step than one-on-one approaches because their colleagues will be engaging in processes that are likely to entice the recalcitrant teacher to join the team. Being rejected by one's peers is a powerful deterrent and is likely to ensure that the teacher in question keeps at least some of the commitments made by the team. Once these teachers are part of the team, the coach can work with them one-on-one, especially if that is the protocol established by the team. If all team members agree to one-on-one coaching in relation to a collaboratively planned lesson, for example, then the teacher in need of improvement does not lose face to agree to her turn at bat.

When thinking about which teachers to start with, consider that the goal is to build momentum and sustainability into the design. Look for teachers who are learners, who are willing to share, and whose practice is already effective. Let the teachers you select know that you think they are good teachers and potential leaders and would like to invest in them, to engage them in coaching to both improve their practice and build their capacity as leaders. Also let them know upfront that we expect them to turn around and support others down the road.

▶ **Build a cadre of teacher leaders and work to develop their classrooms into collaboration sites.** Use coach time to encourage and focus the work of buddy teachers; this can double the coach's impact. You can start by taking advantage of existing informal relationships. Thus, if you begin with experienced teachers who are willing to learn and share and then find ways to invite a colleague to sit in on the planning sessions or to observe the co-planned lesson you will capitalize on their collegial relationship. Providing time for the first round of teachers to meet with those they already informally plan with seeds the culture of collaboration and nurtures distributed leadership. After a while the principal can gradually ask lead teachers to facilitate grade-level meetings or to take a new teacher or two under their wing and help them plan or provide feedback after observing a lesson. (It is imperative that when teachers are asked to take on these extra responsibilities something is removed from their plate. Asking them to add coaching to a full teaching load often results in their coaching falling by the wayside.)

The coach needs to focus on developing and spreading collaborative cultures, seeing the potential in others and working collaboratively with them to release their creativity and know-how. In particular, we suggest developing lab-site classrooms or collaboration-site classrooms. We use these terms to reinforce the idea that teaching is highly complex and we need to collaborate with one another to increase our collective knowledge. We avoid the term "model classrooms" because this connotes the idea that the lab-site teacher will model "best practice" for others, which can make them feel expected to implement it whether or not they understand or agree with it rather than engage with others in thinking deeply about teaching and learning. Model classrooms are part of a competitive structure, whereas collaboration sites are part of an inquiry approach to professional learning.

In this scenario the teacher leader would be coached publicly by the coach, with colleagues invited to witness and/or contribute to the coaching session (plan, teach, and debrief a lesson). This is a powerful way to de-privatize teaching and to spread promising instructional practices. After this initial stage, in year two or so, we imagine small groups of teachers being given the time to meet with the lead teacher (with or without a coach present) to plan a lesson, watch the lead teacher (and coach) enact the lesson, and debrief the lesson in constructive ways that influence teaching practice. The participating teachers then agree to teach the refined lesson in their own classes with either the lead teacher or coach observing and providing feedback. The giving and receiving of constructive feedback is critical for real progress to take place.

▸ **Use student-performance data and teacher-identified goals to find mutual purpose and set personalized goals.** Use information gathered from the survey mentioned previously or through an interview to set a mutual, high-leverage goal or two with each teacher you work with. The goal should be clearly defined and focus on some aspect of the instructional core. It should be specific, descriptive, and involve both process and content. Here is an example of a high-leverage goal that focuses on both content and process: *Identify and incorporate big ideas into lesson plans (content) and increase student academic discourse (process).* Consider benchmarks of progress by asking one another, "How will we know we are making progress?" (See Appendix D.)

▸ **Plan and design lessons and/or units of study collaboratively with individual teachers or in pairs or small groups.** In our view, lesson design is one of the key areas in which many teachers need assistance. Because many teachers think that the lesson plan *is* what is written in their curriculum materials or packaged programs, it is important to help them distinguish what constitutes mindful rather than mechanical lesson planning. Also, when practitioners collaboratively plan lessons using appropriate guiding questions or processes it is more likely that they will internalize these and essentially develop new habits of mind (see Appendix A for updated Guide to Core Issues).

▸ **Co-teach lessons with teachers.** Coaches should be willing to teach the lessons they help design. This means that, when asked, they are able to model the lesson they are planning with teachers. However, in content coaching we do our best to quickly get teachers co-teaching with us because we do not want to create dependency on the coach. When not modeling, coaches should be co-teaching, working side-by-side with teachers and coaching in the moment as needed. Proximity allows us to model specific teaching moves in the moment as necessary. Learning to stay close together during the teaching of a lesson, conferring with one another along the way, sometimes one taking the lead and sometimes the other, is at the heart of content coaching. This kind of co-teaching requires skill, trust, discipline, and focus on the part of the coach.

It is rare for a content coach to teach an entire lesson, except at the very beginning of a coaching relationship, because the coach and teacher should be focused on specifics (e.g., when to ask students to think-pair-share). Watching an entire lesson may give a teacher a sense of the whole process and confidence that her students can indeed do what is being asked of them, but it will not likely give her specific moves to practice. Focusing on the essential elements takes practice and is often best done in small sequences or in the moment in response to something that occurs in class.

➤ **Debrief lessons and provide actionable feedback to teachers; then follow up with teachers to ensure carry through.** After each coached lesson the teacher and coach should debrief and reflect. The postconference is where the coach and teacher pinpoint the specific improvements in practice they are aiming for. By the end of the reflection time they should determine one or two specific things the teacher will try between coaching sessions and agree on what evidence they will collect to document the attempts to implement the new skills. For example, if the goal is to work on improving how the teacher launches lessons, she can videotape herself launching a lesson in which she is trying to incorporate the coach's suggestion to contextualize or personalize the launch. At the next coaching session she and the coach can analyze the video looking for her incorporation of the suggestion and work together to refine the practice further. If a teacher agrees to work on remembering to name the big ideas or essential questions when planning a lesson, she can give the coach a copy of the lessons she planned between coaching sessions.

➤ **Plan and facilitate professional learning opportunities for all forums in which teachers meet.** An important strategy for developing a collaborative learning culture is to utilize every structure presently employed by the school to bring teachers together: grade-level meetings, department meetings, professional learning communities, and faculty meetings. During these various forums, the whole staff or subsets of the faculty can at least be exposed to the in-depth work that is happening with specific teachers.

Time is precious; the coach should carefully plan meetings and be very realistic and specific in setting goals. For example, if a grade-level meeting happens once a week for about 40 minutes, then the coach should ask herself, "What can be accomplished in 30 minutes that will leave the kind of residue that will continue to stimulate thinking and improvement?" We've found two techniques helpful.

First, select one high-leverage activity and do that one thing in depth for the entire meeting. You might plan *one* lesson together rather than skim over the lessons coming up in the next few days. Or you might study one or two samples of student work in depth to develop a lens for looking at all the student work. Maybe consider specific, individualized feedback that would motivate the student(s) to stretch into the next level of learning.

Second, keep the focus consistent. Don't plan a lesson one week, look at student work the next, look at data the next, change content areas each week, etc. Get good at something over a period of time and then move on to another practice and master that. One exception to this might be if the team plans a lesson one week, implements it during the week, and brings student work back to the team the following week for analysis. That cycle of plan, teach, study student work can work well if teams meet consistently and agree to teach the same lesson within a short time frame.

Coaches may move from one-on-one coaching as their predominant activity to more frequent study lessons with small groups, using the classrooms of lead teachers to benefit the practice of visiting teachers. They may come to see that a large group of teachers needs specific content knowledge and facilitate a study group to address this need. As long as coaches keep the tenets of effective professional development in mind and stay true to their purpose of improving instruction and learning they can invent forums and formats that keep them and the teachers they work with on the journey to success.

‣   **Create and implement professional development menus to supplement coaching.** Coaching alone is not going to address all of the learning needs of the teachers on the staff, especially if content knowledge needs to be strengthened. Therefore, coaches, with help from lead teachers, the principal, and/or the district, should also create a menu of other forms of professional learning designed to address things coaching does not address in depth. Here's where mini-courses, study groups, seminars, and so forth can be offered during school or outside of school hours.

Content knowledge is not generally developed to any depth during coaching sessions. You can provide a thimbleful of mathematics or science content in a planning session—enough to get the teacher through a lesson with a bit more confidence. However, at some point teachers who don't know the content they are expected to teach will need to take workshops, classes, or summer institutes to dive into the content. The coach can then work with them to implement their new knowledge into their lesson designs or units of study. In addition, if possible, the district should negotiate with the provider of the content seminars or workshops to "apprentice" the coaches in planning, implementing, and debriefing the seminars or workshops provided in order to develop the capacity of the coaching home team.

It's important for the coach to invite teachers to co-plan and eventually co-facilitate study groups, study lessons, workshops, and courses. When one of the authors was Director of Mathematics in Community School District 2 in NYC, she insisted that the coaches work in pairs when planning workshops. Each coach in the pair selected two teacher leaders as apprentices. Together these six people co-planned the workshop. The apprentices took copious notes during the first offering of the workshop. The team debriefed and refined the plan of the workshop. The next time the workshop was offered the team split into groups of three—one coach and two lead teachers—and each team then taught a session of the workshop. This time the coach did less of the teaching and more of the note taking. After the second iteration, any pair of people from the original team of six could co-facilitate the workshop. If one or more of these people left the district for any reason, there were still several people who could provide the workshop in the following year. Building capacity means investing upfront in people and being very deliberate about how things are done in the short term to ensure success in the long term.

▸ **Maintain trust and open lines of communication.** Many teachers worry that coaches are the eyes and ears of administrators. Desire for confidentiality also stems from fear of exposure or of admitting we don't know how to teach something in a culture that expects that teachers right out of college should be equipped to teach all subjects to all children well. Coaches, administrators, and teachers must work with one another, blur the boundaries between roles, and offer support from a place of trust and respect. Every adult can learn and has something to contribute. None of us have yet figured out how to ensure the success of every student. Admitting what we don't know and questing collaboratively to invent possible solutions is the work.

One simple step toward working together more effectively is for the principal, coach, and teacher to meet together initially to discuss the learning goals and to identify relevant benchmarks of progress. It is also helpful for the team to discuss the coaching process before the coaching cycle begins so that the teacher understands that the goal is not punitive, but rather a means of supporting development—an investment in her career. In these meetings, the teacher should also be given voice so that she can set relevant goals that matter to her. The team—principal, coach, teacher—might also discuss what to do if a disagreement or problem arises between coach and teacher. The team can agree to meet again mid-cycle and at the end of the cycle to check in with one another and to reflect and tweak the plan and goals as needed.

▸ **Document the work and keep progress logs with teacher input.** To many, documentation begins to fall into the arena of evaluation. This is an

COACH NOTE

Coaches often seem to be in no man's land because they are not supervisors and they are not classroom teachers. Teachers often see them as aligned with supervisors and supervisors often see them as aligned with teachers. This tension in how the role is viewed is part of what needs to be considered and attended to in the initial design of the coaching initiative. We'll discuss this tension further later in the chapter.

idea we need to reconsider. If we don't document what we are doing, if we are unable to name signs of progress, how do we (and others) know if we are being successful? Documentation of our work and effectiveness becomes especially critical in budget crunch time when programs and positions are eliminated. Without evidence, how do we convince people that our jobs as coaches are critical to the advancement of the profession and enhancement of student learning?

Documentation is important for other reasons as well. Without it, how will we remember what worked and what didn't? How will we remember what we did with different teachers and how we can build upon it? Surely there must be some way we can document our work without falling into the trap of formally evaluating teachers. This is something we think districts and schools will need to discuss and work out. Coaches are not formal evaluators, more like bridges between the administrators and teachers. Transparency on the part of all players and discussion about specific concerns, agreements, protocols, and so forth can lead to an agreement about documenting the work in a way that benefits all.

We do not yet have clearly delineated coaching effectiveness tools that can be used to evaluate a coach's effectiveness. We would be wise to take a proactive stance and attempt to identify both qualitative and quantitative evidence that would point to coaching success. We do not yet have useful documentation to name the incremental stages of teacher improvement (a teacher developmental landscape, if you will), though new tools for teacher evaluation have recently entered the arena. Charlotte Danielson (2013) and Robert Marzano (2013) have created rubrics for assessing teaching. These rubrics are becoming very popular across many districts. Perhaps the use of these rubrics in conjunction with setting personalized goals for teachers and providing related support, such as coaching, is a possible way to begin. We would caution, however, that these rubrics are not panaceas. They are tools that are relatively new and just being tested on a wide scale. They are also associated with teacher evaluation, which might mean unions could oppose their use in conjunction with coaching.

In any event, we should look to what has been published and study the proposed rubrics with a critical eye to see what actually resonates in practice. Just as with curriculum materials, we want to work with rubrics mindfully not mechanically, from a stance of inquiry, and test their relevance and usefulness. The Danielson rubric has four domains: Planning and Preparation, The Classroom Environment, Instruction, and Professional Responsibilities. Each domain has several components and each component is ranked from unsatisfactory to basic to proficient to distinguished. The descriptions of each component are shorthand for what we might value in classrooms as evidence of effective teaching. However, as Elmore and colleagues have stated,

> It is now fairly typical for principals, coaches, and professional developers to periodically enter teachers' classrooms for various purposes. It is not typical for these various parties to have a common definition of what they are looking for. (City et al 2009, 7)

Rubrics may be a step in the direction of helping us define what we are looking for, but aligning our interpretations of what we witness in practice is another matter and part of the dilemma of codifying practice to meet the criteria of high status professions.

▸ **Provide feedback to district-level administrators.** Just as coaches need to act as bridges between principals and teachers, they also can be bridges that connect school administrators to district administrators. Coaches can provide information about how to improve the work in the school, what additional supplies or supports are needed, what programs are burdensome or missing the mark, which teachers are emerging as leaders, and which classrooms are now open to inter-visitations from teachers and how to use them to spread the work across the district. They can tactfully raise issues that the district might need to reconsider, like conflicting messages in the field, or scheduling conflicts. Because of their unique interactions within the system and because they are not in positions of authority, but do have influence, coaches have a valuable role to play in providing feedback loops to all parts and levels of the system.

What Coaches Should Not Do

Many coaches are saddled with a laundry list of tasks that have nothing to do with the kind of coaching that improves teaching and learning: distributing testing or curriculum materials, inputting data, lunch duty, bus duty, assistance with administrative report writing, and so on. These activities may need to get done, but when principals assign them to coaches, coaches simply cannot focus on their primary purpose.

Classroom teachers can also miss the point when they see coaches as an extra teacher who can work with a small group of students while the classroom teacher works with other groups of students. (What is the teacher learning when the coach is working with a small group of students on the other side of the classroom?) Coaches can also diminish their impact when they spend inordinate amounts of time gathering materials, running

DATA

To clarify our stance on data, there is a difference between data input, which is something a clerk can do, and data analysis. While data analysis is something a coach might engage in, it is important to make sure that the data is timely, actionable, and relevant. This is especially true because we live in a world of data overload. One of the authors worked with a coach a week after the coach met with a teacher. The coach and teacher went over the interim test data and realized where they needed to make some changes. The next week, before there was any evidence that any of the changes had been made, the coach planned to go over a new set of data with the same teacher! Wouldn't it be more beneficial to take action on the data from last week than to look at additional data this week?

It is so much easier to keep looking at data than it is to change practice—which is the purpose of effective coaching. We suggest that coaches roll up their sleeves, plan a lesson based on analyzing last week's data, co-teach the lesson, and reflect on the student work samples to see if any progress was made. (Student work samples are relevant, timely data that should be used to guide instruction.) This cycle may need to repeat a few times before the team will be ready to look at additional standardized data.

off worksheets, or rewriting curriculum units instead of actually coaching. These tasks do not support the goal of transforming idiosyncratic approaches in teaching to more coherent and effective pedagogy. Plus, since coaches generally tend to be more senior staff, it costs the system more money to have them spend time doing unskilled tasks that lesser paid employees can easily accomplish. One solution might be to consider who on staff could do these tasks (e.g., a secretary can distribute materials or input data and an aide can work with a small group of students) without taking time away from the coach's main role of improving instruction.

In some instances principals assign lunch or bus duty because teachers have complained that coaches are not required to take on these duties and teachers, who are also busy professionals, are required to do so. Coaches should acknowledge this dilemma and advocate for themselves. They might argue that bus or lunch duty time slots are precisely when teachers not assigned to those duties may be available to meet with the coach. Coaches might also work in collaboration with principals and teachers to find creative solutions to the conflict.

When coaches work full time in one school, they are more likely to be assigned tasks unrelated to coaching. (This is especially true if coaching is seen as a voluntary support provided at a teacher's request rather than an essential process in which everyone needs to engage. If the coach is seen as a critical member of the learning community, her time is more apt to be valued and respected.) We tend to recommend that coaches work between two schools and report to someone at the district office. When a principal has the coach's services for two days instead of five, she will likely make more strategic use of the coach's time. When the coach reports to the district office and not the principal, there is more likely to be some consistency in what a coach's responsibilities are in each school in the district.

THE ROLE OF THE PRINCIPAL

Where does the principal fit in this picture? Principals are encouraged to be "instructional leaders," but their job descriptions are too packed with managerial and bureaucratic obligations to devote the kind of time and attention it would take to facilitate professional growth of each individual teacher and the faculty as a whole. Principals may coach individual teachers and use a coaching style of leadership when interacting with staff, but that is not their primary function in today's schools.

A coach can really assist a principal in her role as instructional leader, but only if the principal is willing to see the coach as a partner rather than as a subordinate, and recognize the potential influence a coach can have on the faculty. If the principal is willing to learn from and with the coach she will gain the respect of the staff and simultaneously make a strong statement about the importance of being coached. If the principal is willing to think aloud and share information with the coach as they work together to support the faculty—in other words, is transparent in her decision-making process—then both will be pleasantly surprised by their success.

To co-create a partnership relationship with the principal requires taking a proactive stance. It means seeing oneself as a leader who exercises influence, albeit without a traditional kind of authority. One very real way a principal can assist in building the coach's identity as leader is including the coach on the leadership team in the school even if the coach works only part-time in that school.

Aligning and Communicating Goals and Vision

As they begin their dialogue, principals and coaches will notice where they have similar opinions about what they are observing and where their differences lie. Coaches and principals must come to some common understanding of what success looks, feels, and sounds like in that particular school, and agree on terminology and tools. Knowledgeable coaches, particularly those who are knowledgeable in content areas in which the principal is less so, are great assets to principals who are trying to learn to distinguish effective from less effective lessons. Principals who recognize and use the expertise of coaches and lead teachers can go a long way in both cultivating a coaching culture and in ensuring highly effective instruction is occurring in all classes.

Taking the Pulse

Coach and principal will find it useful to visit each classroom in the school together. This can begin as a search for potential lead teachers. The principal can take the coach to visit teachers she believes are doing the best job in the school. As part of this process they should spend at least 15 minutes in each room focusing on evidence of student learning and instructional strategies at play, taking note of the tasks offered students, and verbatim notes of the actual discourse. The principal and the coach can compare notes, share impressions, and begin to understand each other's values, strengths, and goals. In addition, this information sets the stage for thinking about where to begin the work. Do the principal and the coach agree on which teachers have a practice closest to what they want all teachers to develop? In other words, do they agree on the "treasures"? Don't be surprised if the principal and the coach disagree on which teachers have worthy practice. It is part of the work to align images and consider the value of each perspective. It is also this very crucial aspect of the work that is often skipped over.

Setting the Tone and Creating the Climate for Coaching

The principal is instrumental in setting the stage for coaching. She needs to inform the faculty that each individual is expected to set professional learning goals for the year and participate in professional learning opportunities designed to help them meet their goals. Coaching may be one option of a short menu of options to achieve their individual goals. (The survey mentioned earlier in the chapter could be one way to get the ball rolling.)

Principals should also share with the faculty the long-term goals for developing pedagogical coherence across the school, for cultivating a collaborative culture, and for developing teacher leadership. Principals might ask for volunteers interested in working with the coach and inform the staff that she will also be tapping some teachers on the shoulder to encourage them to work with the coach. Principals will also need to inform teachers about the three-period coaching cycle that will be used and work with teachers to carve out time for coaching. She should also let teachers know that the coach will be facilitating some grade-level or departmental meetings and the principal will be attending some of those meetings and soliciting feedback from teachers related to the relevance and focus of the meetings. In other words, the principal needs to put her weight behind the coaching initiative and set clear, high expectations for participation in the work. She must also solicit input from teachers to ensure the relevance and practicality of the design of the work to ensure teacher commitment in the coaching process.

Hiring, Supporting, Encouraging, Promoting

Perhaps one of the most important tasks the principal has is hiring teachers. She may do this in conjunction with a teacher committee, but in the end she is responsible to ensure that every teacher hired to work at the school takes a learning stance and is willing to work at refining her craft over time. Each new hire should work with a coach or lead teacher to ensure their successful assimilation into a coaching culture. New teachers and experienced teachers who are new to a school should systematically be brought into the coaching culture. After the initial launch of a coaching initiative, during which coaches are cultivating leaders, the second most important job of coaches is to ensure that those new to the profession are supported to the degree that they can hold themselves responsible to meet the high expectations of a committed professional.

It is incumbent upon the principal to schedule an initial three-way conversation with the coach and each teacher being coached to establish protocols, schedules, goals, and expectations and to secure a commitment from the teacher to participate fully in the work. Full participation means coming to planning sessions on time, being prepared to discuss and plan the lesson, co-teaching the lesson with the coach, and sitting down after the lesson to reflect upon its effectiveness. It also means setting goals for improving practice and trying to implement some or all of the suggestions offered in coaching sessions. A three-part coaching cycle can be accomplished within the school day or in a twenty-four-hour period if the principal provides coverage. Planning or reflecting sessions can also happen after or before the school day according to the union contract.

The principal should schedule a weekly or twice-monthly meeting with the coach to assess progress, handle scheduling issues, and refocus the work if needed. The faculty should know that these meetings take place and that they are designed to ensure that everyone is receiving the support they need to meet their individual professional goals and collective faculty goals. Transparency goes a long way in building trust. The principal should take care not to use the conversations in ways that might result in teachers feeling unsafe and causing them to back away from the coaching process. In other words, the principal must encourage teachers to take informed risks, try on new practices, and assure them that she knows that it will take time to master the recommended improvements or new strategies. She also needs to recognize and celebrate individual teachers' successes—however small they may be.

When difficulties arise (e.g., a teacher is often late, unprepared, misses coaching appointments, etc.), if the coach is unsuccessful in resolving the problem directly with the teacher, the principal should address the issues with the teacher in a timely manner. It is often best to have a three-way discussion with the teacher and coach; this kind of meeting allows the team to ferret out the real issues and work through them. This requires the capacity and willingness to have difficult conversations and for everyone to acknowledge their part in the problem and find solutions in order for the work to progress.

Scheduling

Scheduling is often challenging because time is at a premium and school schedules are complex and usually overcrowded. Some principals use substitutes on a regular basis to cover teachers for the pre- and postconferences; others schedule an additional preparation period for one of the two conferences and expect teachers to use one of their daily preparation periods for the other. The most important thing is that the schedule is consistent and coverage is provided when appropriate. It is also important to let participating teachers know that their time is valued, that an investment is being made—whether through additional preps or by having substitutes—and they need to make a reciprocal investment in their professional advancement. They are not "giving up" a preparation period, they are using it to prepare a lesson with the assistance of a knowledgeable other. They are investing their time in improving their craft.

In addition, principals must not demand that everyone teach the same content at the same time of day. If everyone is expected to teach math first thing in the afternoon, then what is the literacy coach expected to do during that time? Flexibility is the name of the game. Even if a principal insists that literacy must be taught for 90 minutes each morning, she can exempt specific teachers from teaching at a given time in order to have those teachers work with the math coach on regularly scheduled days.

If there is more than one coach in the building, or the school uses outside consultants as well as in-house coaches, it is wise for the principal to meet with these people collectively once a month or so (which can be in lieu of a one-on-one coach meeting) to ensure that all the people employed to support teacher development are working as a team and coordinating their efforts. We have been in districts where there are both math and literacy coaches in each school. Sometimes the teachers feel really confused because the literacy coach is advocating one thing and the math coach something different. The literacy coach may be asking teachers to cover the walls with student work and suggest that some chart paper or small white board is all the teacher needs to document a literacy lesson. Meanwhile, the math coach is asking for a large white board and lots of space to document the footprint of a math lesson and compare and contrast several student strategies with the entire class. What is a teacher to do? When coaches work together these kinds of double messages can easily be resolved.

Lastly, the principal should keep the assigning of any tasks that are not aligned with the purpose and goals of improving the instructional capacity of the faculty to an absolute minimum. This includes having the coach work with small groups of students. This practice may raise the test scores of a few kids this year, but it will not improve the teacher's capacity to get the same results herself with all her students year after year. At the very least video record the coach's session with the small group and take the time to look at it with the teacher to identify practices that might inform her teaching.

Programs, Formats, and Policies

Many schools use packaged curriculum programs as the basis of their math, science, social studies, or literacy instruction. Often these programs are tied to pacing calendars created by the publishers, schools, or districts to ensure that teachers are moving along at an agreed upon pace. While this drive for efficiency looks good on paper, it perpetuates a notion that learning happens on a schedule and that teaching is a mechanistic act. Anyone who has ever taught and any parent who has had two or more children knows that every learner is different and learning takes place in spurts as well as incrementally.

At the same time that schools and districts push for uniform pacing, they also demand that teachers differentiate instruction to address the wide range of needs and understanding of the students in their classes. These contradictory demands cause a great deal of stress among teachers, confusion in the field, and conflict between administrators and teachers.

Principals must give teachers and coaches permission to use professional judgment to determine the appropriate pace of a unit of study as long as they also attempt to balance and prioritize the demands of the year's curriculum. (An important caveat, of course, is that professional judgment implies that teachers are knowledgeable about the landscape of learning for a given content area.) Principals should give teachers permission to intelligently experiment by adapting lessons in the text, altering the format of a lesson, enriching the task in the curriculum materials, inserting challenging questions, and slowing down the pace to allow students to think, discuss, and write. On the other hand, teachers should be able to justify the changes they make and clearly articulate how these changes support or deepen student learning.

The principal must lead the way in being willing to critically examine and modify school-wide programs, policies and decision-making processes in light of new information, teacher development and student learning. Differentiated expectations of teachers based on their demonstrated know-how, professional learning goals, and expertise is as important as differentiated treatment of students. Coaches are uniquely positioned to provide differentiated treatment of teachers while moving the entire faculty closer to a coherent view of learning and collective use of effective instructional strategies. They need the principal's support and trust to accomplish this mission.

Deliberate Strategies to Spread the Work

As mentioned previously, grade-level and departmental meetings provide opportunities for coaches to develop a collaborative culture and to spread the work among the faculty. Principals should help coaches establish a foothold in these meetings by attending the first couple of meetings with each grade level. The principal, by her mere presence, gives weight to the importance of these meetings. If necessary she should establish the fact that she wants the coach to plan and facilitate the meetings. She should set clear expectations that the teachers are expected to come to the meetings on time, express their needs, desires, concerns, and participate fully in shaping the agenda of the meetings.

When a lead teacher is ready to open her classroom as a collaboration site, the coach can inform the principal that the group is ready for their first study lesson. This will likely mean that the principal will need to provide a couple of periods of coverage for the team involved. In addition to having the team plan, observe, and debrief the lesson, the principal can require that all other teachers on the grade teach the same lesson within a specified timeframe and allow the coach to observe and provide feedback. In this way, the teachers on a given grade begin to build coherent practice and the coach begins to set the stage for the teacher leader to eventually take the lead at the grade-level meetings and with a colleague or two.

The principal and the coach can also think about the faculty as a whole and through their collaboration determine a theme the entire faculty can engage in. The coach and principal can co-design faculty meetings to dive deeply into the theme. One example is the development of rigorous academic discourse across every subject area and at every grade level. Through discussion, the principal can set expectations that all teachers are expected to work on improving the quality and quantity of student academic discourse. The coach can work on this theme with teachers during grade-level meetings, study lessons, and coaching cycles and the principal can support the work by looking for evidence that teachers are working on this school-wide theme in their respective classes.

The Role of the Teacher

We invite teachers to see themselves as professionals working in a complex field in which the work is never done and perfection is a mirage. We encourage teachers to be willing to continue learning throughout their careers and to realize that their personal instructional preferences may not benefit all of their students. It is their responsibility to expand their instructional repertoire, keep up to date with the latest research findings related to learning, continue to deepen their content and pedagogical content knowledge in service of student learning, and collaborate with others to ensure a coherent and excellent experience for their students. Toward this end, teachers welcome the assistance of coaches and take full advantage of professional learning opportunities offered by their coaches, principals, and districts.

Transforming educational culture in ways that de-privatize and professionalize teaching is everyone's responsibility. Teachers willing to share their expertise, raise questions about teaching and learning, investigate the effectiveness of their lessons, and hone their instructional and assessment skills contribute to the development of the field. These teachers use their power of influence to shape our profession and advocate for what's best for students. Engaging skillfully in open and frank dialogues with each other and administrators about instruction and evidence of student learning may not be the present culture, but dialogue is essential if we are to transform the status quo into a vibrant, highly-respected, learning profession.

Teachers need to be willing to admit what they don't know and take advantage of opportunities to learn what they need to in order to improve their practice (and need to be willing to help create environments where this process is safe). This might mean taking courses, working with coaches, participating in study lessons, visiting colleagues, and investing time reading professional texts in collaboration with others. Moving from competitive mindsets into collaborative communities in which everyone has something to contribute and something to learn benefits both the collective and the individual. In a true coaching culture students will learn more than content from their teachers; they will learn how to learn and be able to do so in the company of others.

THE ROLE OF THE DISTRICT

"Although coaching is a highly localized form of professional development, its success at the school level depends on the district. Only if the district shapes the coaches' role, focuses the coaches' work around the district's instructional goals, and articulates the connection between the work and the schools' overall reform strategy can coaching be effective" (Neufeld and Roper 2003). In Chapter 2 we went into great detail about ways to create a successful coaching initiative. Here we will add a few specifics a district must attend to once an initiative is underway.

Articulate a Vision and Provide Common Images

District leaders need to articulate and actualize a vision of effective instruction as illustrated by real-time, in-depth student learning. We are not talking about writing a vision statement. We are talking about having and articulating clear images of success. The vision must be grounded in examples of practice (e.g., video clips) that become familiar to all educators in the district. These common images assist everyone to develop a clear picture of what it is they are trying to create, ensuring a shared vision at all levels of the system. And, like all things in life, the vision is kept alive by allowing it to evolve over time as we gain further insight into what works and what doesn't.

Support Principals as Educational Leaders

A district needs to set clear and high expectations for principals regarding supporting the work of coaches, and assist them in doing so. This means working with principals to ensure that they cultivate a safe adult learning environment in which coaching can take root, encouraging them to work side-by-side with coaches as the coaching initiative gets underway, and to utilize the expertise of coaches to augment their own expertise in evaluating and improving the effectiveness of instruction at their school.

As a coaching initiative proceeds, there needs to be ongoing attention to the work of coaching and forums for the various players to discuss progress, reshape the work as needed, design subsequent stages of the work such as the development and responsibilities of lead teachers, and create processes for dealing with other issues that arise.

Articulate a Theory of Action

If the district intends to use coaching to develop cadres of teacher leaders and collaboration-site schools or classrooms, and use study lessons to bring teachers together from across the district, they are enacting a theory of action which needs to be made explicit, stated and restated until everyone understands it. Principals are expected to seek out potential teacher leaders to work with coaches instead of assigning coaches to work exclusively with struggling teachers, for example. When the district emphasizes that teacher leaders will eventually be supported to mentor colleagues, and that principals and coaches are expected to act as partners, the district leaders cultivate a true professional learning community that uses coaching as a useful learning process.

In our view it is a mistake for a district to focus the work of coaches exclusively on the implementation of packaged curriculum programs. The main focus of the work should be on teaching content well using available resources flexibly and mindfully. This theory of action is counter to what many districts do when they buy new programs and focus all their energy on getting teachers to teach the program with fidelity. Perhaps a more useful focus should be on teaching the *content and children* with fidelity. Our theory of action is to focus on naming the features and cultivating the essence of great teaching and on deepening teacher pedagogical content knowledge, relying less on packaged programs to get the job done.

Define and Specify the Role of the Coach

The district needs to clearly define the role of the coach and in that definition specify how coaches are expected to spend their time and *not* spend their time. District supervisors should continue to work with principals and coaches as they create schedules, select teachers, and design the focus of the work. In our experience, even with centralized models of coaching, individual school leaders often need assistance in utilizing coaches effectively. When principals continue to insist that coaches work with only struggling teachers, or do not provide time for the full coaching cycle, or insist on a volunteer model of coaching, district supervisors need to step in. Coaches alone cannot negotiate their roles with principals who do not agree with the district definition. This is analogous to principals stepping in when coaches are having difficulty resolving issues with a given teacher whom the principal expects the coach to work with.

Create and Implement a Fair Hiring Process

The process and criteria for hiring coaches should be transparent, fair, and equitable. It is imperative that coaches be seen as credible and capable. In many districts where coaches are school based and report to principals, the selection process is uneven and differs from school to school. In some cases principals have selected teachers to be coaches as a way to get ineffective teachers out of the classroom. This practice is clearly problematic and should be avoided. A centralized, district-level selection process with clear qualifications will more likely lead to the hiring of skillful teachers and/or experienced coaches, and garner greater respect for the role of the coach.

Provide Ongoing Careful Training for Coaches

In many cases districts hire coaches from within their system. This generally means that there are many novice coaches among the initial hires, and coaching requires an additional skill set that most people right out of the classroom simply do not have. People new to the role of coach need specific, job-embedded, ongoing training, just like teachers and principals do. The training should include the development of basic coaching skills, including: communication skills, especially the kind needed to have difficult conversations; identifying and working on specific high-leverage instructional strategies such as developing academic discourse; working with special needs, second language, or gifted populations; developing focused lenses for observing classes and providing specific, actionable feedback; facilitating collaborative lesson design and study lessons; working with administrators; goal setting, record keeping, and identifying benchmarks of progress; understanding the change process; and developing leadership skills. We recommend that coaches spend eighty percent of their time in schools and one day a week immersed in their own training for the first couple of years.

Bringing coaches together regularly implies that coaches, like teachers, are expected to collaborate and learn from one another, builds a coherent model of coaching, and ensures that the work done at each school is based on similar principles and aligns with the goals of the district. Coaches can meet within disciplines and across disciplines during these professional learning days. They can identify common threads across content domains such as developing classroom discourse or cultivating metacognitive skills like self-awareness, self-management, and self-reflection in both educators and students. These process goals unify the work and provide a common focus.

When working in cross-curricular teams coaches can also compare the messages they are giving teachers and work to clarify and align these messages. When the coaches gather according to content domain they can delve more deeply into the distinguishing characteristics of the pedagogical content knowledge associated with a particular academic area (e.g., the use of mathematical models in math or the inquiry process in science). Math coaches can do mathematics together using lessons from the curriculum materials they are expected to help teachers implement; science coaches can try out experiments from the curriculum; literacy coaches can read common texts and share reading and writing strategies; everyone can design or adapt assessments and study student work in their respective areas of expertise. By collaborating with other coaches, perhaps engaging in study lessons together, shadowing one another, and coaching each other, they too will be committed to their own professional growth and the uplifting of the profession as a whole.

Finally, coaches can provide feedback to the district-level supervisors about the progress and impediments to the work in the field. They can brainstorm possible solutions to the issues and concerns they encounter in the field and in this way influence district policy and practice.

Summary

We are all in this together. Every educator and administrator in a district has a role to play in creating a coaching culture. The process of coaching one another is the process of learning together and learning is the business of education.

In the next section of the book we turn our attention to the skill set of the coach. We examine the role of self-awareness and social intelligence in building resilient coaching relationships and cultivating an environment for learning.

Know Thyself

The eye cannot see the eye.
—Traditional

We believe that effective coaching hinges on the creation of strong interpersonal relationships and that developing these are directly related to a coach's emotional intelligence. Although there is no consensus among cognitive scientists and researchers as to the definition of emotional intelligence, or EI (or even if it is an actual 'intelligence'), there is no question that having the ability to understand one's own emotions is essential for coaches because the primary act of coaching *is* rooted in social interaction. Within this interpersonal space, any coach who lacks the ability to perceive and use emotions effectively is going to be severely hampered, not only in her ability to work with others but also in her ability to motivate and inspire them to change their beliefs and behaviors.

EMOTIONAL INTELLIGENCE AND LEADERSHIP

Because successful leadership depends on the development and refinement of emotional intelligence (Goleman 2003), coaches have to be aware of their own EI. To do this, it is helpful to use Daniel Goleman's framework for emotional intelligence. Goleman identifies five key components of emotional intelligence: self-awareness, self-regulation, motivation, empathy, and social skills (ibid, 238). Self-awareness, self-regulation, and motivation are self-management skills; empathy and social skills are crucial tools in managing interpersonal relationships (Goleman 2005). While all of these abilities are critical for coaches to have (or develop), the linchpin is self-awareness. Without self-awareness, one cannot hope to interact in meaningful and productive ways with other human beings. This is not to say that self-awareness alone will ensure successful social interactions. One can be highly

COACH NOTE

It is important to be aware that emotions play a major role in learning. Since, in any coaching relationship, there are at least two learners (the coach and the teacher being coached), it is critical for coaches to understand how their own emotions are affecting what they are doing and how what they are doing and saying may impact the emotions of others. For example, when teachers realize their practice is ineffective or that they do not know what they need to know to teach well they may feel embarrassed, inept, or frustrated. In these kinds of emotionally charged situations, learners may become defensive, angry, or resistant. Knowing how to deal with and manage emotions then becomes essential to coaching successfully.

self-aware *and* be socially inept. The balancing act—the art of emotional intelligence—is that one can use self-knowledge as the source for having and maintaining successful social interactions. And this only occurs if one both understands and regulates one's emotions so that they are not the driving force behind one's words and actions.

Self-Awareness Is Key

Self-awareness is a kind of *inner vision* that helps us reflect on and monitor our own reactions and feelings as they are happening (Goleman 2005). When we know our own strengths, weaknesses, emotions, values, natural inclinations, tendencies, and motivation, we are able to discern how these shape our interactions with other people (Goleman 2003). Coaches who are self-aware are able to have an inner dialogue and ask questions like: What is happening here? Why am I feeling like this? Is this about my own 'stuff'? How is my own 'stuff' getting in the way and what can I do about it? When coaches self-regulate like this, they are able to monitor and control their own behaviors. This helps them create and sustain positive learning experiences for the teachers with whom they work.

Self-awareness is essential for developing and maintaining relationships. When we are truly self-aware, we are more easily able to discern how our own beliefs and values are coloring our perceptions and influencing our behaviors. Being self-aware also helps us act in more genuine ways, which in turn fosters trust in the teachers we coach. When we operate from self-awareness, we are in sync with ourselves, which often means there is a greater congruence (Rogers 1961) between *what we think we do* and what we *actually* do.

The narrative below, which was taken from one of the author's journals, illustrates how easy it is for a coach to create a negative working environment. In her reflections, the coach offers a hindsight perspective of her own behavior and the effect it had on a nascent coaching relationship. Her lack of self-awareness and her inability to understand how her own needs and emotions were driving her behavior contributed to a destructive social interaction.

> I was a district-level staff developer and it was my first day of coaching. I was excited and nervous not just because it was my first day, but because I was working in a school where the in-house math person (I'll call her Mary) was very knowledgeable about math. I respected her and wanted her to respect me. Even though she asked the district to have me as a math staff developer, I was still uneasy. This was because I had only worked in an early childhood school and now I was going to be coaching in upper elementary classrooms. This isn't to say I didn't understand the content—I did—I had had years of training to prepare me for this job. I was just not sure how my teaching knowledge, which was so specific to early childhood, would play out in upper elementary classrooms.

On my first day at the school, the expectation was for me to visit all the classrooms with Mary so that I could get a sense of the teachers and the school culture as a whole. Mary insisted we start with her classroom and had prepared a special lesson for the occasion. We didn't plan the lesson together, which was probably my first mistake. She asked me to watch and give her feedback. Although she was a very competent teacher, I noticed right away things I could help her improve. One of the most notable was that she was emphasizing key words, which I knew was problematic because words, phrases, and questions can mean multiple things (e.g., just because the word, total, is in a math problem, it doesn't mean you have to add). I felt elated that I had found something relatively easy to talk about with Mary, something she didn't know, but that I did. I knew I could even cite books and research to support my argument.

When we debriefed the lesson, I brought up everything I knew about key words, including research that could be used as evidence as to why this technique did not help students in problem solving. I was quite pleased with myself until I saw Mary's face. I knew in that moment I had upset her; I didn't know how upsetting it was until another staff member, months later, confided that this was the technique she had emphasized to the entire staff as necessary for problem solving. This teacher also told me that, once I left that first day, Mary ran from classroom to classroom telling every teacher to pull down their key-word charts from their bulletin boards and that they weren't to teach key words anymore.

Although I knew in the moment after I spoke that I had done something problematic, I never realized how one moment of over-reaching ego could affect an entire coaching experience. My year at that school was the most difficult in my coaching career; my relationship with Mary never recovered from that initial session in which my emotions, my needs overruled any concern I might have had for hers. I was so focused on myself I never even considered my 'self' on a collision course with her 'self.'

Years later, I wondered why I had been so eager to share what I knew and why I shared it in the way I did. I realized my actions came from a place of fear and pride. From this experience, I learned something invaluable about the importance of knowing yourself, your own needs, fears, and beliefs. I learned that until you know who you are as a human being, your coaching will be profoundly impacted by your self-ignorance. Until you deeply know yourself, it is impossible to monitor and regulate your behaviors.

COACH NOTE

Here are some key questions for you to consider as you continue to read this chapter and think about how you act and interact in social settings:

1. *What is the inner place, the source from which you operate?*

2. *How well do you recognize emotions in yourself and others?*

3. *What are your own recollections of highly-charged emotions that occurred in social settings? Is there a pattern to these emotions? (e.g., do certain situations trigger certain kinds of emotions?)*

4. *What kinds of situations might elicit the emotions of pride, guilt, embarrassment, coyness, and self-consciousness?*

This narrative illustrates an important point for coaches. We need to be able to identify our beliefs and emotions and understand the ways in which these can be counterproductive in coaching sessions (e.g., if we see that a teacher is resistant have we considered how *our* actions or words might be the root of this resistance?). If we know what brings out the worst in us, we can use that self-awareness as we interact with people and be vigilant of our own emotional state. This self-awareness can help us understand how and why a teacher affects our moods and the real reason certain emotions arise in us when we work with her. Once we know this, we will be better able to self-regulate, to control our impulses and not react in the moment.

How Do We Develop or Deepen Our Self-Awareness?[1]

Becoming aware starts with the act of *noticing* what happens in our own consciousness (Kegan 1982). To do this, we have to be able to fully examine what is occurring as it is happening. For many of us this is very difficult to do, especially if we get drawn emotionally into a situation and are trying to manage our own feelings and fears. In fight or flight mode, we are often focused on self-preservation and cannot clearly and rationally understand what is occurring. If we are too busy trying to manage our emotions or maintain our cool (e.g., "I am so angry right now, but I don't want anyone to see me lose my temper. I'm just going to be quiet until this is over."), our energy—because it is absorbed in self-preservation—cannot be used to understand or deal with the complexity of the situation. This usually means that we are not processing what is happening in ways that will enable us to act coherently or effectively. And when we act emotionally we are usually *reacting* rather than *interacting*.

Understanding our emotions is the first step in being able to manage them. According to Salovey and Mayer, emotional intelligence includes being able to (1) perceive emotions, (2) reason with emotions, (3) understand emotions, and (4) manage emotions (1990). Perceiving emotions is central to understanding emotions and might include being aware of nonverbal signals such as body language and facial expressions. Reasoning with emotions is the ability to use one's emotions as tools in thinking. Managing emotions is the ability to regulate what you are feeling; it helps you respond rationally even when the emotion you are experiencing may not be in sync with responding in this way. Regulating emotions is the ability to respond appropriately to the emotions of others; it is a form of emotional self-management.

Emotions are important to recognize because they help prioritize what we pay attention to and what we react to. Because we respond emotionally to things that grab

---

[1] Activities to help you build self-awareness, and other skills described in this chapter, are found in Appendix C.

our attention, it is important, whether that response is positive or negative, to recognize what is triggering our response.

It is also important for coaches to understand that the emotions people show might have multiple meanings. For example, a teacher comes in, throws herself into her chair, does not make eye contact, is sullen, and barely responds to our questions. How do we respond? How do we react? To be skilled in this kind of situation, we need to be able to *perceive an emotion* from someone's facial expressions or behavior (*Her face is so angry; she practically threw herself into that chair*), *understand* what that emotion is from the inside out (*I've been that angry before; I know what it feels like*), *reason* with our own emotions (*She isn't responding to me and I feel myself getting tense. Should I ask her if she'd like some time alone or if she'd like to cancel our session? Would this help or make the situation worse?*), and, *manage our own emotions* (*This is so frustrating, I feel like screaming! How many times has she come to our planning sessions with some kind of avoidance technique? Today she's mad; tomorrow, who knows . . . Okay, calm down. There's no point in getting angry too; it's not going to help anything. How can I deal with my emotions and support her?*). Notice how the ability to have an inner dialogue can help maintain equilibrium. It is one way to regulate negative emotions and slow down the story so that it does not become the only reality. Also note that the perception and interpretation of the teacher's behavior is just that—the real root of the behavior might be something entirely different. Perhaps the teacher has had other problems that have nothing to do with the coach or the coaching session that are affecting her behavior. This is why it's important to recognize that there may be multiple meanings in any situation, and that other people's behaviors and words may not be directly related to us!

COACHING AND THE NEED FOR SOCIAL SKILLS

Socially skilled coaches have a talent for finding common purpose. They can manage relationships, control their own emotions, and empathize with those of others. Because they are socially skilled, these coaches tend to build strong networks and understand the power of collaboration.

Socially skilled coaches also know how to rely on their networks for support. When something happens that is confusing or upsetting, they know it is sometimes helpful to talk through what happened with a friend who can hear them, help them sort through their emotions, and think about a plan of action that is proactive, not reactive. Sounding boards are a good way to regulate the stories we tell ourselves. One might say, "Here's what I thought happened in that moment. Is that what you saw?" It is likely that two different people will have two different perceptions of the event. If your emotions are triggered and hers are not, then something is clouding how you perceived the situation. This is one way to know when it is your own emotional baggage that you are tripping over and not something in the situation.

As coaches, we need to be able to process our own feelings and emotions while simultaneously monitoring those of other people. In any interaction we have to be able to sort through our own and other people's emotions as well. If we can adequately sift through what is happening (what the underlying emotions are that are contributing to what is said and how people are acting in a given situation), then we can find ways to use this information effectively to guide our actions, behaviors, and emotions (Salovey and Mayer 1990). Coaches who are unable to deal in real time with the interspace of human emotions often focus solely on themselves in relation to what is happening; this kind of emotional focus often clouds their judgment. Thus they may find themselves *reacting* in situations rather than *interacting* because their emotions and the responses dictate their social behaviors. Being aware of what you are feeling and not reacting from that feeling takes a deep level of self-awareness and self-management—two essential traits of the socially skilled.

Let's use the following vignette to think about the role of emotional intelligence in coaching. This transcript was taken from a coaching collaborative facilitated by one of the authors. In this learning community, coaches share their practice publicly. On this day, a first-year coach and a veteran coach had shared their coaching practice with the community. The transcript is from a conversation the facilitator and two coaches had at the end of the day; they are reflecting on their work together.

> **Facilitator:** I want to apologize. I saw how upset you got after we watched your video. I'm not sure what happened, but when I saw you get so emotional earlier, I knew you had to leave the group to calm down. It was a misjudgment on my part to have you share your practice publicly. You're a new coach and that's a really hard thing to do.
>
> **Coach:** I wasn't upset because people watched my video.
>
> **Facilitator** [surprised]**:** You weren't?
>
> **Coach:** No, I was upset from this morning. Something you said upset me so much that I couldn't let go of it all day. It's all I thought about. I couldn't even pay attention to what was going on because all I kept hearing were your words in my head, "No, they're not."
>
> **Facilitator** [bewildered]**:** My words? "No, they're not"—I said that? I don't remember . . .
>
> **Coach:** It was when Donna said that our planning videos were the same and you said, "No, they're not." I felt really insulted. It made me think you thought

one was really good—Donna's—and mine was, well, really bad. [mimics in a snide voice] *No, they're not!*

Facilitator: How awful. I wish you had said something to me earlier. [thinks for a moment before speaking] Why didn't you tell me at lunch that you were so upset? We could have talked things through before we watched your video.

Coach: I couldn't talk about it and I thought the only way I could handle how I was feeling was to keep silent. Obviously, I couldn't—didn't handle myself very well.

Facilitator: Well, let me first say, that I'm sorry that my comment upset you so much. But I want you to know my intention wasn't to insult you. I merely wanted to point out that we had two different videos to share—one was from a veteran coach and one was from a new coach. When Donna said, 'they're the same,' I wanted everyone to know that they were different. Different because of the grade level, the needs of the teachers, the setting, and the experience level of the coaches—not different because one was good and one was bad.

Coach: Well that's not how I heard it. I felt insulted by the comparison.

Facilitator: I'm sorry my words hurt you so much. How you interpreted them wasn't how I intended them. Perhaps next time—one way we can avoid situations like this—is for you to speak to me earlier, don't hold onto something all day, let me know as soon as you can. If you talk to me about what's upsetting you, then we can clear up any kind of misunderstanding. Also, I would love to get to a place where you knew me well enough—trusted me enough—to know that I would never want to hurt or humiliate anyone.

This vignette captures how powerful our emotions are. They can easily shut down our ability to think. It also shows how our perceptions and the emotions that arise from them can trap us into believing that our reality is *the* reality. Notice the differences in the perceptions: the facilitator has no idea the coach is angry; the coach thinks the facilitator tried to publicly humiliate her. The story the coach tells herself over and over during the day becomes *the* story. Her inability to communicate her feelings at any point during the day doesn't quell her negative emotions; it fuels them. These eventually overpower her ability to reason objectively or entertain the possibility that there was another possible meaning behind the facilitator's words, "No, they're not." Not only are the coach's emotions debilitating; they also shut down her ability to engage fully in learning.

Now let's view the scene from the facilitator's point-of-view. Through her lens, she views the coach's tearful expression and assumes she is upset because her coaching session is not as skillful as the previous one that was shared. She is clearly stunned when the coach shares a different viewpoint, stating that the facilitator's words—words she didn't even remember uttering—were the cause of the trauma. What is important to note here is that the facilitator's emotions, which are apparent in her surprise and confusion ("My words? 'No, they're not'—I said that? I don't remember.") do not overtake her ability to discuss what has happened. This self-regulation of emotion and the use of crucial conversation tools (these will be discussed in depth in Chapter 5, "Communication Is Key") defuse a potentially disastrous situation. Had the facilitator responded in anger, said something like, "Come on—do you really think I would publicly insult you?" or "What have I done to you that you have so little trust in my judgment?" the situation would have escalated.

Because the facilitator takes a different course, the relationship is restored. Here are some simple, but powerful things she does: (1) she apologizes (simple words like, "I'm sorry," can sometimes defuse raging emotions), (2) she advocates for herself while acknowledging the perception of the coach ("How you interpreted them wasn't how I intended them"), and (3) she offers a possible solution if a similar situation arises in the future ("Perhaps next time—one way we can avoid situations like this—is for you to speak to me earlier, don't hold onto something all day, let me know as soon as you can"). When the facilitator says, "I would love to get to a place where you knew me well enough—trust me enough—to know that I would never want to hurt or humiliate anyone," she is not only naming her own feelings and desires, but also setting expectations for their coaching relationship.

The vignette is an example of how important it is for coaches to be self-aware and to be able to self-regulate our emotions. As coaches, we need to develop our ability to notice what is happening inside ourselves and then be able to think about this reality intersecting with the reality of others. To be able to recognize our emotions and what is causing them gives us greater control over our reactions. This is one reason why it is so important for us to know our own triggers and to use this knowledge to regulate our behaviors. When we slow down the force of our own needs and emotions and stop to consider those of other people, we self-regulate. And the better we are at self-regulating, the greater chance we have of establishing and maintaining productive relationships with the teachers we coach.

To successfully navigate difficult situations or conversations, we have to develop a kind of super-vision (Tobert 2004). This way of seeing enables us to process a situation with two lenses: we see with our own lens, but we can also shift perspective and see with the eyes of others. This kind of dual perspective is the only way we can reflect "in the moment on the moment" (Schon 1984, 278) and understand how both internal and external factors are impacting what is occurring. Having this kind of processing ability helps us make wise decisions about what we say and how we say it.

Why We Need to Understand Our Own Mental Models

To deal with complex situations and challenge our own beliefs and assumptions, first we have to have a clear picture of what our beliefs and mental models are (Senge 1990). According to Senge, mental models are "deeply ingrained assumptions, generalizations or even pictures and images that influence how we understand the world and how we take action" (1990, 8). To deepen our self-awareness, we need to "unearth our internal pictures of the world, to bring them to the surface and to hold them rigorously to scrutiny" (1990, 9). This self-awareness can have a profound impact on how we interact with others, on how we inspire, and on how we lead.

How Can We Use Self-Awareness of Our Emotions in Coaching Situations?

As coaches, it is critical for us to be aware of our mental models, beliefs, and emotions and think about how they impact our interactions with others. Once we are aware, we also need specific tools to support us in difficult moments. Suppressing emotions, as we saw in the coaching transcript on pages 66–67, is not helpful and can actually hurt the individual who is holding on to the emotion as well as the relationship. The suggestions listed below can be used as tools to help us learn how to use our emotions in ways that are both positive and constructive.

1. **Tune in:** Notice when you start to feel agitated, irritated, frustrated, angry, scared, and take three conscious breaths. Then ask yourself, "What do I want now?"

2. **Assume Nothing; Ask:** When our emotions get triggered, we often have an assumption connected to the emotion. For example, we may be feeling rejected, or that our ideas are not being valued. Frame a question and ask the other person about your assumption(s). (See I Statements below.)

3. **Distinguish Fact from Story:** Say something like, "I noticed that this is the third time you have come late to our forty-minute meeting. I'm beginning to tell myself a story about this. Maybe you don't care about these meetings; maybe you are not finding them useful; and so forth. I'd rather you tell me what is going on so we can get clear and move from there."

4. **Share Your Feeling:** "I need to stop here for a minute, take a breath, and share what I'm feeling. When you said _____, I noticed I felt _____, and I'd like to talk about what you meant."

5. **Use I Statements:** "I felt (hurt, angry, sad) when you (explain in neutral terms what the person did or said) and I would like to (clarify, explain, examine, make meaning of, make a new agreement)."

Summary

Emotional intelligence is essential for transformative leadership. Because self-awareness is a key part of emotional intelligence, to be effective, we, as coaches, have to develop a deep self-perception, one that helps us understand what is at our core. This means we have to be aware of our own strengths and weaknesses and recognize how our own thoughts, beliefs, and emotions impact what we see and how we behave. When we are aware of our own emotions, we can understand those of others. This inner perspective helps us recognize not only how people affect us, but also how they perceive us. When we understand the source of our feelings, we can manage these feelings and use them effectively in social settings. When we can reason with our feelings, we are not ruled by emotions. When we have a deep self-perception, we understand our own mental models and how these inform everything we do, see, and say. It is only in recognizing the limitations of our own mental models that we can transcend ourselves and find the power to inspire and lead.

Communication Is Key

*[If] we wish to move adults to learn together in dialogue,
whatever impedes that dialogue must be courageously
addressed and eradicated. Whatever enables that dialogue
must be fearlessly nurtured and used.*
—Jane Vella

Skillful and courageous communication is the lifeblood of coaching. Coaches need more refined communication skills than most people because part of their role is to question the status quo, nudge teachers into unknown territory, and encourage them to try on new techniques. On the journey teachers may come to see that they might not be as skillful or as knowledgeable as they imagined, or perhaps realize their present practice may be limiting student learning. Such painful discoveries can trigger self-doubt and feelings of inadequacy. This chapter will discuss ways of navigating through the feelings that may arise in others during the coaching process and explore how communication skills help us chart rough waters.

We think that we are skillful communicators because we have been successful in school and as teachers, and tend to get along with family and friends. But if we take a closer look, it is likely that we are good at communication when things are going well and when people agree with us. It may also be true that we tend to seek out those who are similar to us culturally, ethnically, economically, politically, etc. We often handle differences with less skill and avoid and/or judge those who are different from us. The truth is that learning to engage with *all* people in productive ways that actually empower others to do a better job is at the heart of effective coaching and all successful improvement efforts. Most of us simply have not honed these skills to the degree necessary.

Coaching Requires Deep Listening

Margaret Wheatley says, "Listening is such a simple act. It requires us to be present, and that takes practice, but we don't have to do anything else. We don't have to advise, or coach, or sound wise. We just have to be willing to sit there and listen" (Wheatley 2002). Content coaching involves providing the space for teachers to come into deeper relationship with their own authentic questions about teaching and learning. This means staying with the questions, massaging them, walking around them, until we get clarity about the question that is going to open our eyes to possibility. Einstein supposedly said that if he had one hour to solve a life or death problem, he'd spend the first 55 minutes framing the question and then the last five minutes solving the problem.

Listening well and deeply for the questions does not mean that the coach takes a passive role and follows the teacher's lead exclusively, but rather finds the road that *both* believe is worth journeying along. This kind of dialogue requires deep listening (sometimes called active and responsive listening)—the kind of listening that takes effort, empathy, and patience—and a search for common ground.

Listening at All Levels

The way supervisors talk and listen to teachers is often similar to the way teachers talk and listen to students. Coaches need to be aware of hierarchal patterns in the culture in order to shift the patterns of communication in coaching sessions to inquiry-based dialogue between equals. Similarly, the depths of conversation colleagues have about content and teaching strategies closely matches the depth teachers generate in their lessons. To change the relationships in schools we have to change the interactions between the adults, which in turn will change the interactions within the classroom.

When teachers hurry students, interrupt them, tell them how to do things instead of letting them grapple, coaches often advise them to use "wait time" to give their students the time and space to think. We tell teachers how important it is to make student thinking visible in order to know where to go next in the lesson. Yet, when teachers think aloud, grapple with issues, and ponder challenges, how many of us jump into rescue mode and try to give them an answer rather than listening intently as they consider their alternatives? And when we—whether teachers or coaches—engage in these kinds of asocial listening behaviors, what happens to the learners' self-esteem, to their trust, to their willingness to risk not knowing and engage in truly deep investigations? To listen deeply, coaches need to be fully present in each coaching conversation, letting go of preconceived agendas, hopes, and fears. Coaches need to be able to stay silent when there are spaces in the conversation. This is often difficult to do because many of us feel uncomfortable with silence.

Listening Is a Learnable Skill

With a bit of self-awareness and the willingness to monitor and manage our own behavior, we can all improve our capacity to listen. For coaches, learning to listen well is a necessity. By listening well, we mean a deeper, more interactive kind of listening that sparks ideas and keeps curiosity alive. This kind of listening takes practice and stamina.

Identifying Stumbling Blocks

First notice your own listening patterns. When someone is speaking are there two conversations happening simultaneously—the one with the other person and the one inside your head? Is that little inner voice commenting on the other person's appearance or accent, judging the person, listening for commonalities or differences in order to agree or disagree, rehearsing what to say? Alternatively, we may find ourselves getting distracted when someone is speaking; thinking about all the things on our to do list or daydreaming about an upcoming event. In short, we are doing everything *except* listening attentively and objectively. (See the activity "Why Not Listen and Learn?" in Appendix C.)

Once we become aware of what our listening tendencies are, we can make a plan to monitor and refine them. When you get distracted or when that little voice in your head starts wreaking havoc on your focus, notice it and do something to bring your attention back to the speaker. For instance, one of the authors knows that interrupting others is a listening stumbling block for her. She noticed that she interrupted when she was afraid she'd forget something she definitely wanted to discuss; when she was getting impatient and thought she already understood the speaker's point; when she wanted clarity about something the speaker said. To prevent interrupting, she takes a quick note and then refocuses on the speaker. She noticed that the simple act of writing a couple of words keeps her from interrupting because she is now assured of remembering what she wanted to say. This helps her remain focused on the speaker.

We can also do things like face the speaker and adjust our bodies to be open and attentive. Deliberately set aside all distractions (e.g., cell phones, email, close the door if the hallways are noisy). Tune into the speaker and show that you are tuned in by nodding occasionally and responding with an "uh-huh" every now and again. If we do get distracted, admit that we lost focus, paraphrase the part we heard and ask the person to please repeat the part we missed.

Checking for Understanding

Because we tend to listen through our own filters and biases, we often hear something other than what was intended. Therefore, it is important to sincerely check for understanding. While listening, try to mentally summarize what the speaker is saying. When the speaker finishes speaking, paraphrase (e.g., "What I hear you saying is . . . .") or ask clarifying questions (e.g., "I'm not clear what you mean by . . ." or "Can you give me an example, please?"). Ask if she is indeed done or if she has more to add to what's been said. Then summarize the key points you heard and ask the speaker to confirm or edit the summary.

Slow Down and Dive Deep

Coaches need patience and willingness to slow down even though our talk time with teachers may be limited. Slowing down often allows a deeper dive into content, which in turn helps teachers to retain what they have learned. So, take the time to speak fully about one topic, issue, or concern. Each session can then build on the last. Trust that when you fully understand the other person's perspective, concerns, and desires, because you took the time to listen, you will more easily be able to set and act upon goals that are relevant to both of you.

Listening and Talking: Cultivating Dialogue

Dialogue is a unique and rare kind of communication through which we essentially talk our way into shared meaning. We strive for dialogue where there is no hidden agenda and where all parties are able to genuinely explore ideas. We refrain from coercion, and put our own goals and agendas on the back burner and reframe our beliefs into hypotheses, shining a light upon them. We do so through continual discussion rather than through insisting on following prescribed habits, materials, behaviors, or techniques. As Paolo Freire says, "True dialogue cannot exist unless the dialoguers engage in critical thinking . . . thinking which perceives reality as process, as transformation, rather than as a static entity—thinking which does not separate itself from action" (Freire 2000, 4). To have purposeful dialogue with teachers, coaches need to have authentic interest in their ideas, findings, and conclusions. We also need a profound humility and a good dose of self-awareness. Teachers gravitate to this kind of positive energy and are more willing to learn and challenge themselves publicly.

The Importance of Mutual Purpose

Finding and acting on mutual purpose is one key aspect of cultures in which people learn through discourse. This requires someone to take the lead in ferreting out mutual purpose during discussions. This is not easy and requires a shift in thinking. When we ask coaches to express their concerns or frustrations about coaching, it is not uncommon to hear:

> ➤ "How do we get stuck-in-the-mud people to change their practice?"

> ➤ "What do you do about people who are resistant to working with a coach?"

> ➤ "People don't seem to care about this work and it is so frustrating."

> ➤ "How do you get a teacher to be more professional?"

> ➤ "My principal wants me to work with the struggling teachers and they don't want to work with me. Half of them don't even show up for our meetings."

Every coach—if we're being honest—has probably uttered some version of one or more of these questions and comments at some point in her career. These statements express the kind of thinking that needs to shift.

The moment you think your role is to get other people to do what you want them to do, think again. Coaching is about encouraging, empowering, and inspiring *others*— bringing out *their* genius. In order to empower someone, you have to understand what matters to them and think about what kinds of support might help them in accomplishing their goals. Before you can communicate with others, you need the capacity to see your own bias and admit that you, like everyone else, see the world through your personal filter.

Different Perspectives Offer Opportunities

You may be wondering, "What if what matters to the person I'm coaching is different from what matters to me?" Vive la différence! Difference often means you will need to find a third way or new perspective in order to find common purpose. Coaches need to be skillful enough to engage in inquiry with their colleagues and be willing to acknowledge that different points of view are not only possible, but contain the ingredients that cause innovation and growth.

Here's a typical example of what appears to be irreconcilable differences when it comes to mathematics education (note that similar philosophical differences hold in every content area). It is also an example of why dialogue matters. The teacher is interested in making sure the students know all their multiplication facts by heart and doesn't want to focus on anything else until they do. The coach wants students to work through rich math problems that require multiplication in their solution and believes this problem-based approach will assist students in learning their facts. They seem to be at an impasse. These differences are based on different ideas about what matters in mathematics, different interpretations of standards or tests, and different beliefs about how people learn and the role of the teacher, not to mention the teacher's comfort level with mathematics.

If we can reframe the debate (a big if!), we can move from a stance of knowing to one of mutual inquiry. A stance of knowing essentially means we think we know what is best and try to convince the other person of our perspective or to use our suggestions. In contrast, in a process of mutual inquiry, we can notice that we both want students to learn math well enough to use multiplication fluently and appropriately. We can notice that we seem to have different ideas about how to get that outcome, and agree that we may have to gather some evidence from our practice to see what is and is not working for specific students. We disagree on which comes first, learning facts or engaging with contexts that get us to think multiplicatively—but we can concede that these two approaches are not mutually exclusive and probably some of both are needed. Maybe by creating a little bit of space for both perspectives, we can create a third perspective that actually meets the needs of a greater range of students.

What Is Your Motivation?

To communicate successfully and authentically means that we have to be very clear about our own motives and beliefs. Are we secretly trying to get someone we see as resistant or inept to do what we think is best (a manipulative framework)? Or are we seeing the other person as worthy, caring, intelligent, and capable—someone with her own ideas (a respectful framework)? Being clear about our own motivations and judgments is critical because people can usually tell when someone is trying to manipulate them. This kind of manipulation usually leads to resistance, frustration, or anger for the participants. The more entrenched we become in our positions and the more we label others, the less likely we are to have a true dialogue.

Dealing with Disagreement

In the transcript below (from a coach learning community facilitated by one of the authors), the coach and teacher reach an impasse very quickly. The coach's motivation (to get the teacher to use a specific model) comes in direct conflict with the teacher's desire (to use something she favors instead).

> **Coach:** So let's look together at the anchor problem that kids will be working on during this lesson.
>
> **Teacher:** I'm skipping that one.
>
> **Coach:** Can you help me understand why you would do that?
>
> **Teacher:** They're never going to have to show division on the open array. I hate that model. The kids never understand it. That's why I'm skipping it.

Before reading the rest of the transcript, think about what your response might be to the teacher's last statement. Remember the discussion of emotional intelligence in Chapter 4: we need to think about what we say, how we say it, and why we say it *before* we speak. If your motivation is to *convince*, your talk moves will be focused on convincing.

If your motivation is to *understand* the reason why the teacher responded in the way she did, your talk moves will be more exploratory. It is also important to consider the other person's motivation. She says it's about her students not understanding the model, but could it be that she has limited understanding of how and when to use this model herself and that's why she's avoiding it? How would recognizing this affect your response?

Read how the coach continued and think about her motivation and the effect it has on the quality of the conversation.

> **Coach:** That's interesting that you feel the model isn't relevant to division, because a few minutes ago you told us how successful the partial quotients strategy has been in your classroom, and I think the open array can be a really useful model for representing that strategy.

> **Teacher:** I don't think it is. As I see it, the open array just confuses the kids. They don't know which numbers go where and I'm not bothering to explain that to them when I have more important things to do like teaching them how to divide.

> **Coach:** Which model do you prefer to use then to help students understand the partial quotients strategy?

> **Teacher:** No model. They don't need one. They just need to learn how to divide. And that's what I want to spend my time doing: teaching them how to divide.

> **Coach:** I agree that kids need to learn to divide. However, the standards do state that the area model needs to be understood by students. And in 2014 our students will be expected to know this.

> **Teacher:** Not my problem. I'll be out of here by then. [spells out] R-e-t-i-r-e-m-e-n-t!

> **Coach:** Well I'm glad you find that satisfying, but it's really no consolation to me especially when the students that are in your class currently will be tested to those standards.

> **Teacher:** [snorts, rolls her eyes, folds her arms, and sits back in her chair; does not speak again for the duration of the grade-level planning meeting]

In this conversation, the coach and teacher reach an impasse. What causes the resistance? First, the coach fails to understand the teacher's point of view. Genuine curiosity about what the teacher says and a simple question ("What did your students say or do that made you think they didn't understand the open array?") or paraphrase ("Let me see if I understood what you said. You dislike the array and your students struggle to use it . . .") might have shifted the dynamic and prevented a stalemate. If the coach had taken the time to understand the teacher's point of view, she could have begun to find common ground. It would have signaled to the teacher that she was interested in her ideas and could understand and empathize with her concerns, which is certainly one way to build trust. By letting go of her own agenda and calming her rising emotions, the coach could have opened the dialogue space and might have found mutual purpose ("We both want your children to succeed and be successful in division."). When the coach cites examples of why the teacher needs to use the open array, she is pushing her own agenda, which is a form of coercion. And the teacher responds to this force with resistance and hostility. (See the Role Plays activity in Appendix C for ways to practice communication moves.)

Active and responsive listening is more difficult when someone is expressing views that are diametrically opposed to our own. The first step is to know that this is *not* personal, so don't take it personally! But it's hard to stay focused and neutral when someone is pressing our buttons. Whatever reactions you are having, whatever emotions you are feeling, belong to you; the other person is not causing you to feel that way. As we discussed in Chapter 4, we need not only self-awareness (e.g., "What am I feeling?"), but also the capacity to manage our emotions and reactions (e.g., remain calm, use neutral language, use an even tone, take a couple of deep calming breaths). Couple the capacity to manage our emotions with skillful communication skills and the likelihood of successfully navigating difficult situations improves exponentially.

An Example from Our Experience

One of the beliefs that presses our buttons—"These kids can't"—we often hear expressed in myriad ways: "Not my kids!" or "Jeremy is limited because of his learning disability" or "They're second language learners; all this talking is too hard for them." Depending on how it is said, and what is happening at the school, the authors' impulse is to immediately challenge the other person and defend our own perspective and righteously stand up for the kids. Instead, because we are aware that this is *our* tendency and that these emotions arise in us with such utterances, we are learning to take a breath, paraphrase, probe the belief once it surfaces, and then turn it into a hypothesis and design an inquiry around it. Here's an example from an actual coaching session one of the authors facilitated:

> **Coach:** What's a possible inference from the observation that kids are not talking to each other about the math when asked to turn and talk? My inference might be that they are not used to doing so.
>
> **Teacher:** Or it could mean they just don't have the skills. In this group there are a number of students who are significantly low. They can't contribute.

Coach: From my perspective, there wasn't one kid in the class who couldn't contribute. Not always what I was looking for . . .

Teacher: Well in terms of dialogue in math, some are very limited and that is a work in progress.

Coach: There were kids who needed more help and needed coaching to contribute.

Teacher: We have some kids who are significantly low, don't have basic skills; there's the writing piece, the reading piece.

Coach: I'm wondering how much of the "can't" is coming from our eyes and how much is coming from the kids? When are we limiting kids because we think they can't?

Teacher: I'm not saying that. I'm saying there are kids that are going to have a hard time talking no matter how much we try to give them the skills.

Coach: Okay, and I'm saying that is your hypothesis—some of the kids don't have the social skills—the life skills—to do what we are asking them to do. I'm suggesting we use this hypothesis as our inquiry and think about what we can try in order to get them to develop these skills.

Teacher: That's what we are working on.

We have come to understand that generally the teachers who state these beliefs often blame the children for not learning because it is easier to project their discomfort on the students than to own up to the fact that they are at their wits' end in terms of how to reach the particular children they believe "can't" learn. Our job as colleagues/coaches is to join with them in an exploration of how to give every child access to whatever content we are expected to teach. We do this by getting very specific. Becoming specific is one way to help teachers think about how to support student learning (and improve their practice).

The conversation continued and the teacher and coach came up with four specific strategies to develop student capacity to talk and listen to each other and engage in academic discourse:

Coach: What specifically are you going to work on? You have a hypothesis, which may be correct. I don't know. Some kids are more skilled at this than others. We have observed that. They don't necessarily talk about whatever it is you want them to talk about. As the instructor, now that I've observed that and I have a hypothesis, my next question is: "What specific moves am I going to make to make sure that these kids can have these conversations?" When I say, "turn to a neighbor," they know what to do.

Teacher: What I do is sometimes have some of those children be my partner.

Coach: Okay that is one strategy.

Teacher: I noticed you look at the group, finding someone you didn't think was doing what you wanted them to do, and you would go and join the group. Get them talking and then invite them to be the first to share with the whole group.

Coach: Yes, that's another strategy.

Teacher: Also, I noticed when Simon didn't have an idea at all you took him to the board to look at the visuals and asked him about what he was seeing. When he described a square number, then you told him to write that in his book and be ready to share it.

Coach: Strategy 3. Anything else?

Teacher: Sometimes, when I do turn and talk I ask the students to tell me what their partner said.

Coach: Strategy 4. Now we have four different, specific strategies we can practice to assist students. We can also get more specific. For example, when I started the meeting I told kids what I expected. "I expect you to listen carefully to what your classmates are saying. To listen so well that I can call on you to repeat what was just said." I then reminded them of that expectation throughout the lesson and gave them opportunities to practice meeting that expectation.

Specificity is the name of the game. When we honor each other's perspectives, and then get specific about ways to inquire into that perspective, we can assist each other to hone our repertoire of instructional moves and regain our faith that all students can learn.

A couple of other things to note in relation to the above dialogue: The teacher's opinions were turned into hypotheses that would allow for her and the coach to investigate their merit. The coach also used the pronouns *our* and *we* when challenging the coach's perspective. She said, "I'm wondering how much of the can't is coming from our eyes and how much is coming from the kids? When are we limiting kids because we think they can't?" If she had said, "I'm wondering how much of the can't is coming from *your* eyes," the confrontation might have become personal. Both parties in this case are using the pronoun *I* to own their own ideas and opinions rather than the universal *you*. The use of *I* statements is generally more effective in building trusting relationships in which people can speak honestly to one another. Owning our opinions and being willing to examine them begins with *I* statements.

QUESTIONS ARE THE KEY
TO SUCCESSFUL COACHING

In order to understand what a teacher wants and values, her goals and struggles, and how to be of assistance, coaches need to ask lots of probing questions. Coaches need to make sure that their motivation in doing so comes from a place of genuine curiosity and willingness to support learning. Questions that are thinly veiled interrogations, that back teachers into corners or make them feel exposed and ignorant, will quickly damage any coaching relationship. Trust can be built through questions; it can also be destroyed through questions.

Getting Started With Questioning

One way to ease into the role of questioner is to let people know that you will be asking questions and telling them why. It is important to let a teacher (or principal) know in the first session that you will be asking lots of questions, and that your questions come from a genuine interest in the other person and a desire to find mutual purpose. Also invite the other person to ask you questions and to challenge your thinking. By framing the conversation in this way, you create safety. When people feel safe, they are more likely to open up and tell you what is on their minds.

For example, we might say, "I'm genuinely interested in how we might learn together. In order to do so, I need to ask a few questions to find out what you want to learn or what you have found challenging in your work. I really want us to be able to work together in ways that feel good to both of us and I don't want you to think that I'm here to convince you to do things you may not agree with or want to do." Notice the contrast in this statement. I want this and I don't want that. Contrasting statements like this establish safety in an exchange (Patterson 2002).

Here are some questions we can ask teachers and supervisors early on to help us understand the culture in a given school:

- ‣ What matters to you?
- ‣ What issues are most vital to you?
- ‣ What are you grappling with and what is your current thinking?
- ‣ Can you describe a few critical incidents in your work to help me understand the situations you face?
- ‣ When you have a question about teaching, whom do you turn to?
- ‣ What are the tensions you feel?

> ‣ What do you wish you knew how to do better?

> ‣ If someone had an idea for how to improve things, and that idea might challenge the present way things are done, what should that person do?

> ‣ If you could fix/change one thing around here to make things better, what would it be?

By exploring the perceptions, concerns, and contexts of others we create safety and build trusting relationships. When people feel safe, they are generally willing to share their perceptions and consider new ideas and ways of doing things.

When Questions Are Difficult

Sometimes in our questioning, we uncover gaps in a teacher's content knowledge or limits in their repertoire of instructional strategies. These gaps and limits expose ignorance, incompetence, or imperfection—to most people, these are unsettling revelations that make us feel vulnerable and may challenge our identity as competent professionals. Reestablishing safety is called for in circumstances like this. Humility on the part of the coach is often a good move here. "I am having trouble myself trying to figure out how to reach Sammy. I know you care about him, so maybe we can figure something out together."

Most people do not welcome failure and can become angry, scared, embarrassed, or defensive when faced with their own ineptitude. These attitudes often require coaches to engage in the difficult conversations that most of us avoid. Maintaining safety while having a difficult conversation is often challenging, but can be done. One way to maintain safety during a difficult conversation is to state aloud what you are observing. For example, "I noticed you seem a bit angry and you suddenly got quiet. Are you upset about something?" Or "I noticed you seem a bit upset, please help me understand what you are feeling." These kinds of moves may feel a bit scary because we often think we are the cause of the problem. One time when one of the authors asked a teacher who suddenly began to cry what was upsetting her, she expected the teacher to say, "You are interrogating me!" or something to that effect. Instead the teacher said, "I just realized I don't know how to plan a lesson." This "aha" moment, though painful, was the turning point for that teacher.

A Culture of Questioning

Einstein admonishes us to never stop questioning (1955). Dewey said curiosity is the foundation of all thinking (1933). Teachers are encouraged to ask open-ended, higher-order questions to cultivate students' capacity to reason. Yet coaches often shy away from asking colleagues provocative, probing questions, and teachers who question the new initiative, mandate, policy, or program are often seen as resistant or insubordinate and are sometimes sanctioned. When this happens, people tend to whisper in the teacher's room instead of speaking up during a meeting. How might we create an environment in which asking one another genuine, thought provoking questions is the welcomed norm?

We are describing a significant shift in culture. Shifts like this begin with small steps and generally start with us. For example, if we want others to welcome questions, then we need to encourage others to question us and when they do, we need to receive those questions with grace and humility. We can ask permission of others to question them and give them permission not to have answers. This creates safety. For example, "I have a question that I'd like to ask you, and it may be one you can't answer easily or right now and that's okay. Are you open to me asking it?" This approach is respectful and freeing and also provides safety. If the person chooses to answer, respect that answer, being careful not to criticize or reject it. Maybe ask a further question. If the person chooses not to receive the question or not to answer, be graceful then too.

We can also acknowledge that uncertainty or being unable to answer a question is often anxiety provoking. We can empathize with each other's angst and learn to breathe into the place of uncertainty and let it percolate. Reminding people of the larger purpose in asking questions—to broaden our horizons, find better solutions, be more creative and innovative—can provide motivation to engage in questioning.

Make it safe and playful to question. Perhaps have a question box or a question bulletin board where people can post questions (anonymously or not). Maybe share in a newsletter the most interesting, useful questions of the month. In other words, find ways to value the questions.

DISCUSSING THE UNDISCUSSABLES

Who do you avoid talking to? When do you say nothing, even though you are about to jump out of your skin in response to what a colleague is saying? It is usually the conversations we avoid having that are causing the greatest obstacles to real progress in education (and in life!) (Patterson et al. 2002).

Why do we avoid having difficult conversations? Most of us fear that others will get angry if we challenge or disagree with them. We are afraid to upset other people and do not want to hurt anyone's feelings. We want to be liked and want the approval of others, especially our colleagues and the principal or authority figure to whom we report. Some of us are afraid we will say the wrong thing and not be able to take it back once it has flown out of our mouths. Others value peace and harmony and fear that conflict will damage relationships in irreparable ways.

Worse, it is difficult for many of us to remain confident when others disagree or are angry with us. We think that if we remain quiet and say nothing the problem will go away of its own accord, and if it doesn't we just grin and bear it because there is nothing we can do about it anyway. We are often much better at silently suffering and finding endless ways to cope with difficult circumstances than we are at productively engaging others in finding solutions to what appear to be intractable issues.

Coaches experience these feelings just as much as everyone else, and yet as agents of change, we must learn to face these fears and start and maintain challenging conversations through to resolution over time. Say, "No" to ending at an impasse where we agree to disagree, and make it safe for others to do so as well.

Dealing with Skeptics and Cynics

When we are not particularly skillful at communicating with skeptical colleagues, we sometimes choose to avoid the skeptics or cynics and work with the few people who are open and responsive. While this reaction may allow us to feel more confident, it ultimately widens the gap between those teachers who become more skillful through coaching and those who don't engage in coaching and defeats the purpose of coaching as a process for developing school-wide coherence in instruction.

The skeptic is actually a very valuable member of the team. The skeptic, being more cautious than those of us who tend to be more enthusiastic, usually raises issues we might not have considered. The cynic, on the other hand, is likely to be someone who cares very deeply but has been disappointed along the way and now prefers cynicism to getting burnt again. In either case, it is incumbent upon the coach to develop a collegial relationship with every member of the staff. It is sort of like insisting that students work with every other student in the class, whether they happen to like each other or not. To do so, remember first and foremost what Lucy's former Superintendent, Anthony Alvarado, used to say, "It is NOT personal. It is about the work!" Here are some suggestions:

> ▸ Do your best to see the person as a worthy human being. Find out who they are, what they value and care about, which teachers on the faculty they hang out with, and how they view teaching and students.

> ▸ Include them in the secondary formats of coaching, such as grade-level meetings, study lessons, book studies, and the like. If during the meetings the teacher says something that you find irritating or voices skepticism, breathe and try paraphrasing. Once you have confirmed that you understand the point, then decide whether to respond yourself or to throw the response to the group. "What do the rest of you think about _____ concern?" Sometimes throwing the response to the group is a really useful choice. It validates the person's right to have a concern and it nudges the group to address each other's issues. Also, coming from peers, the response may be given more weight than coming from the coach, especially if the coach is an outsider.

> ▸ In the event that the team is not willing to speak up, you might ask a probing question of the speaker or note the speaker's concern and thank her for raising it and suggest she help the group think about possible ways to avert the outcome she's concerned about. Suggest putting time in the agenda for the next meeting for her to bring her solutions forward. In other words, be respectful and make sure that you are not dismissing someone's idea or concern because you are feeling irritated or taking it personally.

> ▸ Look for points of common interest. Lucy worked with a teacher who was quite critical of the work and was also the union leader. When Lucy found out that this union leader had a background in mathematics, she was able to find an entry point to build a relationship. Eventually the union leader became an advocate for the work.

> ▸ In working with someone who has become cynical, reigniting passion is the key. Sometimes those who seem the most recalcitrant are harboring the greatest passion. Lucy once worked with a group of high school social studies teachers in a chronically failing district. The teachers were at a summer institute that they were obligated to attend, and none of them wanted to be there. They were asked to tell the story of the thing they were most proud of in their careers. Some of them had been teaching for forty years! The stories told of the extraordinary things these people had done to engage their students or to provide them with experiences that would broaden their horizons or assist them in solving relevant issues. Yet these were the very teachers the district leaders had described as having no capacity. The frustrated leaders at the district level were trying harder and harder through more coercive means to get teachers to improve their instruction and in so doing actually making things worse. The teachers felt beaten down, disrespected, and worn out. What might have been different if the leaders had come to the teachers and asked them how they would solve the problems facing the district?

For a coach working with teachers in similar circumstances, it is imperative to ask the teachers for their ideas and solutions, uncover their passions, and support them by being a conduit between the administration and the teachers. Give teachers permission to use their creativity and encourage them to take a chance. Then be sure to celebrate their efforts and to buffer them from criticism from administration.

None of this is easy work, and yet improvement, change of any kind, is all about relationships. Coaches must find every means possible to develop caring, trusting, respectful relationships with everyone they encounter in their work.

Communication as a Way to Equalize Power

It is important for coaches to equalize power in their opening meetings with teachers. We can start by stating explicitly that we *desire* to do so, letting teachers know that we want to explore teaching and learning with them, side-by-side; and thereby signaling that we respect their expertise as classroom teachers. We have also noticed how a subtle change in wording—from *you* to *we*—can have major impact on how teachers receive us. For example, rather than saying, "What are *your* goals for this lesson?" say, "What are *our* goals for this lesson?"

Coaches also need to be able to equalize power with the principal and other administrators. In other words, we need to get over our unwillingness to raise tough issues with our supervisors. We encourage teachers to speak up to us, yet we may shy away from speaking up to those we perceive to have authority or power. Even if the principal is not our direct supervisor, we may feel inhibited about being proactive.

The techniques are essentially the same no matter whom we are dealing with. The most important thing is to inquire into the other person's thinking and preferences. Kerry Patterson, in an email exchange, went so far as to suggest that supervisors actually teach their subordinates how to speak to them about the things they notice that are not working (2002). While it is unlikely that all our supervisors will take Kerry up on his suggestion, we can be proactive by asking our supervisors to share with us how they prefer to receive suggestions, complaints, or less than positive information.

The activities in Appendix C, "Why Not Listen and Learn?" and "Role Plays," are designed to help you put some of the ideas in this chapter into practice. Communication is key and it is our responsibility to become as skillful in this arena as possible.

SUMMARY

If we coaches can be courageous and find our own unique voices, if we can learn to communicate clearly and effectively, we can have a powerful impact on those with whom we work. By simply changing the conversation, we can ultimately change the cultures in which we work! All global change begins locally. If we start influencing the school or district in which we work, before we know it, we'll have created a movement that reshapes twenty-first century education.

6

Assessing Teacher Development

The Starting Place for Coaching Teachers

*You have to start where people are, because their growth is
going to be from there.*
—Myles Horton

We believe that the mantra—all children can learn—should also be applied to teachers: *all teachers can learn.* The coach's role is not merely about examining teacher practice, it is about assessing teacher development as a vehicle to support teacher learning. This means that we, as coaches, have to think deeply about teachers on a developmental continuum, and use this assessment to determine the choices we make in our work with them. With some teachers, we need to focus more on deepening content knowledge; with others, we may be able to explore more sophisticated aspects of practice such as pedagogical content knowledge or how to use discourse to promote student learning. Whatever the focus of our work, we have to tailor our coaching to meet the developmental needs of teachers. Doing this ensures that whatever experiences we offer teachers will ultimately improve their practice in ways that contribute to enhancing student learning.

ASSESSING TEACHER DEVELOPMENT

Having the right starting place for our work with teachers can make all the difference in our effectiveness as coaches. To frame our work with a teacher, we have to have a clear picture of who that teacher is. We need to gather evidence and weigh it to think about how to begin our work. As we think about how to work with individual teachers and teams of teachers, here are a few questions that may be helpful in planning.

1. What do teachers need to know in order to teach well?
2. How do we identify what teachers know and then use that to inform our coaching?
3. How do teachers learn what they need to know in order to teach well?
4. Are there specific things coaches do (e.g., co-teaching in the classroom) that produce results more quickly?
5. What opportunities are there for teachers to learn (e.g., workshops, grade-level meetings, one-on-one coaching, professional teaching-learning communities)?
6. Are *all* learning opportunities beneficial to *all* teachers?
7. If teachers need different learning experiences, how do we differentiate what we do so that we meet their individual needs?

These questions are critical for effective coaching because until we learn to assess teachers accurately—not evaluate, but assess their needs—we cannot determine how to work with them or have legitimate reasons for how we are working with them. Having teacher learning at the heart of what we do also pushes us to be creative and think about how we can design our work to meet each teacher's specific needs. And we firmly believe that when we meet teachers' needs, we see growth. One size does not fit all—especially in coaching!

PAINTING A TEACHER PORTRAIT

One major challenge coaches confront is how to determine a just-right starting place for coaching individual teachers. Because finding a just-right starting place has implications for the success of one-on-one coaching, we think coaches should spend some time gathering information *before* they begin coaching teachers. We call this information gathering *painting a teacher portrait*.

To paint a teacher portrait is to look probingly at the individual, to find the essence not just of her practice, but of her beliefs and her values as well. Because it is not easy to know a teacher, we suggest that coaches use both narrow and wide lenses for painting teacher portraits. For us, the narrower lens is for looking at classroom practice; the wider lens is for looking beyond an individual's pedagogy to a teacher's social connections and how she fits into the school culture. Gathering a variety of information will help you think about the best starting place for your work with her.

As you gather information, it is important to focus on the positive because approaching a teacher from a deficit model (*There is no rich academic talk in her classroom. We'll have*

COACH NOTE

Understanding another human being is not an easy task, and painting a teacher portrait will require time and effort. You may find that you revise your initial assumptions and perceptions as you get to know a teacher. For example, a teacher's resistance and negativity at grade-level meetings may turn out to be about fear of change or fear of trying to change and failing. Going below the surface (this is what she does—resist) and finding reasons for why she is doing it (she is afraid) will give you more options for coaching. Here, something as simple as a personal narrative (your own story of when you were afraid of trying something new) might give you more leverage because shared stories are one way to find common ground.

to work on changing that.) can set the stage for negative interactions. Often, when a coach focuses on what a teacher does not (or cannot) do, she might fall into the trap of trying to fix the teacher. In our experience, there is no faster way to create friction in a coaching relationship than to have a teacher perceive your work as something that is being done *to* her rather than as something that is being done *with* her. This is why looking for and using the positive is helpful. Being positive helps us build from strength (*This teacher has developed a lovely classroom community—children speak respectfully to each other. I wonder how we could build on this? Perhaps we could use it as an entry point into developing rich academic talk?*).

We will explore key features of and skills required for painting a teacher portrait in depth in the ensuing pages. However, we also know that reading alone will not fully develop this skill set. To become truly skillful at portraiture, coaches have to develop a keen eye for analyzing teacher practice. To this end, in Appendix C (on page 204), we have included some activities and questions to help you develop your ability to paint teacher portraits.

Begin By Painting Your Own Portrait

Assessing teacher development is not an easy task because, as we discussed in Chapter 3, educators do not yet have codified standards of practice that are universally accepted. This means that educators watching the same lesson might be noticing very different things! Because what we value influences *how* and *what* we see, we need to be aware of how our own beliefs impact our understanding and assessment of teacher practice (Senge 1990).

We suggest painting your own portrait before attempting to paint a teacher portrait. Doing this cultivates a deep self-awareness, which can help us recognize when and how our own needs and fears color our perceptions and sift through what we notice about the teachers we work with. For example, if we are highly sensitive to equity and gender issues, we might have to take time to sort through our observations and make sure to keep to factual evidence when issues of equity or gender arise in a classroom. Being able to put an observation in neutral terms (*He called on Ken ten times*) rather than in evaluative terms (*He values male opinions more than female's; that's why he's called on Ken so many times in this discussion*) may be the difference between having an effective crucial conversation around teacher choices (and practice) and one that veers off into recriminations that might damage the coaching relationship. (For more information on self-assessment and self-awareness see Chapter 4, "Know Thyself." For more information on crucial conversations see Chapter 5, "Communication Is Key.")

Using Developmental Frameworks as Tools for Painting a Portrait

The more completely you know the teachers you work with, the more likely you will find ways to help them grow as professionals. But what does *know* a teacher mean? When we, as coaches, assess teacher development, how do we know what we are looking for and what do our findings tell us about a teacher? How do we distinguish among novice, competent, and expert teachers? (Berliner 2004)

Here are some questions currently being grappled with by educators everywhere:[1]

1. Is there a developmental landscape for teaching? If there is, what are the critical big ideas in teaching?

2. What are important strategies teachers need to develop to support student learning?

3. Is there a specific skill set, a way of behaving in the classroom, that distinguishes a novice from an expert teacher?

Charlotte Danielson, in her book, Enhancing Professional Practice: A Framework for Teaching *(2nd edition), provides one example of a developmental framework for teachers. She lists four domains for assessing teacher practice: (1) planning and preparation, (2) classroom environment, (3) instruction, and (4) professional responsibilities (2007). These four domains are broken down in specific ways. Danielson offers elements and indicators of each domain that can be helpful to coaches as they assess teacher development. They can be used to help coaches consider which aspects of teaching to focus on as they paint teacher portraits.*

These questions, while important, are not easily answered. And even though different educators are creating protocols and frameworks (Danielson 2007) for analyzing teacher practice, it is important to remember that we, as a profession, do not yet have universally accepted standards of practice. So while we recommend that coaches be aware of the different protocols and frameworks that are available to assess teacher development, we also suggest that coaches remember that these protocols and tools are only useful if they inform *how* you coach a teacher.[2] For example, some of the frameworks are set up like checklists. Checking off what a teacher does or does not do and how well she does or does not do it is only useful if you can use that information in the service of teacher learning. Because content coaching is about both naming *and* doing, if you are going to help a teacher grow, you have to be able to identify strengths and weaknesses and coach from a place that is both accessible and transformative. (For an example of how a coach sets specific goals for teacher development and weaves them into her one-on-one coaching, see the case study in Chapters 7–9.)

UNDERSTANDING A TEACHER'S VALUES AND BELIEFS

In education, our tendency to compartmentalize often obscures the bigger picture. If we engage with our colleagues only on a surface level, if we do not seek to know anything about their professional interests or understand other facets of their lives, we can only have

---

[1] For an example of a framework currently being used to evaluate teachers, visit the website, http://www.danielsongroup.org/article.aspx?page=frameworkforteaching.

[2] We recognize that Danielson's framework is being used in some districts and schools as a tool for evaluation; we are not encouraging this. What we are suggesting is that the framework is *one* possible tool for thinking about how to paint a teacher portrait.

a very limited view of them. By taking the time to paint a more complete picture, we can often gain deeper insights—a perspective that can be used to find mutual purpose in our professional lives. For example, a colleague and I disagree about which style of teaching is best. When I find out that this colleague went down to New Orleans after hurricane Katrina to help out on her summer vacation, my lens widens because I now see what we have in common: we both care about humanity. My revised portrait of my colleague helps me keep the differences in our teaching philosophy in perspective because I now know her in a broader sense. Because I see her more completely as a human being, I am less likely to trivialize her as a person and to dismiss her ideas. In our coaching experience, we have found that the more we seek to know about one another, the more likely we will find commonalities between us. And commonalities can be the bridges that support difficult, crucial conversations.

In order to see our colleagues as people and not as vehicles or obstacles to our own professional agenda, it behooves us to learn how to inquire into *their* beliefs and values. But how do the beliefs and values of others manifest themselves? And how can we use the evidence we gather about teacher beliefs and values to support our work with them?

Use Student Learning as Evidence

Because student learning mirrors teacher beliefs about teaching and learning, coaches can analyze the data they collect and gain insights into teacher beliefs and values. How and what students learn, their level of engagement, the quality of discourse and the lines of communication, the opportunities provided for their questions and confusions to surface, and the quality of the artifacts they are asked to create can all be used to benchmark important aspects of teacher practice. For example, first graders are having a whole-group discussion and the teacher calls on one child, who replies incorrectly to her question. The teacher says, "No, that's not it," and turns to another child and says, "Can you help out?" What does this snapshot tell you about classroom culture? Although this is not the complete picture, it certainly gives some information about what is valued (correct answers) and how mistakes are handled (they are ignored or "fixed"). But the fact that the incorrect answer was not explored might be interpreted in different ways (the teacher holds to a tight schedule or the teacher doesn't yet understand the value of misconceptions and mistakes in learning, perhaps). Remember, one snapshot is not a portrait!

Go Beyond the Physical Environment of the Classroom

Although looking at the physical environment of the classroom (e.g., room arrangement, student grouping, a meeting area for sharing ideas) may seem like an obvious starting point, this may not necessarily give a deep insight into teacher beliefs. The external view may not match internal beliefs. For example, many classrooms in NYC now have a cooperative learning setting—today's norm for how classrooms look. Students are seated in groups of four or five or six. There are meeting areas in classrooms where whole-group discussions can occur. The appearance hints at communities of discourse. However, if one peers below the surface (e.g., are students actually collaborating? Talking to each other? Or are they working individually while seated in what appear to be collaborative groups?), it is easy to discern that this cooperative setting may actually be a façade, and that students are just as boxed in, controlled, and powerless as in more traditional (desks in rows) classroom settings.

Coaches can get a more accurate reading by broadening this lens and thinking of environment not just as a physical space, but as an emotional one. Try answering one of two questions: *Would I want to be a student in this classroom and why?* or *Would I want my own child to be a student in this classroom and why?* Here, coaches might focus more on: (1) student affect, which is a mirror of teacher affect (Are students responsive? Happy?); (2) the ways in which students and teacher speak to each other (Are students respectful to all members of the classroom community? Do they listen to each other or only to the teacher?); and (3) the kind of energy in the classroom (Are students engaged or passive learners)?

While classroom culture is important to notice and can help coaches gain perspective on teacher values and beliefs, there is one caveat. It is possible for classrooms to be vibrant, joyful places, places of mutual respect, where students exhibit positive learning behaviors and speak freely *and* also places of superficial learning! For this reason, coaches need to look beyond student engagement, and explore what teachers are actually asking students to do (*What is the nature of the task students are engaged in?*) and how teachers are supporting student learning (e.g., *How do they conference with students? How do they facilitate whole-group discussions?*).

Tasks as a Source of Evidence

The kind of tasks teachers give students and how they use them can give a coach information into teacher content and pedagogical content knowledge (Shulman 1986) as well as insights into teachers' beliefs about teaching and learning. Here are a few questions to consider as you examine a task and how it is used in a classroom:

> ➤ Is the task rich? By this we mean
>
>> ◆ Is it differentiated (does it have multiple entry points)?
>>
>> ◆ Is it developmentally appropriate? If it's too difficult, children will shut down; if it's too easy, children will not be challenged. When the task is too easy, you'll see students breezing through it. While they may seem engaged and be both happy and talkative, their intellectual engagement may only be superficial. A developmentally appropriate task gives

children the opportunity to grow intellectually and emotionally: Intellectually when the task challenges and expands their knowledge base; emotionally when they, as learners, have to persevere, have to deal with disequilibrium, have to develop specific learning habits to complete the task. On the other hand, when a task is too difficult, you may see some students not participating or relying on their peers to do the work for them. Frustration levels may be high and students' emotions may be negative.

> ▸ How does the teacher anticipate and deal with divergent strategies and perspectives? How does she predict and deal with student misconceptions?

> ▸ How are students grouped (hetero- or homogeneously)? What's the rationale behind this grouping? For example, when teachers say things like, "The one who gets it is going to help the one who doesn't," a coach has information that can help her determine where to begin her work with that teacher. Just examining what a teacher means by *helping* and gathering evidence around what this help entails for each learner can be eye opening to teachers when they begin to realize that one child does the work (is actively learning) and the other child watches (is passive in the learning process).

> ▸ As they work on the task, are students free to move around the room or do they need to ask permission to get out of their seats?

> ▸ Are students able to get up and select their own tools or has the teacher preselected the tools and/or manipulatives? Are these tools appropriate for the task or do they limit thinking?

> ▸ What is the nature of student talk as they work on a task? If they are partnered, do they question each other, or work in tandem with little or no talk?

Analyzing Classroom Discourse

One way to gain insight into teacher beliefs about teaching and learning is to script classroom discourse. For this reason, we suggest that coaches visit classrooms and, if possible, transcribe the conversations they hear.[3] Try to gather information from a variety of conversations; these might be whole-class discussions, teacher-student conferencing,

---

[3] We recognize how difficult it is to transcribe classroom conversations. However, we also know how helpful it can be for coaches to have exact quotes of what transpires in a classroom when they are talking to teachers about their practice. For this reason, we suggest that all coaches become skilled at accurate notetaking; transcribing as much of a classroom conversation as possible is a part of this important skill.

and/or student-to-student conversations. Taking the time to analyze the patterns and quality of talk (e.g., do students talk in complete sentences or give one word responses) can be enormously helpful as you try to get a clear picture of a teacher you are about to coach.

Here are some questions to think about as you observe classroom talk:

> Who *owns* the learning? Where are children's voices in the conversation? If we think of the conversation as a dialogue ball, does the ball always go back to the teacher? Do students pose their own questions to other students or is the teacher the conduit for talk?

> How do students talk to each other? Are they respectful of each other's ideas? Do they listen to each other? Do they look at each other when they are speaking?

> What kinds of questions do students pose? Do they slow down the learning process by asking questions when they don't understand?

> How does the community deal with mistakes—are they avoided or embraced as learning opportunities?

> What *talk moves* (e.g., use of wait time, pair talk, paraphrasing) does the teacher use and how effective are these moves in supporting learning (Chapin, O'Connor, and Anderson 2009)? Does the teacher use talk moves to

 ◆ slow down the learning around big ideas or conflicting perspectives?

 ◆ bring children who are struggling into the conversation?

 ◆ challenge students' ability to reason and communicate that reasoning?

> How does a teacher use the share (whole-group conversations)? Is it unstructured, as evidenced in the question, "Who wants to share today?" or is it carefully mapped out to support student development of key ideas (Fernandez and Yoshida 2004)?

Gathering Big-Picture Evidence

To help paint a teacher portrait, be sure also to gather big-picture evidence. This big-picture evidence can be gathered in a number of ways and from a number of different sources. You can ask the principal or other administration about the teacher you will be working with; you can observe her in a variety of settings (lunchroom, staff room, at school functions, to name a few). As you gather big-picture evidence, here are a few questions to keep in mind:

> What does the leadership team (principal, assistant principal, other coaches) think about this teacher's practice and willingness to learn?

- ▸ How does this teacher fit into the big-picture hierarchy of school dynamics?

- ▸ How respected is she in her particular grade? Is she someone others go to (and how frequently), or do her peers avoid her?

- ▸ Who does she network with on the staff? Does she have cross-grade collaborations? With which teachers?

- ▸ What is her affect toward learning? Is she someone who signs up for different professional development offerings? Tries on new teaching practices? Seeks out the latest professional reading materials to help her improve her practice?

- ▸ How do students view her? Is she beloved?

MAKING SENSE OF THE EVIDENCE

So how *does* a coach weigh this evidence, know which piece of information to choose and use in her first coaching session? It is critical to select an aspect of practice that has the potential to engage the teacher and, when explored over time, impact that teacher's craft. It is also helpful to find an area of focus that might also connect you in mutual purpose. For example, if both you and the classroom teacher are passionate about equity, this might give you an entry into examining aspects of her practice that might be affecting poor, minority, or female students' ability to achieve to the highest levels. For more about choosing a starting point for a teacher, see Chapter 7, where we discuss how one of the authors gathered evidence and used this in her initial coaching session with the classroom teacher.

SUMMARY

Painting a portrait is about coming to know a teacher from a variety of perspectives. Taking the time to paint a portrait will help you determine the best starting place for your work with a teacher. Gathering information will also help you determine what the most productive, mutually aligned approach might be for coaching. As you gather information, as you try to capture the essence of a teacher and what her needs are, stay focused on the positive. Remember, the more detailed the picture you paint, the more specific you can be in how you coach a given teacher. The depth of your knowledge about an individual will directly impact the depth and effectiveness of your coaching.

The Preconference

Lesson design is nothing less than an art form.

Previous chapters focused on ways to assess yourself as a coach, to assess the teacher you are working with, and how to use these assessments to set realistic goals for your coaching. While all of this prep work is foundational for effective coaching, it will not, in and of itself, transform teacher practice. To do this, coaches have to focus their work with teachers on the instructional core. At the center of this work is planning lessons (the goal of the preconference or planning session), enacting these lessons in the classroom (the goal of co-teaching), and gauging the effectiveness of these plans in light of student learning (the goal of the postconference or debriefing session).

Of the three components in the coaching cycle—planning, co-teaching, and debriefing—we believe that in the initial stages of working with teachers, planning has the most potential to affect practice deeply. Here's why: in planning, a coach is able to explore salient aspects of lesson design. This includes helping teachers understand the content they teach, how children learn that content, how to craft questions when conferencing with students, how to anticipate and support student learning in the classroom, and how to assess student learning. Having a clear and detailed plan also helps coaches know when to co-teach (when to enter and exit a lesson in the classroom) and how to structure the postlesson conversation (what to focus on in the debrief).

INFLUENCING TEACHER PRACTICE

In crafting lessons, content coaches help teachers anticipate student learning paths and misconceptions and think about how they *might* address these, what questions they *might* ask, and what challenges they *might* pose to learners. Teachers who have a sense of what *might* happen and how to use this knowledge in the act of teaching are able to shift the focus from self to students, which is so essential in effective teaching. As teachers shift their focus, they get better at facilitating the flow of learning because they are able to consider which ideas they want to come to the fore, and which ideas can remain in the background. When teachers are able to weigh student responses in relation to important ideas in the content, they can decide how to use students' comments or questions in discussion (whether to connect or juxtapose ideas, whether to create disequilibrium, or whether to scaffold learning for the entire community).

When a lesson has been carefully planned, teachers can anticipate what *might* happen in their classrooms. For many teachers, having a mental map is pivotal for changing practice. It is easier for them to take risks and shift their behaviors in the classroom when they have developed a map of possible student learning routes. With a clear picture of what might happen, what students might do or say, teachers can better anticipate which teaching decisions might best support learning.

> **COACH NOTE**
>
> *Teaching is both an art and a science. Great teaching requires people to think deeply about what it is they are teaching and how they are influencing the lives and minds of their students. Part of the art of teaching is directly related to lesson design.*

THE ROLE OF CURRICULUM MATERIALS

The art and science of lesson planning, using curriculum materials well, and designing units of study and individual lessons is the work of the profession of teaching. One of the major questions facing all teachers and coaches is: how do we take curriculum materials, units of study, and individual lessons and make them come to life, make them meet the needs of our students?

To respond to this challenging question, teachers and coaches have to give themselves permission to engage with curriculum materials in ways that give them opportunities to understand (1) the learning theory that underpins the materials (assuming there is one), (2) the way the materials are constructed, and (3) the reasons for that construction.

Educators also need to have the liberty to adapt the lessons in a given set of curriculum materials to meet their students' developmental needs or to slow down or speed up in relation to those needs. To plan lessons successfully coaches and teachers have to consider questions like: What is the learning trajectory of this content? What are the big ideas? Supporting ideas?

KEY QUESTIONS FOR PLANNING LESSONS

What, why, who, and *how* questions are essential in any planning session with teachers. These can be framed as either big- or small-picture questions. Although both big- and small-picture questions should be addressed for successful lesson design, not all questions need to be addressed at all times. For a coach, this is part of the skill of knowing what aspect of lesson design to focus on with a given teacher.

COACH NOTE

It is sometimes a challenge to keep teachers from jumping over the what, why, *and* who *questions. If this happens, remember that once teachers have gone through a preconference or two, they become more accustomed to the process and realize that the* how *question is better addressed if the other questions are crystal clear.*

THE *WHAT, WHY, WHO*, AND *HOW* OF LESSON DESIGN

Lesson design focused solely on implementing curriculum materials is frequently inadequate because the planning focuses on only one aspect of lesson design, the *how* (*How will I teach this lesson?*), and fails to address *what*, *why*, and *who* questions. We have found that it is the *what*, *why*, and *who* questions that essentially change teacher thinking and trigger more reflective lesson planning habits of mind. This is not to say that the *how* question is not important; it is. However, it is not the sole purpose of lesson design, and spending too much time on the *how* is often the root of flawed instruction. Because the coach's primary role is to facilitate reflection and growth, *what*, *why*, and *who* questions serve to empower educators to think more deeply about their curriculum tools, assessments, and what constitutes ongoing evidence of student learning.

Here are some examples of *who*, *what* and *why* questions:

> ▸ **What** is the content to be learned by the students?

> ▸ **What** strategies, habits of mind, or learning dispositions are to be practiced by students?

> ▸ **Why** is this specific content being taught at this particular time?

> ▸ **Why** will this content be taught in this particular way?

> ▸ **Who** are the students being taught? **What** are their developmental needs?

> ▸ **What** understanding do they bring to this topic?

This sample list is by no means exhaustive; each of these questions has several sub-questions that can be explored by coach and teacher to refine the actual lesson plan.

How do you know which questions to address and when to address them in a planning session? We will explore this critical lesson-planning question in greater depth in the ensuing coaching case study. (To read more about this, see the "Revised Guide to Core Issues in Lesson Design," which provides a list of questions worth pondering when designing lessons or units of study.)[1]

---

[1] The "Guide to Core Issues" from *Content-Focused Coaching* has been revised by the authors and can be found in Appendix A. This tool can be used in lesson design.

Focusing on Big Ideas and Essential Questions in a Domain

To plan lessons effectively, teachers must consider the big ideas in their domain of study. Without this perspective, lessons often skim the surface. This means that for teachers to answer the *what* question, they have to know their content from two perspectives: a conceptual one (what are the essential underlying and/or unifying big ideas of this unit of study?) and a skill-based one (what are the critical skills, facts, and procedures in this lesson or unit of study?).

Because many teachers have skill-based understandings of teaching and learning, the big, conceptual ideas remain elusive. How might one define *big idea*? Here are two different yet similar definitions of big ideas. Randall Charles' definition for big ideas pertaining to mathematics:

> A *Big Idea* is a statement of an idea that is central to the learning of mathematics, one that links numerous mathematical understandings into a coherent whole. . . . Big Ideas should be the foundation for one's mathematics content knowledge, for one's teaching practices, and for the mathematics curriculum. (Charles 2005, 1)

Catherine Twomey Fosnot and Maarten Dolk in their seminal book series, *Young Mathematicians at Work*, describe big ideas thus:

> Big ideas are the central, organizing ideas of mathematics—principles that define mathematical order. They are characteristic of shifts in learners' reasoning—shifts in perspective, in logic, in the mathematical relationships they set up. (Fosnot and Dolk 2001, 10)

Change the word *mathematics* in the above examples to science or social studies or any other academic domain, and the definition still works! In social studies, a big idea might go something like this: *Civilizations develop in ways that are impacted by their geographic location.* In this example, a teacher planning a social studies lesson might consider how to help students understand how a culture's geographic location affects the evolution of the culture. Sometimes teachers are expected to write *guiding questions* in relation to a unit of study or a lesson. Guiding questions are based on big ideas. Take the example above from social studies. Here is a possible guiding question: How is the economy of a society impacted by its geography?

Turning to science, an example of big ideas related to sound might be that there is a relationship between sound waves and energy. Sound waves have energy and can travel through different media. When the wave encounters an object, the energy of the wave can be transferred to the object. This is an unobservable, underlying cause for the observation that an opera singer can sometimes shatter a glass with her voice. A guiding question might be: How can sound cause objects to distort, shake, or break (http://tools 4teachingscience.org/tools/Big_Idea_Primer.pdf)?

Here is a scenario: a coach is working with a teacher to plan a lesson that begins with the problem 19 × 7. When the coach asks, "What's the mathematical goal of the lesson?" and the teacher responds, "multiplication," there's a misconception here: that the topic (multiplication) names the goal or that the topic *is* the big idea. For example, when a student solves 19 × 7 using the standard algorithm for multiplication, what does he actually understand? Can he explain how the partial products (9 × 7) and (10 × 7)—the distributive property—make this algorithm work?

$$19 \times 7 = (10 + 9) \times 7 = (10 \times 7) + (9 \times 7) = 70 + 63 = 133$$

What this example highlights is that to plan a successful multiplication lesson, teachers have to be clear about what big ideas (e.g., distributive property), strategies (e.g., creating partial products), and models (e.g., open array) relate to this topic. They also have to know how these ideas are connected, and how students develop them.

In thinking about big ideas, strategies, and models, and how they are developed (what Fosnot and Dolk call a mathematical "landscape of learning" (2001, 15–31)), teachers can consider how any given lesson will build upon and extend children's multiplicative understanding. For example, the distributive property might be thought of conceptually and students who understand how it works might say things like, "You can break numbers apart, multiply the smaller parts, and then add them all back together to get the product of the original problem." While the students may be describing a strategy for solving a multiplication problem, the underlying big ideas are not specific to this problem but are fundamental structures *in* multiplication that make this strategy work. The generalization of big ideas is what supports moving away from algorithmic use of strategies to more creative ways of thinking about numbers (e.g., A student might say, "The product of 19×7 is equivalent to the product of $(20 \times 7) - (1 \times 7)$.)." This use of the distributive property over subtraction as a strategy is rooted in the generalizing the distributive property as a big idea, which is a critical component of numeracy.

Big-Picture *What* Questions

Understanding the big ideas and/or essential questions is at the heart of effective lesson design. One big-picture question that should be considered thoroughly is: *What is the specific content in this lesson? Is the lesson designed to develop big ideas or explore essential questions? If the lesson is focused on specific skills, is the teacher aware of the underlying big ideas related to those skills?* Being able to think about lesson goals in terms of big ideas and skills (is this lesson going to develop a big idea or to help children master a specific skill related to a big idea) is an important framework that helps coaches and teachers map out learning objectives, create realistic timeframes, and find appropriate ways to assess student learning.

Framing Student Learning

One way to frame the conceptual/skill question is to connect it to another big-picture *what* question: *What will students have learned as a result of this lesson?* The answer to this question relates directly to the depth of one's understanding about both content and children's development of that content. Because learning is not linear, there may be multiple goals: different goals for different learners and ultimately different degrees of understanding among individual students. To articulate exactly how the lesson will support all students' thinking is a necessary component of any well-crafted lesson.

Other *What* Questions

Here are some more big-picture and small-picture *what* questions and how they might play out in lesson design:

> ▸ *What is the nature of the task?* Is it open-ended? Closed? Skill-driven? A task that is too broad might need to be narrowed; one that is too closed may need to be opened. Both types of tasks need to be carefully considered when one is thinking about the time frame for the lesson: How long will the introduction be? How long will students need to complete the task? Will there be a whole-class discussion at the end of the lesson or will this be done on the next day? Will there be time for student writing and reflection?

> ▸ *Given the content, what will student strategies, misconceptions, and partial under-standings be? What kinds of difficulties will they encounter? How will their struggles*

be connected to big ideas they are developing or have not yet developed? Understanding child development is important to successful lesson implementation. For this reason, as part of lesson design, coaches should help teachers identify each learner's present understanding and also identify the collective understanding of the group. This means taking time in the planning session to map out where students fall on a developmental continuum. In doing this, the coach can help the teacher think through individual and group learning. However, this is not possible if one does not understand content in ways that help one ponder things like *what does a beginning (or advanced) understanding look like in a given domain? Sound like? Are there places when conferring with individual students where a just-right question might pivot those students to a new place in their thinking? How might I identify and then, in the classroom, respond effectively to emerging ideas as expressed by children orally or in writing?*

➤ *Given the content in this lesson, what will the time frame be for executing it successfully?* A rule of thumb might be: the richer the task, the more time children need for exploration, for writing, for discussion. In a skill-type lesson, the time frame may not be problematic and can follow a fairly predictable pattern (e.g., introduction, work-time, share). If the content is rich, however, children might need more than one day to explore and complete the task. If children are expected to write, create products (e.g., picture books, websites), work on projects, or create solutions to share with their peers, additional time might be needed for them to prepare this writing. Some key questions here are: how much time do children need to reflect on their work before a discussion? Will I use a gallery walk[2] for children to get feedback from their peers and then offer them an opportunity to revise their writing?

➤ *What does it mean to complete this task successfully and how will student learning be assessed?* Because assessing student learning is one of the most difficult tasks confronting teachers, it is essential in lesson planning to map out how the learning will be assessed. There are many different ways to do this (e.g., a teacher might take notes as students work on the task or might analyze student written responses for evidence of learning), so what needs to be

---

[2]A gallery walk is a powerful learning tool that is used to share different ideas that have arisen in a classroom in relation to a specific task students have been exploring. In this process, students share their written ideas in a public forum, reflecting both on each other's work (they write comments or questions on Post-it notes and put these on each other's posters [writing]). As part of this process, students are given an opportunity, after the gallery walk, to reflect on what was written on their poster, and to revise their writing if necessary. This iterative process gives students an opportunity to develop and reflect on what it means to communicate with clarity.

explored by coaches as part of lesson design is what is to be assessed and how to assess it.

The *Why* and *Who* Questions

In addition to *what* questions, content coaches work with teachers to think about *why* questions. Here are some big-picture and small-picture *why* questions and how they might play out in lesson design:

> ▸ *Why am I teaching this particular lesson? Why are we using this particular lesson with our students at this particular time?* In considering the *why* questions, *who* questions naturally arise: who are my students and what are their developmental needs? Is this lesson connected to what they know? Will it build upon and deepen their existing knowledge? Will it be too difficult? Too easy? If the answer to "Why this lesson?" is "It's next in the curriculum," that is not sufficient to explain why this lesson is necessary at this particular time from the perspective of learning as development. For coaches, it is important to help teachers understand that they must consider how a lesson fits into a sequence of lessons, what kind of prior knowledge is necessary for children to be successful with the task at hand, and how this lesson will support their development or understanding of big ideas in the domain.

> ▸ *Why are we choosing to teach a given lesson in a particular way?* Content coaches explore how lessons are structured and why they are designed that way. Questions here might focus on how to introduce a lesson (*why are we introducing it like this?*); what materials are to be used (*why are we putting out these materials (or manipulatives)? How will this tool support student learning?*); how students are grouped (*why are we grouping students in pairs?*). As part of lesson planning, coaches help teachers not only think about their choices, but also justify their decisions (*I know this is the best way to teach this lesson because . . .*).

> ▸ *Why are lessons in a curriculum organized in certain sequences (and are those particular sequences the best way to develop student thinking)?* Content coaches ask *why* questions to help teachers dig into the materials they are using and learn to use them in more reflective ways. Exploring why questions in relationship to the curricular materials can help teachers learn how to make more informed instructional decisions so that the curriculum becomes a tool, not a script. With a teacher, a coach might explore the following questions:

>> ◆ *Why* might the lessons in a curriculum be sequenced the way they are?

>> ◆ *Why* is the curriculum suggesting a particular sequence and set of activities?

- *How* would we know if the activities would actually develop the ideas or skills they're intended to develop?

- *Why* does the curriculum suggest telling students how to do something rather than using exploration and immersion to develop their capacity to think?

- *What* do these choices tell us about the authors' underlying beliefs about how people learn? Do we agree with this philosophy? If not, how can we adjust these lessons to reflect our own ideas about learning?

The *How* Question

The *how* of lesson design is often much easier to handle than *what, why,* and *who*; in fact, it's usually what's in the curriculum materials! In many models of coaching, the *how* question is the one that gets the most attention and the *what, why,* and *who* questions are glossed over or neglected.

If we revisit our multiplication example (see page 100), a teacher may decide to teach the distributive property by giving students a sequence of mental-math arithmetic problems that might prompt the use of partial products, followed by discussion of why a partial-products strategy works and whether this strategy will work for any given multiplication problem. The teacher might plan to encourage students to use array models to represent their ideas and prove generalizations about the distributive property, deepening their understanding.

The *how* question also addresses whether students will work in groups, in pairs, or individually. Timing, management, and so on also fall under the umbrella of how.

Here are some other big-picture and small-picture *how* questions and the ways in which they might play out in lesson design:

▶ *How will this lesson support the developmental needs of all the learners in my classroom?* If the lesson is too difficult or too easy for some children, there will be frustration or boredom or both, which often leads to management issues. Is the task one that provides entry to all students and has enough complexity to challenge more sophisticated learners?

▶ *How will I launch this lesson?* The coach and teacher may consider questions such as:

- Will the launch be a minilesson or will we go directly into a major task or activity?

- Where will the students be sitting (At their desks? In a meeting area?)?

- *What* will I write as I introduce the lesson? (Will I put key information on the board?)

- Will I have students restate any part of the information I am presenting?

- Will I then write key elements of what they say on a board for everyone to see?

- How long should the introduction be?

- Should I build in time for pair talk as a way to ensure that all students understand the task before they work independently?

- If I have students paraphrase the task or directions, should I give time for them to also pose questions?

- If there are children who I know will struggle with this content, should I give them extra support before sending them off to work? And what is the nature of this support? *How* scaffolded should this support be?

▶ *How do I use my understanding of content and development to anticipate the kinds of pedagogy I need to use to support learning?* In lesson design, coaches have to explore pedagogical content knowledge with teachers. Here, understanding student strategies, struggles, and oral communications can help predict how to work with ideas or confusions as they come up, how to link or scaffold specific ideas related to content, and which ideas are needed structurally to support learning. For example, in lesson design, coaches can help teachers think about pedagogy using the lens of discourse, which can be orchestrated by specific pedagogical moves (e.g., pair talk, think time, and paraphrasing).

▶ *How will I use questions to support and challenge student thinking?* A major component of lesson design is to help teachers learn how to anticipate and create the kinds of questions they will use in their teaching. In this regard, the coach assists the teacher in being able to anticipate student responses to the task at hand. Doing this helps teachers develop confidence in their ability to control the flow of the lesson, to know when to dig deep, when to create disequilibrium, and when to move on.

▶ *How will students be grouped? Will they work independently or in small groups or both? If in small groups, what kind of grouping will be used (heterogeneous or homogeneous, and based on what criteria)? How might one's knowledge of children's social relationships affect any grouping?* For a content coach, an important part of lesson planning is the exploration of the ways in which teachers envision students working on a given task. This includes whether children are expected to work alone some or all of the time, whether they are paired or asked to work in small groups, and the rationale underlying these groupings. How a teacher groups students is a window into a teacher's beliefs about how children learn and who the players are in the classroom. Exploring these kinds of teacher choices during lesson planning is important for short-term (the immediate lesson) and long-term (how do I refine this teacher's practice) goal setting. Because teachers' opinions about their students often become the views children internalize about themselves (e.g., *Oh, she's the smart one; I'm not!*), having this information gives the coach invaluable insights into teacher beliefs and understanding of child development that can be used in future coaching sessions.

Big-Picture *What, Why, Who,* and *How* Questions: An Example

What would thinking about the *what, why, who* and *how* questions sound like if we were planning a poetry lesson? To answer this question, we might have to first consider big-picture questions like: *What experiences have my students previously had with poetry? Who are my students as readers and writers and how would this lesson (these lessons) support their learning?*

In planning the lessons, one would have to consider big-picture questions like: *What would I like students to understand about poetry?* Possible answer: Poetry has salient features that distinguish it from prose. Examples might include: use of metaphor and simile, that poetry can rhyme or not, that poems have white space and line breaks, and that poems have different rhythms.

Another big-picture question to consider might be: *How do students develop a deep understanding of the genre?* Possible answer: Because reading and writing of poetry are necessary for developing an in-depth understanding of the genre, we will have to build this into our lesson/s. In thinking about how students learn to write poetry, the coach and teacher may have to consider the importance of immersion, that students need to read a variety of poems silently and orally, listen to poetry, analyze poetry, and study the writing styles of different poets. Critical for students' own writing may be having time to spend gathering images and anecdotes and listening to speech patterns and rhythms, which they can later use in their own poetry.

To help children understand this genre, a teacher might gather a variety of poems that utilize metaphor to a great extent and have children compare and contrast them to understand how poets utilize metaphor to create powerful poems. She might use reading strategies that help the reader make meaning of the poem.

THE ROLE OF COLLABORATION

Lesson planning as part of content coaching is often done with small groups of teachers, and this collaborative model has proven to contribute to the growth of all involved. By planning and trying activities and strategies in the company of others, we sometimes discover that there are many ways of approaching or thinking about the task. When divergent ideas arise, teachers gain insights into the variability of human thought. For teachers who can imagine the solution only as their solution or from what's written in the text (curriculum), it can be very surprising (and enlightening) that there are other ways to think about a given task. As teachers listen to the reasoning of their peers and justify their own thinking, they develop habits of mind critical to developing students' thinking. In their classrooms, this may translate into being more open to the possibilities of different interpretations or solutions. It also may mean that when they are better able to anticipate different responses or ideas, they become better able to question student thinking. And because teachers will have explored the big ideas underlying a lesson and thought about how those ideas are developed and connected, they may, in their own classrooms, find ways to juxtapose critical big ideas to deepen student learning.

A Case Study[3]

Background on the Coaching Session

David, a third-grade teacher at a charter school in the South Bronx, has been teaching for eight years. In the past year, Toni (the coach in the transcripts) worked with him in grade-level meetings where the team mapped out units of study. Although Toni visited David's classroom several times over the course of the year, she never coached him one-on-one.

In preparation for coaching David, Toni visited his classroom the day before the coaching session and took notes on his instruction and his children's learning habits. As she observed the lesson (he was facilitating a small-group multiplication minilesson[4] while the other children were playing a math game, Factor Bingo[5]), Toni observed two things to focus on in her coaching. First, she realized that David had altered the game, and, in doing so, removed the math challenge. Second, as she watched his mental-math minilesson, she realized that his knowledge of how to pace the lesson and how to model student thinking needed to be examined and refined. These two snapshots taken from a brief classroom visit impacted her goals for coaching David.

COACH NOTE

Although our case study focuses on mathematics coaching, we believe connections and generalizations can be made to all content areas. We invite readers who coach in other content areas to examine the coaching moves in the case study and think about the implications for their own coaching practice.

---

[3] We highly recommend that you watch the corresponding online video *before* reading the case study sections of Chapters 7 through 9.

[4] The kind of minilesson described in the ensuing pages is specific to mathematics instruction and the development of computational fluency. It differs from the kind of minilesson often used in literacy. For more information on this kind of math minilesson, see Chapter 5 in Fosnot and Dolk's, *Young Mathematicians at Work: Constructing Multiplication and Division*.

[5] Factor Bingo is a multiplication game. There are different variations of this game. The goal of the game is to help children understand factor-product relationships as well as develop automaticity with their basic multiplication facts.

PLANNING TIP #1: *Hit the Ground Running*

Because time is of the essence in teaching and coaching, coaches should hit the ground running. One way to do this is to collect evidence to use in coaching (for an example of one way to do this, see the activity, *Painting a Portrait*, in Chapter 6). This could be as simple as emailing the teacher the day before a coaching session to get information on the lesson being taught or as complex as spending time in the teacher's classroom, taking notes on both teaching and learning, and then using one's observations to plan and set goals for coaching. However, if this is your first time working with a teacher, taking notes can be disconcerting especially if he has never worked with you before or if he is unfamiliar with the coaching process.

COACH NOTE

A major question confronting coaches is: How do I address important issues of practice and challenge thinking without alienating the person I am coaching? *In the case study, transcript segments will be used to highlight possible ways to address specific issues and concerns about teacher practice.*

PLANNING TIP #2: *Set Specific Goals for Coaching*

Determining how to start a coaching session requires the coach to consider the following questions: (1) How much time do I have for this session? (2) What are my goals for this planning session? (3) Are some things (e.g., content knowledge, pedagogy, pacing) more important to address than others? (4) How do I bring up difficult but crucial ideas and issues? (5) What do I know about this teacher's style of teaching, personality, and interests that might help me coach?[6]

Where to Begin the Coaching Session?

In the initial coaching session, three challenges confront coaches: (1) how to begin a coaching session, (2) how to weave in one's goals for developing teacher practice, and (3) how to address issues and concerns about teacher practice. The segment below shows how Toni began the coaching session.

> **Toni:** I was amazed yesterday when I was in your third-grade classroom for a number of reasons. I was amazed by the level of math they were doing—because I remember where they were in September. And I was also amazed by the community you've developed. I thought that that was incredible. So one of the things we're going to be working on is we're going to be looking at minilessons . . . like mental-math minilessons in multiplication and that's what our lesson is going to be based on. And then the other kids are going to be playing . . . ?

---

[6] More suggestions for collaborative goal setting can be found in Appendix D.

David: A just-right math game, Factor Bingo.

Toni: And how is that game going?

David: I think the kids are having a good time with it; they're getting to practice a lot of multiplication facts that we didn't necessarily have them memorize, but they were using their work and now they're really focusing on their facts that they want to challenge themselves with.

Within the first two minutes of the coaching session, Toni uses a number of coaching moves to set the framework for the coaching session. First, she *names the positive*. Second, she *frames what they will be focusing on* (a mental-math minilesson with a small group of students). Third, she *opens up the conversation to explore a teacher choice* that she had found problematic. This third move sets the stage for both exploring the rationale underlying David's choice to change the game's rules, and helping him understand that, when played correctly, the game has the potential to develop mathematical reasoning. By taking the time to gather information about his understanding of the game and his choices, Toni can decide whether to explore this with him in the coaching session. David's response, "I think the kids are having a good time with it . . ." and his affect (he is relaxed and confident), signals to Toni that this might be a good time to continue to explore his choice. She continues:

COACHING MOVES & TOOLS

1. *Name the positive*
2. *Frame the lesson*
3. *Gather information*
4. *Offer specific suggestions or solutions*
5. *Offer choices*

> **Toni:** All right. So I noticed you had changed the game a little. Did you do that so there wouldn't be the competitive piece or you didn't realize the game was one game board between two players?
>
> **David:** A blend of both.
>
> **Toni:** Okay.
>
> **David:** So, no, I didn't realize it was one game board for two players, but it kind of went along with all the other games we've played in the year where you have your own space basically in front of you . . . but you have to help each other out and use accountable talk when helping the other person out.

By giving David the opportunity to explain his choices, Toni gathers important information: his reason for separate game boards makes sense. He wants to remove the competitive element of the game, which might lead to problematic social interactions (behavior issues). This is a legitimate concern if he is trying to do a small-group minilesson and does not want to be interrupted. For this setup to work, children playing the games have to be independent. Any social issues that children cannot resolve on their own are ones that will disrupt his small-group minilesson and thus undermine his teaching goal (to refine children's computation strategies in a small-group lesson).

Using this information, Toni can decide to move on or to continue to explore the game with David. Because she is not sure if David fully understands the mathematical goals of the game, she continues to explore it with him and makes this explicit when she says, "a big part of it is the strategic use of . . . . How do I know which factor I'm going to make because I want to cover the multiple . . . . I also want to think about getting five in a row and blocking you. . . ." In the next segment, Toni uses the coaching move *offering specific suggestions or solutions* to support David's goal (accountable, friendly talk) and the mathematics (challenging a strategy based on factor-multiple relationships).

> **Toni:** What if we set them up in partnerships, so you'd have the partnership talking and they'd be playing another partnership? Would that be possible?
>
> **David:** That—yeah.
>
> **Toni:** I think the one-on-one creates tension between the children.
>
> **David:** It does. Mhmm.
>
> **Toni:** And they're really not talking that much.
>
> **David:** Right.
>
> **Toni:** But if we put them in pairs . . .
>
> **David:** Yeah, two partnerships. I think, yeah, that would be, I think that would work out.

Even though David agrees with her suggestion as a possible solution, Toni recognizes that this may not be the moment to initiate change. If she wants to focus her work with David on how to facilitate an effective minilesson, changing how the game is played might mean having to shift the focus of the lesson because David might need to support his children, monitor their interactions, and deal with any social issues that arise as a result of this change. Her coaching move, *offering choices*, is directly related to this understanding.

> **Toni:** Now do we want to try that today or no? Because I know there's enough other things happening. It might be something for you to think about.
>
> **David:** I think moving forward and modifying the game, so when they build enough of a routine with the game, we can then switch it up.
>
> **Toni:** Okay, so keep it as it is today and then . . . ?
>
> **David:** Keep it as it is today. I'm already noticing yesterday one strategy that many of them used was immediately multiplying by 1, so many of them were already winning in covering that first row.

Toni: So there's no challenge.

David: So I mean, right, so the modification will come soon.

Toni: All right, so then we can work on that, we can talk about that in our debrief.

David: Okay.

Toni: The other thing I was watching you do was a string[7] with a small group of children.

David: Mhmm.

Toni: And I think that's where we'll spend our time in this session.

Within five minutes, Toni has gained invaluable information about David's choices for the game (taking out competition and trying to support accountable talk between partners) and his understanding of what was happening as children played the game (that there was no mathematical challenge in the way children were playing it). By taking the risk and bringing up what she noticed, Toni has helped David think about how to structure the game in the future.

PLANNING TIP #3: *Map Out the Lesson*[8]

One of the key goals of coaching is mapping out the lesson that will be done in the classroom. The *what, who, why,* and *how* questions outlined in the previous part of this chapter become crucial here. Equally critical are the coach's choices for how the lesson is explored. This includes: (1) where to start mapping the lesson, and which planning questions get addressed (remember, not all questions can be addressed in a coaching session), (2) how to document the planning (Do I have a written document we can refer to in the debriefing session? Do I just take notes for myself?), and (3) how to weave your coaching goals for teacher learning into the session (if I am helping a teacher develop a better introduction to his lessons, I have to make sure I focus my coaching in ways that bring this goal to the fore).

---

[7] A string is a guided mental-math minilesson in which a series of interconnected problems are used to develop flexible computation strategies.

[8] It is important to note that the board space used both to plan the lesson and teach the lesson was not adequate for a true mapping or modeling of student thinking. This board was chosen for film-making purposes; a larger board was desired by both coach and teacher.

Mapping the Lesson

A good deal of time (20 minutes out of a 30-minute planning session) is spent mapping out David's minilesson. This entire coaching segment is focused on getting a picture of David's content knowledge, what work he has done with children prior to this lesson, the children's mathematical development, and an assessment (how David groups his children is an example of how he is assessing their development). All of this information is essential for planning the lesson.

In mapping the lesson with David, Toni uses specific coaching moves that will be highlighted with transcript segments from their planning session.

> **Toni:** And I wanted to start by thinking about what multiplication strategies have you worked on with your children?
>
> **David:** So one of the earliest ones we worked on was skip counting, repeated addition, doubling. We've . . .
>
> **Toni:** What do you mean by *doubling*?
>
> **David:** Doubling, so when the kids have set up their repeated addition, one of the strategies many of them use is to immediately recognize those pairs, they can then have a bigger number to work with.
>
> **Toni:** [writes on chart paper] All right, so, strategies. So they have early multiplication strategies like skip counting . . .
>
> **David:** Skip counting, repeated addition, from repeated addition, we pulled out doubling.
>
> **Toni:** And can you give me an example of what you mean by "doubling?"
>
> **David:** Sure. If the kids are multiplying something like 6 × 4, and this was early on . . . as they were setting up, adding 4 six times, so they'd write out the 4 six times, then they started recognizing that if they added two 4s, that they'd have three 8s then.
>
> **Toni:** Ah! Like a repeated doubling strategy.

Two questions address two critical issues for coaches: How do you know what a teacher knows about content? and How do you collect information about children's development and prior experiences? To explore these questions, Toni uses four coaching tools: she (1) *gathers background information* on teacher knowledge and student development; (2) *builds a content map* with David to document important big ideas, strategies, and models; (3) *uses a recorded map as a tool* in planning; (4) *develops specificity of language* ("what do you mean by doubling?"), and *loops back* (when she is unclear about doubling, she again poses the question, *what do you mean by doubling?*). As they continue to map out their lesson, Toni continues to gather information to get a clear a picture of David's students' mathematical development. This kind of clarity about student development is critical for planning effective lessons. Prior to this transcript segment, David has been talking about a very sophisticated strategy: students halving one factor to solve a more difficult multiplication problem (e.g., 6×4 can be solved by doubling the product of 3×4).

Toni: So do children actually do this or it's something you're working toward?

David: We're working toward. There are, I would say maybe one or two scholars who recognize it and they've been using that strategy to help them with bigger multiplication. With the rest of the class I would say it's an idea that many of them are not seeing or we're just, we're still working with it.

Toni: So are you, how clearly can they articulate what's halving and how it affects the product?

David: So two scholars, in their explanation, they can talk about looking at the number of groups . . . and if you know that that number of groups is another number's double then you know that you can, when you halve that amount, you're left with half of that group.

Toni's question *pushes for specificity* (another coaching tool): when we're saying children are using this strategy, how many children are we talking about? Ten percent? Fifty percent? Eighty percent? For a coach, this kind of information is invaluable because when teachers over-generalize what children know (or don't know), lessons are often created that are either too easy or too difficult. When the team has a clear picture of the development in a classroom (only two children in David's classroom are using the strategy under discussion and can articulate their thinking clearly), this becomes useful in sculpting the lesson.

In this segment, Toni uses another important coach move: *anticipating student talk*. When teachers can predict what student ideas sound like, they are better able to predict the underlying misconceptions or ideas children are using. This kind of understanding helps a teacher craft questions to promote student thinking.

In addition to big-picture questions, Toni also explores some small-picture questions related to *who*, *what*, and *why?* The segment below explores David's choice for grouping students and his reasons for that choice.

Toni: Some children are going to be playing games, I'm wondering which groups we're going to be working with and what strategies we're going to be developing. All right?

David: Okay. I already have my kids in four . . . in four groups . . . based on their math work—mental-math work specifically for the past few months. And so my two groups who are in the middle . . . one group I worked with yesterday—they're pretty similar. So I was thinking, when we did group these two groups, my second group, I thought, didn't have many strategies or weren't very fluent in using a lot of these strategies. I was surprised when my third group, group number three, they were actually a little bit more confused when they were using these strategies in their computation. And so I'd be interested to see where we go with that group today.

Toni: How many children in these groups? So you have two groups, could you put those groups together if they're working in a similar place?

David: Each group is either four or five scholars. So today's group has five, five kids.

Toni: Okay, and why five kids? Is that management? Social?

David: Management, thinking about the social dynamic among the kids, who also supports each other's learning and thinking.

Toni continues by addressing the social/emotional aspect of learning and names a behavior that might be problematic. Using notes from yesterday's observation of David's teaching, she names what she would like to focus on in the lesson. Because Toni wants to address issues around pacing, it is important to help David understand how specific aspects of pedagogy affect student learning.

Toni: Yeah. Alright, 'cause I saw that one little girl shut down and dig in her heels and she was having none of it. She wasn't ready to entertain that her thinking was flawed somehow.

David: Exactly.

Toni: And so, does that happen a lot? 'Cause then you have to be aware of it, when kids are getting stuck, how do we . . .

David: Work with . . .

Toni: . . . work with the emotional . . .

David: Exactly.

Toni: . . . and not shut down the whole conversation.

David: Right, right, and I mean we have that in every group and so it's just really being aware of how far . . .

Toni: We can push?

David: . . . push, how far they're, they're going to be, they're going to have space to continue with, with their line of thinking before I then kind of step in and redirect. . . .

The question: how to address one student's emotional needs without losing the other students is an important one for David to consider. This is because, on the previous day, his minilesson ground to a halt when he tried to help one student understand the error in her thinking. When other students disengaged, it was difficult for him to regenerate their motivation and thinking.

PLANNING TIP #4: *Have Specific Coaching Goals for the Teacher*

In every coaching session, it is important that the coach have clear goals for developing teacher practice. The question, *What are the developmental needs of this teacher?*, can help a coach set the parameters for her work with a teacher. It is also helpful not to have too many goals because this can overwhelm both coach and teacher. A few carefully selected goals are easier to weave into a coaching session. And setting just-right goals (these are goals that are not so unreasonable a teacher will have difficulty attaining them) and weaving them into the coaching session is the best way to change teacher practice quickly.

Have Specific Coaching Goals for the Teacher

In the ensuing coaching segments, Toni weaves her goals for David (how to pace the minilesson and how to model student thinking) into the lesson planning. She is using the three coaching moves, *naming what's problematic*, *offering specific suggestions*, and *modeling pedagogical content knowledge* to support him.

Toni: And that took a good fifteen minutes.

David: Yes.

Toni: Why do you think it took so long?

David: I know in the end, there was the one student who didn't see the relationship between the other two. Some of the other kids in the group, I think were seeing the relationship or they came to that understanding after a few different tries and showing it in different ways. But with her, I, she added another group of 7 to the problem, and that's where . . .

Toni: She just got stuck.

David: I think we all got stuck.

Toni: All right. So one of the things we might want to think about working on today is the facilitation of the minilesson around when do you open it up, and when do you move on? So the pacing becomes really critical because if you have three or four groups and you want to do at least two or three minilessons a day . . .

David: Right.

Toni: . . . it's got to be capped at like ten minutes.

David: Yeah.

Toni: If you're going fifteen and twenty minutes, then . . .

David: It's, it's lost.

Toni: And also the kids shut down after a while too, 'cause . . . it becomes too much.

In the next segment, Toni works with David's understanding of modeling; she is developing his ability to represent student thinking. As in the previous segment, she begins by naming and offering specific suggestions to help him attain this goal.

Toni: I also noticed that you weren't modeling[9] . . .

David: In the beginning?

Toni: Yeah.

David: Some of these they know like their name, and so we would just write down the response.

Toni: But I think getting the model up right away is actually going to help.

David: Okay.

Toni: So that they say, 2 groups of 7, you just put up, if you're using the open . . .

David: Gotcha.

Toni: . . . number line, right?

---

[9]For an example of how the open number line is used to model the connection between 2×7 and 4×7, see the video of the case study.

David: Mhmm.

Toni: And so here's one group, two groups, here's our 2 groups of 7. And that's 14, right?

David: Yeah. And in my strings, that's something I definitely need to work on, is just having that visual up. I tend to get stuck in just writing it out with numbers, and some kids will follow and then I'll have a few other kids not seeing it, so I need to be flexible enough in resorting to either the open number line or ratio table.

Toni: Right. So working with the model is one way to help build some of the big ideas.

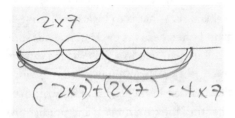

She also models student strategies for him to demonstrate what this might look like in the classroom.

Toni: . . . and help kids understand the connections. 'Cause I know when you went from 2×7, right? [models this on the open number line] So here's 1 group of 7, 2 groups of 7 . . .

David: Mhmm.

Toni: Right? And then the double number line, what's happening when we go to 4×7? [models with the double number line] Right? You're going to have this [points to the 2×7 on the top of the double number line] and it's going to get doubled.

David: Right.

Toni: Right, and now we have 2 groups of 7 plus 2 groups of 7 . . .

David: Mhmm.

Toni: Right? And that's where you got your 4 groups of 7. So this seemed to be like a just-right place for where the children were in that group. Is that who you're working with today? Or a different . . . ?

PLANNING TIP #5: *Do the Lesson You Will Be Teaching!*

In the previous segments, Toni is also doing the math with David. We believe that it is critical that teachers actually do the lesson they are planning to give students. This is an essential, and often neglected, step in lesson planning. To a content coach, doing the lesson is a critical part of lesson planning. Teachers may argue that they know the content and therefore don't need to do the activity, but this misses the point because exploring and understanding the content is just one reason to do the activity; the other is to think through all aspects of lesson design. Doing the lesson with the teacher also helps a coach understand the depth of the teacher's content knowledge, and given this understanding, where he might need support in the classroom as the lesson unfolds.

What does this look like in practice? If a teacher wants students to do twenty-five practice math problems, then she should actually do the task she is assigning and look for the cognitive demand in this task. What is to be learned from doing this task? If there is little or no cognitive demand, then perhaps the lesson needs some revision. If the teacher is using a new set of curriculum materials in science which call for a particular experiment, then the teacher ought to try out the experiment prior to giving it to students in order to think through the ideas embedded in the experiment, work with the materials, discover any issues related to conducting the experiment, and predict probable student responses to the experiment. If a teacher wants students to write poetry, then it makes sense for the teacher to have a poetry notebook of her own in which she tries out some of the techniques of the craft.

Here are a few things that may arise as a teacher tries to do the lesson he will be asking students to do:

> The time frame for the lesson may need to be adjusted; either the time needs to be extended to account for exploration or the task needs to be opened up because students can breeze through the lesson with little thought.

> The structure of the lesson may need to be tightened or rethought because the sequence within it is flawed.

> The entire lesson may need to be restructured because the intended learning goal is not clear.

Placing teachers in the role of learner is important because it is in this role that they can come to understand the lesson from the learner's point of view. Doing the task is one way to help them anticipate students' needs and adjust their lesson design using this understanding.

PLANNING TIP #6: *Rehearse the Lesson*

One step in lesson planning is to revisit the plan with the teacher. This can be as straight-forward as having the teacher rehearse the introduction (by rehearse, we mean do the introduction as she would in the classroom). Teachers often resist this coaching move because they feel uncomfortable acting out the lesson. We have found that this small move is often the difference between a successful lesson and a flawed lesson. Why? It is often in this practicing of the lesson (or revisiting of the outline of lesson) that both coach and teacher realize they are not on the same page. Often the coach realizes that (1) the teacher has not fully understood what has been discussed, (2) the teacher needs more time to internalize the plan, and acting it out gives him time to absorb things like pacing, questions, representation, and (3) where in the lesson the teacher might need specific co-teaching support (if a teacher is having difficulty keeping the introduction within time limits, the coach might have to find ways in the lesson to liven the pace).

Rehearsing the Lesson

In the coaching segment below, Toni revisits the lesson plan with David, beginning with the question, *What did we say we were going to do?* As she revisits the lesson they have constructed, however, she also helps David anticipate places where his pacing might shift, where he can move more quickly and where he might slow down and explore children's thinking, and when and how he might model student thinking. Note that this is a very guided segment: Toni is very explicit and names what they are doing, why they are doing it, and how they are doing it. This is also a coaching interlude that shows Toni emphasizing important goals for David (pacing and modeling). By having David anticipate and be aware of pacing and modeling, she is also setting the stage for her co-teaching in the classroom. Because Toni knows that these might be places where David will need support in the classroom, she is highlighting the moments where she may have to come in and co-teach. This coaching tool, *helping a teacher anticipate co-teaching*, is very useful to both coach and teacher, and prepares both for what may happen in the classroom.

COACHING MOVES & TOOLS

16. *Helping a teacher anticipate co-teaching*
17. *Practice representing*
18. *Rehearsing*

Toni: So 2×7, then 4×7. So what happens—because this is a place [marks 4×7 on the chart paper] where you have to sort of open it up.

David: Mmm.

Toni: So [points to problems on the chart] Kids know it like they know their name.

David: Right.

Toni: We move on.

David: Mhmm.

Toni: What happens here?

David: So I think the majority of the kids will see that, okay 2×7 to 4×7, we're doubling it. So we're adding 2×7 plus another 2×7 to get 4×7.

Toni: So then this would be the perfect model to show that, right?

David: Yeah.

Toni: [indicates problems on chart] So 2×7 plus another 2×7 gives us 4×7.

Toni also helps David practice modeling. This includes how to model student thinking and how to highlight the different ideas students are working with (how and why to use different colors). Because this kind of modeling is relatively new to David, Toni knows he needs some time in the planning session to try this new tool. She also knows that modeling student thinking as it happens in the moment of teaching is very difficult for many teachers; the more they practice hearing what students might say and having opportunities to model this, the better able they are to represent student thinking as it occurs in their classrooms.

Toni: Now do you want to model it, so the 2×7 and then the double on the bottom?

David: Yeah.

Toni: And then do we need a different color? 'Cause I think the colors . . .

David: Yes.

Toni: . . . become . . . so all this here, this is kind of sloppy—we'll do it better when we actually teach, but that would be your 4×7.

David: Right.

Toni: All right.

David: Would you, in, in drawing with the blue line, what you did down there, is, 'cause I mean, looking at all this information visually for, I'd say for a lot of the kids, I'd say that is a lot . . .

Toni: Is it too much? So what would you take out?

David: Probably the blue line.

Toni: These? So then this would be 2×7 . . .

David: Yeah.

Toni: . . . plus another 2×7.

David: Another 2×7 . . .

Toni: I guess what's . . . what I'm trying to think about here is the stamp . . .

David: Yeah.

Toni: . . . that this image is like being stamped again . . .

David: Mhmm.

Toni: And if you take out this inner group, you lose the stamp. It just becomes a bigger group.

PLANNING TIP #7: *Establish Signals for Interacting (Co-Teaching) in the Classroom*

It is also important to establish signals to use in the classroom when co-teaching. This is especially critical in the first coaching session, when there is more possibility for a teacher, who is not used to co-teaching, to be thrown (or unnerved) by a coach entering into the lesson or posing a question.

In a planning session with teachers it is important to set clear boundaries for the work you will be doing in the classroom. This means establishing norms for entering into the lesson as well as establishing signals for doing this. As part of this conversation, it is helpful to establish your respective roles in the classroom: Will I be taking the lead? Will I be taking notes on your teaching? Will I be co-teaching? If the teacher would like you to model some part of the lesson (e.g., the introduction), it is important for the coach to set expectations for what the teacher will be doing. Giving the teacher a focus is one way to support development. For example, if you are focusing on helping a teacher learn how to pose open-ended questions and deal with student responses, you might have her take notes (and by this we mean transcribe the dialogue verbatim) on the questions you ask, when you ask, and how you handle student responses. These notes can then be used in the debriefing session as a tool to focus conversation and develop a pedagogical skill or content understanding.

Establishing Signals for Interacting in the Classroom

In the segment below, Toni addresses issues around co-teaching.

Toni: Okay, and then one thing, if we're going to co-teach . . .

David: Yeah.

Toni: . . . you're going to have to give . . . let's just have a signal and . . .

David: Of course.

Toni: . . . and we'll be . . . whatever . . .

David: Okay.

Toni: . . . 'cause, you know, I don't want to get to the place where someone is shutting down or getting angry . . .

David: Right, frustrated.

In this brief segment, a number of things are addressed. First, Toni lets David know that she plans on entering the lesson. Second, she lets him know that they need an agreed upon signal. Third, she lets him know that she will need his help with the social and emotional behaviors in his classroom. This latter move signals to David that they are equals in this teaching partnership: he is as much a resource to her as she is to him. While she may be bringing a level of expertise in terms of pacing and modeling, he is an expert in terms of knowing his children's needs.

Establishing Co-Teaching Boundaries

In the following segment, Toni and David continue to negotiate their roles in the classroom.

> **Toni:** So this is our minilesson; other kids are going to be playing games.
>
> **David:** Yup.
>
> **Toni:** Okay, and you and I . . . I'll be coaching you, and you'll take the lead?
>
> **David:** Gotcha.
>
> **Toni:** And you're comfortable with the modeling?
>
> **David:** Yes.
>
> **Toni:** Okay, great.
>
> **David:** Yup.
>
> **Toni:** And comfortable with the questioning?
>
> **David:** Uh—yes. And if something . . .
>
> **Toni:** Okay.
>
> **David:** . . . is slipping by, then please . . .
>
> **Toni:** All right. I'll try and take some notes, but if I really feel I need to . . .
>
> **David:** Yes.
>
> **Toni:** . . . interject, I will.

Here, Toni brings up two key components necessary for facilitating effective minilessons: modeling and questioning. Although she anticipates that David will need support with these, this gives him the opportunity to take the lead. However, she also indicates that she plans to enter the lesson in relation to his modeling and questioning if (and when) the need arises.

SUMMARY: PLANNING A LESSON

Because we believe that planning a lesson is the starting place for all effective teaching, we used this chapter to outline important big-picture and small-picture *what*, *who*, *why*, and *how* questions that might be used in a planning session (preconference). Because we also realize that there are many ways to use these questions (and that not all questions have to be addressed in every coaching session), we also included a coaching case study to examine how these questions play out in real-time. As part of this case study, we also gave and illustrated specific coaching tips. While we realize these tips are by no means definitive, we do believe that they outline some critical tools that will help coaches (and teachers) plan more effective lessons.

Co-Teaching the Lesson

Knowing is one thing; knowing what to do with the knowing
is something entirely different.

Although content coaches use a variety of coaching techniques (e.g., they model lessons, they observe lessons and take notes to provide feedback to the teacher in the postconference), their primary in-classroom work is focused on co-teaching. Why the strong emphasis on co-teaching?

Content coaching is fueled by one maxim: immediacy. If our goal is to improve teacher practice as quickly as possible, then we cannot wait to broach tricky or delicate topics. Our failure to act has major implications for children. If children's learning experiences are only as effective as the teacher providing them, then content coaches cannot wait to ask the hard questions. We have to address teacher beliefs, their use of pedagogy, and their content knowledge from the outset of our work with them. This is the primary reason why content coaches focus on co-teaching in the classroom, why they find key moments to pose more rigorous questions of students, why they advocate for changes in teacher practice. Their ultimate goal: impact teaching to improve student learning.

CO-TEACHING: WHY, WHEN, AND HOW

Co-teaching is one of the prime ways coaches can influence teachers' practice as it happens—*in the moment of teaching*. Although entering into a lesson as it is happening may be a controversial practice to some educators, for us, when done skillfully, it is a way to shift a teacher's practice both radically and quickly. Radically and quickly? Is this possible?

In the field of teacher development, changing teacher practice quickly is, for many educators, an unrealistic goal. Underlying this notion is a wide-held assumption that it takes a long time for coaches to shift teacher practice. Why? Because before delving deeply into the work of coaching, one has to first build trust. Many coaches will say, "trust cannot be rushed; it takes a long time to develop." So they wait to go deep; wait for trust to develop. And while they wait to change teacher practice, children wait too.

But what if this belief about how trust develops is not true? What if trust can be developed more quickly? The question then becomes, what builds trust?

Building Trust

We believe, as do others, that establishing trust is key to affecting teacher practice. We do not believe, however, that trust has to take a long time to develop. In fact, we believe that trust can be established in the first coaching session. How does this happen? It happens in the act of coaching. It happens when content coaches engage in public learning, when they model a learning stance. In this stance, coaches share what they think and admit what they don't know or are puzzled by. In this regard, content coaches become learning partners; they take risks and are willing to expose themselves as learners. Public learning—this walking the walk—has the potential to forge trust and invites teachers to take learning stances as well. To create trust and dialogue, content coaches must be honest and open. They must ask probing questions about teacher choices and beliefs, and not hesitate to share observations.

This is not to minimize how difficult it is to open dialogue space. Initiating deep conversation (i.e., dialogue that does not dance around critical issues and concerns) is difficult because the very act of speaking honestly is often fraught with the possibility of negative emotions coming to the surface. Once emotions rise, coaches have to have well-developed social and communication skills to deal with the situation. This is one of the reasons novice coaches often shy away from difficult conversations.

To create honest dialogue, one has to speak honestly. Often, the very act of taking that first step is what creates a safe space and builds trust. Because skillful coaches know this, they try to create an open dialogue right from the beginning of their coaching work. They can do this because they hold several fundamental beliefs. The first is that to create trust one has to believe in the goodwill of the other. Second, coaches who trust in the potential of teachers to learn and grow, often find that their expectations for learning and collaboration are met. Third, the mutual purpose held by coaches and teachers—to improve the learning of all students—is stronger than their differences (background, beliefs, etc.), so they are able to use this belief to effect change. Coaches who believe in the capacity of teachers actually create the capacity for teachers to believe in themselves, too.

Because content coaching (and co-teaching) is a recursive practice, coaches build teacher expectations for the work from the first session. For this reason, when content coaches address issues of student learning, when they do not look away or pretend things

COACH NOTE

Perhaps a tenet to consider is that nothing builds fear like fear itself. The reality often is that coaches who fail to create a space for honest discourse, who fear the outcome of their words, confine themselves to work in superficial ways until they find the courage and wherewithal to raise important issues.

are fine when they are not, when they have the courage to speak frankly, teachers expect this to be the essence of their collaboration. And it is in this content-focused collaborative discourse that trust develops and deepens.

Trust also deepens when content coaches' genuine questions about a teacher's thinking demonstrate that the coach is not there to judge but to partner with the teacher. Trust deepens in a co-teaching relationship because the very act of collaborative teaching requires trust. It demonstrates that the work is about developing and improving the craft of teaching, not spying or enforcing mandates for the administration. Trust deepens in a co-teaching relationship because content coaches assure teachers that their collaboration is about developing and improving their craft. When coaches challenge teachers to think about their practice in relationship to student learning (*Have students learned? What's our evidence?*), teachers must examine their craft to answer those questions. And if teachers are not satisfied with the outcome of their teaching, if students do not seem to be learning to the highest levels, the question becomes: What can we do to ensure that this can happen?

Because content coaching is rooted in an *us-model* of learning—we are in this together—trust is established by confronting the tough questions head on. *If your children are silent and you say you want them to speak, let's look at what's causing this. If you'd like to ask better questions, but are unsure of how to do this, let's explore places in the content where certain kinds of questions might be raised, and then, let's find places in the lesson where these might be used.*

Although opening dialogue, examining practice, and finding solutions are ways to build trust, the act of co-teaching in the classroom is never easy. One reason is directly related to the complexity of classroom teaching. To successfully co-teach, coaches have to be aware of the complexity of teaching and use this knowledge to their advantage.

Teaching Is a Complex Act

There is no question that teaching is a complex act (Davis and Simmt 2003). A teacher is faced with a multitude of decisions in the act of teaching. And because teaching is a "performance" art—it is happening in real time with real students—there are a multitude of things to consider. It is not easy to illustrate this complexity. There is an ongoing debate across the profession as to what constitutes effective teaching. While we are not going to resolve this debate here, we are going to use two analogies to help us consider just how difficult skillful and effective teaching is.

Let's think of actors in a play. They have learned their lines; they have been directed (where to stand on the stage, on pacing, on the nuances of their character as an individual character, and as a character whose thoughts and actions affect other characters in the play). Through rehearsal (practice), this knowledge is then woven to create a real-time performance in front of an audience. Here, what actors do and how they interact is directly related to both the practice (how they have integrated what they have learned as a result of rehearsing together) and to the moment, adjusting what they are doing based on what is actually happening on stage and in the audience.

Now, think of jazz musicians performing; each knows his part, has practiced his riffs. However, they interact in the moment based on what they are hearing—they may adjust their playing based on what is happening around them. They are in the moment, using what they know, applying their skill (which can only come through practicing their craft), but fine-tuning their part in relationship to that of other players.

So, how is a teacher like either of these other performers? Well, to be effective, much like the actor or the jazz musician, "a teacher must be reflecting on action while she is in action," adjusting her thoughts, actions, and language to what is happening around her (Schon 1984, 8–9). The teacher is both the director of the play and an actor in that play simultaneously, but with a significant added layer of complexity. The teacher does not have a script; there has not been a rehearsal of what will be said by all the players (teacher and students). Even though the teacher might have anticipated some of this in planning (e.g., *if I ask this question, here are some possible responses*), there is no guarantee that any of these predictions will actually happen. This means that when things are said, they have to be interpreted in the moment. The teacher has to understand both the text and the subtext. Not only must she consider what she is trying to teach, but she simultaneously has to consider individual students—their emotional and intellectual needs—and the entire class as a community. The teacher also has to have some understanding of how to use students' ideas, clarify what they say, or deal with their confusions as they are happening.

Sound overwhelming? There is more; there is an additional challenge for teachers. The coherence of the play depends not only on her participation, but on her direction, on how she coordinates her actions and ideas in relation to those of the other performers (students) around her. In fact, the coherence of discourse rests on her actions and inter-actions, on her timing in relation to other performers, and her response to what occurs. Similar to a jazz musician as a performer, a teacher needs to improvise, has to be attuned to the other players, and adjust what she is doing in relation to the ideas that arise in discussion.

The described complexity of orchestrating a lesson in real time is just one of many layers of complexity. We have not touched on content knowledge and pedagogical content knowledge and interweaving these with external pressures such as high-stakes tests, changing standards, and conflicting demands from administrators, parents, and policymakers. It is not surprising that the teaching profession has high attrition rates. When left to their own devices to develop expertise, many teachers become frustrated and disillusioned. For this reason, it is important for coaches to help teachers understand this complexity, and to engage with them in real time in ways that enable them to operate within the "blooming, buzzing confusions" that confront them in the classroom on a daily basis (Sherin and Star 2010, 69).[1] Co-teaching, as a model of in-class coaching, is one way to address this complexity head on.

Co-Teaching Is an Art Form

To be an effective co-teacher is not easy. Why? To go back to our performance analogies, the content coach is now part of the play, but her role adds yet another dimension. She is *teaching the teacher to notice*. She is directing the teacher's attention, but she is not directing the entire play. This means a content coach has to be aware of the layers of interaction: of the teacher with the students, of the students with the students, and of her coaching moments in relationship to these. While the teacher may be noticing children's strategies, making interpretations about their understandings, and thinking about how to respond (Sherin and Star 2010), the coach is doing the same, but with the added perspective of thinking about the teacher's thinking in relation to students, considering effective tools of practice (e.g., discourse moves, and moments when pedagogy might be shifted to improve teaching and increase student learning) (Jacobs et al. 2010). Sound complex? It is.

Because of this complexity, content coaches might find it helpful to have at their disposal a teacher development toolbox whose co-teaching tools will be described in the ensuing pages.

The Challenge for the Coach

Co-teaching has major implications for the coach too. A coach has to be able to walk the walk. This means that if a coach suggests that a teacher use talk moves, the coach also has to be able to find moments in the lesson when those talk moves might be used productively, and, through co-teaching, model how this is done. If a coach suggests that a teacher use more open-ended questions, she has to be able to model the use of those kinds of questions in the co-teaching moment.

Co-teaching puts as much of a burden on the coach as it does on the classroom teacher. Both have to be willing to learn publicly—out in the open. Both may feel awkward in this learning position. A teacher may feel uncomfortable or may worry about student perceptions (*Will my students think I'm incompetent if someone else starts to teach?*). A coach may feel awkward entering a lesson, especially when she knows that every entrance will not necessarily be effective. Both teacher and coach need to understand that even if a co-teaching moment is not effective, it can serve as a powerful learning moment to examine in the postconference.

In reflecting on co-teaching, the coach can share what her intentions were, and whether or not the intended effect was the actual effect; if the effect was not what she

---

[1] Quote is taken from W. James, 1890, "The principles of psychology," New York: H. Holt.

intended, then the coach needs to share this with the teacher. It is in this very act, when teacher and coach open themselves to the scrutiny of the other, that collaborative bonds are built. A coach's courage, her willingness to take risks and learn publicly, signals to the teacher, we are in this together; together we learn; and together we improve. This kind of collaboration cements a coach-teacher relationship; it's what makes the hard work, the risk taking, the difficult questions, and the exploring of practice possible.

Pitfalls

As coaches attempt to co-teach, they need to be aware of major co-teaching pitfalls. These can be broken into three major mistakes: (1) failing to establish a clear signal, (2) over-using co-teaching, and (3) entering into the lesson, but failing to hand the reins back to the teacher.

Establishing a Clear Signal

From the beginning of her work with a teacher, a coach should establish clear signals about how she will enter the lesson. In so doing she eliminates the kind of surprises that can derail lessons (i.e., the teacher loses focus or becomes frustrated because she is not ready for the coach to enter the lesson). Establishing clear signals is often done in the planning session. Some teachers are comfortable with the coach just entering the lesson; others need signals like a raised hand.

Choosing a Co-Teaching Moment

Even though a coach has established a signal with the teacher, she still has to selectively pick the moment to enter the lesson. The act of co-teaching is strategic, so it is important to enter the lesson with a clear-cut goal. This means that a coach must weigh the co-teaching moment and think about two important questions, *Is this the right moment for co-teaching? How will entering the lesson at this moment support our goals for improving practice?*

Handing Back the Reins

Having entered a lesson, a coach must find ways to hand the reins of the lesson back to the teacher. Often, when a novice coach tries on a co-teaching strategy, she may forget to give back the reins, with the outcome being she has taken over the lesson. Even for a seasoned coach, entering and exiting a lesson is not an easy thing to do. This is especially true if her entrance has shifted the tone or focus or if the teacher, unaware of where to go with the changes made by the coach, can't take up the reins to continue the lesson.

It is important then for content coaches to be self-aware, and to find every opportunity to help the teacher re-enter the lesson. Failing to do this can undermine, demoralize, or frustrate the classroom teacher and have major implications for the coach-teacher relationship.

In summary, the art of successful interjection into a lesson is dependent on three main things: (1) finding the appropriate moment to enter into the lesson, (2) entering into the lesson without upsetting the flow of what's happening to the degree that the teacher becomes lost, and (3) finding ways for the teacher to re-enter the lesson after the co-teaching moment has occurred. This means empowering the teacher to re-enter and also giving her a direction for when (and maybe how) to re-enter the lesson.

How Do Coaches Know When to Enter the Lesson?

Unfortunately, there is no recipe for knowing when to enter a lesson, but there are some signals or signs that coaches need to be aware of. How do you recognize optimal moments for co-teaching? Here's a short list:

1. **Pacing**

   Depending on the cognitive demand of a lesson, it may need to be sped up or slowed down. A content coach may recognize that the lesson needs to be slowed down because a big idea has come to the surface and the moment is ripe for exploring this idea through discourse. Slowing down a lesson around a big idea can help a teacher hear the big ideas in children's comments, questions, or strategies; think about how to use what has arisen in relation to the other ideas under discussion (e.g., how to build upon ideas, weave them together, or use them to create disequilibrium); and think about ways to invite other children's voices into the conversation about the idea/s being examined.

2. **Improving Teacher Practice**

   A coach identifies that a moment in a lesson is ripe with possibilities for improving teacher practice. For example, a coach recognizes that a teacher ignores comments that don't fit into her plan (a common behavior of teachers who are afraid of losing control of the lesson) or fails to explore a wrong answer (a common behavior of teachers who focus on right answers as the goal of the lesson). When this happens in a lesson, a coach might enter the conversation to focus on a specific comment (or incorrect idea) that the teacher has ignored. By doing this, the coach signals specific beliefs and values:

   - All children's ideas have worth and exploring student reasoning deepens thinking and promotes further discourse; and

- Wrong answers may have as much potential to develop thinking as right answers.

- With this kind of focus, comments and answers are not the end of the conversation, but the continuation. By placing an emphasis on the process by which the comment or answer was derived, the focus of learning becomes the reasoning and communication of that thinking. By exploring the individual's thinking with the group, the emphasis becomes not just on the individual's reasoning, but on the group's justification and refining of that reasoning through discourse.

3. Bookmarking Moments to Highlight in the Postconference

The coach identifies a critical moment in which entering into the lesson might be used in the postconference to highlight the ways in which teacher actions are rooted in beliefs about students. For example, if a teacher tends to call only on certain students (the high-performing or vocal students), a coach might pick a child who has not been invited into the conversation or who is reluctant to speak (and who has become accustomed to playing this role in the classroom), and ponder, "I wonder what _____ thinks about this?" Changing the discourse pattern in this way can have a stunning impact on both the teacher and her students because both have to adjust to these new expectations: teachers realize that because every child matters, it is important to find a way to involve each child, and students understand that learners don't sit back, hide out, or expect others to do the work for them; they own the process of learning.

4. Developing Clarity in Teaching

A coach may also enter the lesson if the teacher has omitted something critical to students' understanding of the content, such as if the teacher

- is about to send the students off to work but has failed to introduce the lesson clearly (e.g., the question students will explore is unclear, there is missing or conflicting information, etc.);

- has not asked for a paraphrasing of the question to be explored (or task that is to be performed) and paraphrasing is needed to check for or solidify student understanding;

- uses inaccurate or misleading words (e.g., ones that might have multiple meanings) which need to be clarified;

- has not written or provided enough visual information to students;

- has not accounted for students with special needs or special language issues.

Using Teacher-Student Conferences to Support Development

In addition to whole-group discussions, co-teaching can occur when teachers are conferencing with students at work. The coach does not act as a second teacher (e.g., going off and working with one group of students while the classroom teacher works with another), but joins the teacher as they confer with students. Co-facilitating conferring gives a coach insights into how a teacher conferences with students, the kinds of questions she asks, the ways she explores or shuts down thinking. In this co-conferencing, a teacher can also observe how the coach interacts and questions students. In these situations, there are opportunities for both coach and teacher to gain new insights into their respective crafts.

If the coach wants to interject in the teacher-student conferencing, she has to be aware of the pitfalls. It is helpful to think about: *Is this a good moment for me to interject? How will my interjecting at this particular moment support the goals we have established for our work?*

There are several ways to set up co-teaching during conferencing. First, it is helpful to set boundaries for this work: who does what, how it is done, what the signals are, etc. One way is to set the structure for the work. Here's an example of a coach setting these boundaries in a preconference so that their roles in co-teaching are clear:

> **Coach:** I think it would be helpful if we looked at our use of questions when we're conferencing with students. Last time, we worked separately; you worked with some students and I worked with others.
>
> **Teacher:** Yeah, that really helped me know what everyone was doing. It's not usually possible for me to get to every group, so it was great to have you as an extra hand in the room.
>
> **Coach:** It did give us a good picture of what everyone was doing, but I thought this time, we might look at how we are working with individuals or pairs of students, and for us to go around the room together—to be joined at the hip so to speak.
>
> **Teacher:** We could, but I'm not sure how that would actually help me.
>
> **Coach:** Maybe it would help us think about why it's so hard to get to every student or group of students.
>
> **Teacher:** I can tell you why; there's not enough time and there are too many kids.
>
> **Coach:** Maybe. But what if it was something else, something that had to do with how we question, or maybe the fact that we don't need to question every pair, and if we don't need to do this, how would we know when to walk away?

Teacher: I never thought of it that way.

Coach: So I was hoping what we could try this time is to stay together in the classroom and listen to each other's questions. We can take turns; one of us will ask the questions and the other one can take notes on the questions. And we'll try to script the questions and student responses verbatim. Then we'll step back and discuss our noticings.

Teacher: That sounds really hard.

Coach: It is, but I think it would help us think about our questions, if they're effective, if we can improve them in any way. Would that work?

Teacher: I don't know, but we can try it and see.

Coach: Would you like to work with the first group we go to or should I?

Teacher: I'd feel better if you started. I could see what you're doing and then try to do it too.

In this short coaching conversation, the coach identifies how she would like to work with the teacher in the classroom and offers reasons why this might be effective. There are several crucial things in the subtext of this conversation: (1) we need to be together (i.e., I am not an extra hand; that's not the job of the content coach), (2) we need to explore our practice (e.g., what kinds of questions are we asking and how are these questions supporting or impeding student thinking), and (3) we need to explore the beliefs underlying our questions. Focusing on the types of questions and using conferencing notes to explore these questions are powerful tools in a content coach's repertoire. For example, a teacher's questions may focus on leading students to an answer; that might be one reason she is not able to conference with many students while they are working—she stays with one child until he "gets it."

To help a teacher understand how her questions are impacting student learning, it is helpful for the coach to juxtapose her questions with the teacher's. In the postconference, a coach and teacher might consider the following questions:

1. How are our questions similar? Different?

2. Why do we ask certain kinds of questions? What is our goal in doing this?

3. Is it okay when we see that children are beginning to work, to use a strategy, for us to walk away or do we need to stay until their work is complete?

4. How can we identify an optimal moment to move away from students? Could moving away at a certain moment actually empower student thinking and cultivate autonomy?

Developing a Co-Teaching Toolbox

To be an effective co-teacher, it is helpful for coaches to have a repertoire of strategies. We have outlined some major ones in the ensuing section. These will be further illustrated in the coaching case study that follows.

Co-Teaching Strategy #1: Set Clear Goals for Teacher Learning

Effective co-teaching begins with setting clear, mutually agreed upon goals for teacher development. In order to set goals for her work with a teacher, a content coach has to think about teacher practice from a developmental perspective, and within that framework, use her knowledge of a teaching landscape to support learning. (See Chapters 4 and 6 for more in-depth information on developing a lens for assessing teacher practice, where to start, etc.)

Setting clear, reasonable goals for teacher learning is critical for a number of reasons. First, if a coach has correctly identified (in collaboration with the teacher) a just-right goal for teacher learning, the teacher will shift her practice. Since pivoting teacher practice, from one place of understanding to another, is one of the key reasons to co-teach, developing the skill to pinpoint these developmental linchpins is crucial for effective coaching.

Co-Teaching Strategy #2: Use Communication Skills to Influence Thinking and Practice

How does a coach know what to say and when to say it during the lesson? The art here partially lies in her ability to express her ideas with clarity. Other aspects are subtle and have to do with a coach's ability to understand the social setting; the skill to communicate in ways that positively affect someone else's thinking and behavior. A coach has to read the cues given by those around her, and within that social setting choose what to say and how to say it. The choice of words, the phrasing, the nuance, the tone of voice has as much to do with the context of the situation and who is in that situation as it does with what needs to be said. (For more in-depth analysis of the role of communication in coaching, see Chapter 5, "Communication Is Key.")

This communication skill is critical in co-teaching because a content coach has to choose the optimal moment to speak and have the ability to clearly articulate the reasons for this choice in a debriefing session with the teacher. Knowing when to enter into the teaching moment and how to exit it is deeply rooted in a coach's understanding of the social context and how her words will affect what is happening. Being able to weigh and predict the effect of her words (e.g., *If I say this, then that may happen*) is critical for co-teaching to be effective. (This is explored further in the case study in pages 138–148.)

Co-Teaching Strategy #3: Consider Both Content and Pedagogical Content Knowledge

An effective content coach needs to have intertwined content and pedagogical content knowledge. This means a coach's ability to enter into a lesson is in direct relation to both how well she understands the content of what is being taught (the underlying big ideas and how they are connected in a developmental framework; what strategies students might use; the critical tools or models within this content) and how well she understands that content within the framework of teaching (What pedagogical tools might make this content come to life in the classroom? What confusions might students have and how might one address these?). The art of co-teaching is to know how to use what is happening in a teaching moment in multiple ways.

For example, if a coach is working with a teacher on hearing the mathematics in a child's thinking and how to create discourse around an idea a child expresses, she might wait for an opportune moment to bring this up. A child says, "Nine is an even number," and the classroom teacher tries to fix the answer, saying, "Think about it. What does an even number end in?" The teacher's response does not explore the complexity underlying the child's thinking, but focuses on fixing it, using the mindset that there is one way to understand even and odd numbers (e.g., they end in 0, 2, 4, 6, 8).

The coach, on the other hand, recognizes that there may be some interesting thinking underlying the child's response (e.g., you can put nine things into equal groups; you can divide it evenly) and that this particular misconception may not be exclusive to one learner.

To help the teacher consider the complexity of the student's response, the coach might enter the conversation at this moment by asking the child, "Why do you think 9 is an even number?" The goal here is not to only address the thoughts of an individual student, but to also engage all the students in discussion once the explanation is given. Questions like, *Do you agree? Disagree? How can we convince each other whether 9 is an even number?* can address the complexity of the situation by challenging the thinking of both the individual and the community (Askew 2008).

In the example above, the coach is addressing content, pedagogy, and discourse simultaneously in one co-teaching moment. She must have enough content knowledge to recognize moments in a lesson that are ripe with possibilities, the pedagogical knowledge and tools (some of these may be related to managing discourse and disequilibrium) to effectively facilitate teacher and student learning, and the courage to engage in the lesson in real time.

Co-Teaching Strategy #4: Maintain Equilibrium by Keeping a Focus on Goals

In the classroom, coaches are often surprised by teachers' choices, especially when these have not been discussed in the planning session. As disconcerting as these moments can be, it is important for coaches to maintain equilibrium. One way to do this is to stay focused on the coaching goals and to think about these in light of teacher development. As part of this process, a coach might look for opportunities to weave these goals into what is occurring in the lesson—planned or not. This means, no matter what direction a lesson takes or how surprising this direction might be to the coach, the goals for supporting teacher development should always be foremost in her mind.

Co-Teaching Strategy #5: Carefully Pick Your Moment of Entry into the Lesson

Co-teaching requires the coach to be attuned to what is happening in the lesson and to be aware of moments in the lesson where she can support teacher development. This means carefully weighing what is happening and deciding (often on the spur of the moment) how to use what is occurring in the classroom as a tool for supporting teacher learning.

Co-Teaching Strategy #6: Quickly Return the Reins of the Lesson to the Teacher

Any time a coach enters a lesson, she needs to find a way to return that lesson to the teacher. This can be tricky if the teacher does not understand why the coach entered the lesson or is confused about how to use what the coach did to continue teaching.

Co-Teaching Strategy #7: Gauge Your Effectiveness as You Are Co-Teaching

Any co-teaching move should be gauged immediately in terms of its effectiveness. How might a coach know she is being effective? One way to determine the effect of the co-teaching moment is to see how the teacher responds to it. If the teacher understands what has happened, and can, so to speak, pick up the ball and run with it, a coach has instant feedback that the move was supportive and useful to the teacher.

Co-Teaching Strategy #8: Respect Boundaries

In any co-teaching situation, it is important for coaches to monitor the number of times they enter into a lesson. It is helpful to remember that too many interruptions can actually hinder teacher learning, especially when the teacher starts to feel incompetent (*How did I miss that students don't understand this?!*) or confused (*Why did the coach just ask that question? I don't understand.*). One way to test whether a teacher is becoming overwhelmed is to ask the teacher directly, "Might I pose a question?" This question is helpful in two ways. First, it demonstrates a respect for the teacher and honors his choices. Second, it is a very useful tool to use in co-teaching because it marks a moment in a lesson where co-teaching might have been possible. This means that even if the teacher responds, "I'd rather not" the coach has now marked a part of the lesson that they can return to in the debriefing session. Why she wanted to enter the lesson, what she might have said, can be then discussed at a future time (e.g., *Remember when I wanted to ask a question? Here's what I was noticing . . .*).

Co-Teaching Strategy #9: Bookmark the Lesson

As we've discussed, co-teaching can also help a coach *bookmark* key moments in a lesson. Because these key moments can be very useful in the debriefing session, coaches should carefully determine where and when to bookmark. Although any moment in a lesson can be bookmarked, it is often better to choose ones that are directly related to goals for teacher development. For example, if you are working on how a teacher paces a lesson, you might slow down or speed up the lesson at opportune moments and bookmark these moments in your mind to use in the debriefing session.

Co-Teaching Strategy #10: Use Co-Teaching to Build on Teachers' Strengths

It is important in any co-teaching session to find moments where teachers are using powerful teaching techniques and to highlight and build upon these. In these moments, it is sometimes helpful to use a mirroring technique to reflect back to the teacher what is powerful. To do this a coach might find moments in the lesson where she can mirror back the teacher's use of language, questions, or representations. This mirroring can act as a positive signal to the teacher (*Wow! I thought that was really effective. I'm going to mirror that back to you so you can see what I see.*); it is also a way to bookmark the lesson (a moment to be used later on) for the postconference.

Co-Teaching Strategy #11: Take Highly Scripted Notes

Because postlesson discussions often rely heavily on a coach's notes, we suggest that whenever possible—when she is not co-teaching or modeling a lesson—the coach transcribe the classroom discourse. Having an accurate record of what transpired during the lesson has two major benefits. First, carefully scripted notes can help a coach reflect on what happened in the classroom and think about how to structure the postconference. Second, these notes, when shared with teachers, are often very powerful because they provide a window into their teaching practice. For example, it is not uncommon that when coaches share verbatim classroom dialogues teachers express surprise (*Did I actually say that!?*) and become reflective (*I'd like to stop talking so much.*). As teachers become aware of specific practices (*I ask a lot of yes/no questions!*), they can begin to think about why they are doing this (*I just realized I use lots of questions when I get nervous that kids aren't talking!*). As part of this process—hearing their classroom practice in a coach's notes—teachers can begin to think about what they would like to change or improve in their practice and brainstorm ways to do this.

In summary, co-teaching is an art form. Doing this well requires coaches to consider a number of key areas in teaching: content, pedagogy, child development, and discourse. We will use the ensuing case study to explore co-teaching strategies used by one coach.

A Case Study: Co-Teaching a Lesson

Background on the Co-Teaching Session

In the planning session, Toni drew David's attention to specific things they would focus on in the minilesson. These were: pacing (how to pace the lesson to keep it within a 10 to 15-minute time frame), modeling (how to model student strategies using the double number line), and discourse (how to facilitate student talk and develop more precise ways of communicating). At first glance, it might seem unrealistic to work on three major goals in one co-teaching session, and you might wonder, *won't this overwhelm or frustrate the teacher*? The point here is that all of these goals are not separate, but interrelated.

First, facilitating student talk is critical to the pacing of any lesson. Without clearly established discourse norms, students often struggle to communicate with clarity and to listen to each other's ideas. When students are unclear in their explanations, the pace of the lesson gets bogged down with long-winded and/or confusing language. To remedy the situation and to keep the lesson flowing, teachers often resort to paraphrasing student comments or questions. But teacher paraphrasing of student ideas takes away the ownership of learning and creates a kind of learned helplessness. Speakers and listeners alike do not have to attend to what is happening because they know that the teacher will ultimately fix it. *Why do I have to speak clearly when my teacher will fix whatever I say, and say it better, louder, and more clearly? Why do I have to listen to another student's ideas?* Other students may not feel compelled to listen and think, *Whatever is said, my teacher will repeat it. I'll listen then.*

Second, modeling student strategies is one way to make their thinking visible. Representing a student's strategy using a model like the double number line can help students communicate clearly and understand each other's strategies and reasoning. The model can also be used to ground conversation, build connections between ideas, or help students work through their confusions.

Keeping Teacher Development at the Center of Co-Teaching

David begins his lesson by reviewing the game and soliciting children's experiences from the previous day. Although beginning the lesson in this way was not discussed in the planning session (and was a bit of a surprise to Toni), she finds ways to support David's choice without losing sight of the goals for developing his practice. She is able to weave these goals in when she realizes children are not articulating their ideas clearly and David is accepting their comments without expressing and naming clear expectations for the ways in which children are expressing themselves. A teaching-learning behavior like this directly impacts the pacing of the lesson, and working on pacing was another goal they set for their work together.

David: Factor Bingo; you guys have played it a couple of days, correct?

Children: Yes.

David: Talk to me about Factor Bingo. What's been going on? Nyrassia, we'll start with you.

[the conversation continues in this fashion for several minutes]

Ketshira: . . . because, the ratio table helps you with time [*sic*] table.

David: Okay.

Ketshira: . . . only time table and maybe division?

David: Mhmm.

Ketshira: You use ratio table like putting the five groups, like 1, 2, 3, 4, 5 and then counting by 9s, like 9, 18 . . .

David: Got it. And that's what you were writing on your white board while you were playing Factor Bingo.

Toni: And so, could I ask a question? 'Cause I heard you use the word, "product." And I'm wondering, where on the board was the product? Were there products on the [game] board? And I hear people using the word, factor, and I'm wondering, where were the factors? And so, why is it Factor Bingo? [to the teacher] I don't know names of the children.

With one interjection, Toni (1) highlights specific words she would like children (and the teacher) to use, (2) poses a puzzlement about what these words mean in relationship to the game (where are the products and factors on their game boards?), and (3) hands the reins back to the teacher saying, "I don't know the names of the children." The latter is a helpful co-teaching tool that can easily bring a teacher back into the lesson because the coach needs his assistance to call on children who want to respond to the question posed.

COACHING MOVES & TOOLS

1. *Be flexible.*
2. *Keep your goals for teacher development in mind.*
3. *Find key moments to enter the lesson.*
4. *Give the reins of the lesson back to the teacher*

Affecting Teacher Practice

After Toni highlights important language to be used by students, David immediately begins to hold them accountable. He is also visibly surprised by one child's initial response to the coach's question.

Toni: And so, why is it Factor Bingo? [to the teacher] I don't know names of the children.

David: Kyasia?

Kyasia: I think it's called Factory Bingo because it's sort of like a factory with numbers.

David: Not factory. It's *Factor* Bingo.

Toni: [hands David a marker]

Kyasia: Oh.

David: So where are the factors on this bingo board . . .

Kyasia: Ah!

David: . . . and then where are the products?

Kyasia: I think . . .

David: So where are the factors on the board and where are the products? [writes these words on the chart paper] So, Kyasia, you got us started. I'm going to call on someone else. Yes? If you have another idea, put your hand up. Adrian?

In this short segment, Toni highlights specific language to be used in talking about the game and hands David a pen so that he can write these words on the chart paper for children to use as a reference. That one child thought the game was called *Factory Bingo* surprises David, who is now aware that some of his children may be playing the game without connecting what they are doing to multiplication. One of the big ideas underlying the game is for children to think flexibly about the factor-product relationship so that they can use this knowledge to deconstruct the numbers on the board into factors (e.g., 36 can be thought of as 4×9, 6×6, etc.), so clearing up this confusion is critical for learning. Without this understanding, the game loses its mathematical purpose.

Keeping Track of the Number of Co-Teaching Moments

In this transcript segment, Toni re-enters the conversation within two minutes of her previous co-teaching entry. Although she wants to challenge students' thinking in respect to the game, she is also worried that she is dominating the teaching and wants to make sure the teacher welcomes this intrusion. She also does not want to undermine or derail him.

> **Toni:** So can I ask a question?

> **David:** Go ahead.

> **Toni:** So if we had 30 on our board and we'll just fill this in and pretend it's here and I want to think about what factors are going to make the product of 30, I have to actually use these numbers up here and think about, hmm . . . I want to make 30 . . . does somebody have a way to make 30 with 2 factors?

> **David:** Peter? What are you thinking of?

> **Peter:** I think it's 5 and 6 because if it's 4, if it's 4 groups, times 6, it's going to be 24, plus another, plus another group it will be 30 because 4 plus 6 equals 10.

> **David:** So Peter right now figured out while he's going to put his paper clips on 5 and 6, what was the strategy that he just used? What was his thinking to figure out it's 5 and 6? What was the thinking he just used right now? Mariel, did you hear?

COACHING MOVES & TOOLS

5. *Make sure the teacher welcomes your entry to his lesson.*

6. *Model the kinds of questions you would like the teacher to use to support student reasoning.*

Toni enters the lesson at this moment because she feels students—even if they now understand that some numbers on their game boards are factors and other numbers are products—may not understand how to use this information, that it might be helpful to model how students might think about the products and how to move their paper clips (e.g., the two factors) as they play the game. Since one of the challenges students will have as they play this game is to deconstruct the numbers on the game board into factors, Toni uses this co-teaching moment to model a way to think about the game, and also demonstrate how to use a specific strategy (e.g., what do I know about 30 in terms of its factors?).

It is also interesting in this short segment to note a change in David's use of talk. While he has been using wait time (he waits patiently for students to express themselves), he has yet to hold other children accountable to what has been said. That he uses this moment as an opportunity for other students to paraphrase Peter's comments indicates that he is aware of how important this strategy is for students' mathematical reasoning, This high-leverage use of talk to support student learning is important for a coach to note.

Using Puzzlement to Support a Teacher's Challenge

David has picked up on Toni's move (e.g., posing the question, What factors would make 30?), which is, in essence, a challenge to student thinking. In the next transcript segment, Toni builds on David's language and gives students an example of what his challenge might mean for their thinking.

David: I want you to challenge—I want you to challenge yourselves today. Yes? So yesterday you used one strategy that helped you fill in this first row, I'd like you to see if you can find another way so that you can have a row down here or a column or a diagonal going across your board.

Toni: So would a challenge be, the number 63 is over here.

David: Mhmm.

Toni: I'm going to challenge myself to think, what two factors are going to make 63. 'Cause I noticed a lot of you were doing 1×2, 1×3 . . .

David: Yup.

Toni: That's not a challenge, right? Even 2×2, 2×3 . . . not a challenge, but 9×8, whoa! That's hard.

7. Monitor and assess your effectiveness through teacher actions, questions, and behaviors.

To support David, Toni mirrors what a child might do who is taking up his challenge. This short back-and-forth between teacher and coach shows that they are aligned and that the co-teaching moves made at the beginning of the session have moved David to (1) use more precise language, (2) hold his students accountable for their use of language, (3) check for student understanding by asking them to restate what other children have said, and (4) challenge them to think more mathematically as they play the game.

Using Co-Teaching Moments to Weave in Goals

David now turns to the minilesson discussed in the preconference. From the start of the minilesson, Toni realizes that David has not internalized their planning discussion about how to facilitate the first problem (to quickly get an answer because children should know the product to know 2×7) and why to model this problem on the double number line (the model will serve as a tool to build connections and promote discourse as the minilesson continues). When he asks a student after he writes 2×7 and gets the product, "How did you know?" he has already begun to slow down the minilesson. Toni bookmarks the lesson at this point by stating that there are times when students will be expected to just know the answer (especially to an easy problem like 2×7) and to give it without explanation. The coach has modeled two important things for the teacher that can be returned to in the postconference. The first is how to set clear expectations for students (sometimes it's okay to just give an answer; you will not always be asked to explain your thinking). The second is how to pace the beginning of a minilesson.

David: Okay, so we'll start off with 2×7, volunteer? Dushawn?

Dushawn: 14.

David: And how did you know?

Dushawn: 'Cause I know that anything times two is a double.

David: Okay, so you have 2 groups of what here?

Dushawn: 7.

David: Okay, and move on to our next one.

Toni: And did you just know it?

Dushawn: [nods, yes]

Toni: So if you just know something, okay? You can just say, "I knew it." 'Cause that's okay; 'cause 2×7, you might know it like that. [snaps fingers] Right?

David: Like you know your name. Going to put up, 4×7. Ketshira, what are you thinking?

After visiting David's classroom the day before, Toni also knew she wanted to help him develop more rigorous discourse in his classroom. While his classroom culture is lovely and supportive, his nurturing of students has a downside: they rely on him to articulate their thinking with clarity. As Toni watches him teach the minilesson, she realizes students are not being held accountable to communicate with clarity and that part of the problem is that he is doing most of the paraphrasing for students. Toni bookmarks this moment in the lesson and uses specific talk moves (pedagogical tools) to slow down the conversation and to establish discourse norms for children's talking and listening.

In the transcript segment below, Toni interrupts David before he can paraphrase what Ketshira has just said, and checks for student understanding. She also points out that because Ketshira spoke so quickly, others might not understand. Here Toni models how to set norms for sharing ideas (e.g., speak loudly enough for everyone to hear you, speak slowly and clearly, make eye-contact).

Ketshira: I didn't even know what's 4×7, so it's like 2×7, 4×7. 'Cause the 7 is the same and the 4 is the 2, double it.

David: So you . . .

Toni: Who understands what she said? She said it so fast.

David: Mariel?

Toni then focuses on having children paraphrase Ketshira's strategy. She uses this talk tool at this moment because a big mathematical idea has come up and she wants to be sure students are attending to this idea.

COACHING MOVES & TOOLS

8. *Bookmark segments of the lesson to use in the postconference.*

9. *Model teaching behaviors you would like the teacher to develop.*

Mariel: I think she means double the 14. I think she meant, I think she meant double the 14.

Toni: So not what you think she means, but what did she say.

Ketshira: But . . .

Toni: Wait, wait. What did she say? Did anyone hear her and can put it in their own words?

David: Jasia?

Jasia: She said that, I think she said that . . . 4, 'cause there's 4 7s and that you could, double the 7s. 'Cause you have 4 7s and 2 plus 2 is 4.

David: Right.

Jasia: So you could double, you could take the 7s, you could put them together and that will equal 14.

Toni: I'm going to stop you. [to Ketshira] Is that what you said?

Ketshira: I, I . . .

Toni: Wait, wait. Is that what you said? 'Cause we've really got to listen to each other. All right. [to Ketshira] Say what you said again and I'm going to say the first thing I heard you say and then I got lost.

Ketshira: Okay.

Toni: But I did hear you say, "I didn't know 4×7."

David: Hmm.

Toni: I loved that you would recognize, I don't know this and then you were thinking about something else. So start again [to the other children] and we're all going to see if we understand what she's saying and if we can put it in our own words.

Ketshira: So I didn't know what's 4×7, but I was thinking that the 2×7. . . .

When Mariel says, "I think she meant double the 14," Toni holds her accountable for paraphrasing what was said. This talk move challenges all the students to reflect on and/ or shift their listening behaviors. The goal becomes not merely to talk, but to listen to someone else's ideas and to respond to those ideas. These discourse boundaries need to be established for children to internalize learning norms. By setting discourse boundaries, students learn that they need to attend carefully to the ideas of others, and that listening precedes responding. Toni's question, *Who understands what she said?* establishes some of those boundaries for students: our job when someone speaks is to listen, to understand what is said, and to be able to paraphrase each other's ideas.

In this discussion, Toni then loops back to Ketshira (the original speaker) to hold her accountable to the child who is paraphrasing her ideas. Because Ketshira has not been attending to what is being shared, she does not know if Jasia has accurately paraphrased her ideas. Toni sets another discourse boundary: when someone honors you by restating your thinking, you need to be listening to that person to see if what they say is accurate or not.

Because Toni is also working on mathematical modeling with David, she intervenes again in the lesson when she realizes he is reluctant to model student strategies. In the segment below, she challenges him to model what is being said.

> **Toni:** So could we just draw this here?
>
> **David:** Sure.
>
> **Toni:** 'Cause it sounded like you said your 2 groups of 7 is 14 and your other 2 groups of 7.
>
> **Jasia:** Yeah, 'cause . . .
>
> **Toni:** I saw you do this [indicates pairs of fingers on each hand] so that would be like this and this, yeah?
>
> **Jasia:** Yeah, 'cause first I had 4 7s, but it's easy for me to break it down so I can understand it more better. So I put 7 plus 7 equals 14 plus 14 equals 28. Then I was going to split it to put 10 plus 10 and 4 plus 4 and it made it 28 again.
>
> **David:** Got it.
>
> **Toni:** So we heard a couple of different things that came up in what you were saying, and one of them was "one stayed the same." What's that "one"? Can we use really precise language?
>
> **Jasia:** The 7 stayed the same.
>
> **Toni:** And what is the 7 called in multiplication?
>
> **Jasia:** The 7 is called the . . .
>
> **Toni:** What's the 4 called? What's the 14 called? Let's label these things.
>
> **Child:** 4 is the factor.

10. Be consistent in your focus (keep your goals in mind).
11. Use writing to help ground teacher and student learning.
12. Recognize and work with teacher discomfort as they try on new pedagogy.
13. Hold the teacher accountable to the goals discussed in the planning session.
14. Challenge teacher practice.

Doing this actually helps the children understand what happens to the product when one factor doubles and the other one stays the same.

David: So this is called the . . .

Child: Product.

Jasia: Wait—the product?

David: This is the answer, but when we're multiplying . . .

Jasia: Oh, the product . . .

David: We're being precise . . .

Jasia: So that's the product! That's the product for 14 plus 14 . . . and 2×7 is a . . . and 14 is the product for 2×7.

Toni: There you go. Could you sit? So, let's go back to your first statement which was, "when it stayed the same," it's not an 'it,' it's when one . . . we're going to try and write this as precisely as we can. So let's rewrite . . . can we squeeze it up there?

David: All of this?

Toni: Maybe we could squeeze it up there.

David: Sure.

Toni: So what are we calling these numbers in this problem?

Child: Factors.

Toni: So when one factor stays the same, what happened to the other factor?

Child: It doubled.

Toni: So when, if one factor stays the same and the other factor doubles, what happened to our product?

Child: Oh.

Child: It doubled.

Toni: It doubled too. So let's hold onto that. That seems like a really cool strategy.

Toni continues to challenge David to model, and at the end of the minilesson it becomes apparent that he is not fully comfortable using the double number line to model how some students solved 4×12 by using an easier problem (they doubled the product of 2×12).

Toni: [to David] So maybe let's just draw the 12 and show it on the double number line, what would happen on the bottom. And then we're done.

David: So scholars, what we're hearing is that we have 2×12, another 2 times 12 . . .

Toni: I was going to do it on the bottom.

David: This is what we heard you say. [models on the double number line] Mariel and Dushawn, is that what you were saying when you said, you would double?

Mariel: Yeah.

David: So you'd have 2 groups of 12, another 2 groups of 12 . . . is this describing it? So then we have 2 here plus another 2, you would be doubling those, correct? Is this making sense?

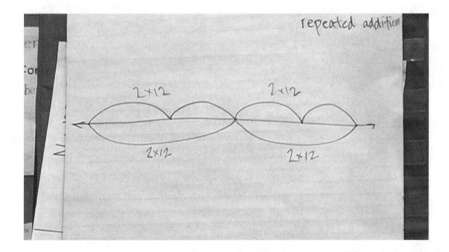

Toni also spends time helping David think about how to use talk signals (e.g., wait time, using a quiet thumb signal when you have the answer, etc.).

Toni: So I'm going to ask us to use a quiet thumb signal. 'Cause all this waving of hands, I get really nervous. So quiet thumb—'cause you look like you need more time to think. So quiet thumb might be helpful here too. When you're ready . . . you want to think of a problem you could use to make this easier if you think it's hard . . . could you use our doubling strategy?

David: Quiet thumb.

Toni: Quiet.

David: Ketshira, what do you think?

In summary, Toni models these pedagogical moves in this minilesson:

▸   having students paraphrase an important idea that has come up;

▸   moving away from students who are not able to paraphrase what's been said (e.g., when the child said, *I think she means double the 14.*);

▸   holding the child who shared a strategy accountable for listening to other children's paraphrases of that strategy (e.g., saying to the child, "Is that what you said?").

Toni also models holding the other children accountable by giving them very explicit instructions as to what their learning roles are: *So start again, and we're all going to see if we understand what she's saying and if we can put it in our own words.* Toni also models how to emphasize what is important in a child's strategy (what is clear): "I didn't know 4×7" and how powerful it is to recognize what you don't know and that you can use what you do know to solve a problem you don't know.

By making all the children responsible for listening to each other's thinking Toni is helping David consider how to develop more rigorous student talk in his classroom. However, when a teacher initially holds students accountable for speaking and listening, the lesson often grinds to a halt. What Toni has to help David understand is that this kind of talk will initially be difficult and frustrating for students and teacher, but in the long run will have major implications for student learning. When students become better skilled at listening and speaking, lessons will move more quickly. When students have ownership of their own learning, when they learn to advocate for themselves, they will raise questions or ask for clarification when they do not understand. This will make the pacing of the lesson about student generated learning. In this kind of teaching, the flow of the learning speeds up or slows down in direct relation to what students know.

The Postconference

You have to start where people are, because their growth is going to be from there, not from some abstraction or where you are or where someone else is.

—Myles Horton

We come to the final segment of the coaching cycle—the postconference. Our goal in the postconference is to leave the teacher with something specific and generalizable to work on. We hope that, whatever we recommend in the postconference, our suggestions positively impact the teacher's future practice. While it is not always possible to have a postconference on the same day as planning and co-teaching the lesson, it is critical that a coach debrief the lesson with the classroom teacher. This debriefing session should be done in a timely manner and in a way that is conducive to reflection.

Successful postconferences are dependent on a variety of skills. First, a coach needs deep-working knowledge of content (what is taught) and pedagogy (teaching skills needed to enhance [or ensure] learning in the classroom). Second, a coach must also possess the social and communication skills to discuss aspects of a teacher's practice and evidence of student learning. Third, a coach needs to have both the courage to have difficult conversations and the finesse to maneuver through them.

Of all the segments in the coaching cycle, the postconference can be the trickiest one for a coach to facilitate. We think the problems that arise for coaches are interrelated and can be distilled to four main causes: time (having an insufficient amount of time to hold the postconference), focus (not keeping the conversation focused on the instructional core), structure (not knowing how to facilitate the conversation), and social and discourse skills (not having the skill set to be able to provide crucial feedback to a teacher).

TIME

In the best of all possible worlds, there would be adequate time for the entire coaching cycle (planning, co-teaching, and debriefing) to occur in one day. In our experience, this is often not the case. Even when sufficient time is set aside for planning and co-teaching, there is often not enough time for the postconference to occur on the same day or even the next day. As a result, coaches find themselves having hurried postlesson discussions. If the debrief is done *on the fly* (e.g., talking to a teacher in the hall or briefly using time during their prep period or lunch), it is difficult with so many distractions to have a conversation that explores important issues or topics and promotes deep reflection. And when coaches do not have rich or crucial conversations with teachers about their craft they forfeit opportunities to help teachers develop insights into how they might improve their teaching.

One possible solution to these time constraints is for coaches to email their postconference notes and reflections on the lesson to the teacher. However, there are several caveats to be aware of with emails. First, writing reflections is a kind of documentation about practice that some teachers might find invasive or troubling. This may especially be true if you are copying administrators on the email to keep them informed of the work you are doing, if there is a culture of fear in a school, or if the environment is not conducive to public learning. Second, even a well-written email does not have the benefit of all of the other clues available in a face-to-face encounter. It is not cushioned by the nuance of voice, use of eye contact, facial expression, and gesture that take place in a conversation. In fact, a coach's postlesson notes that might be accepted when said face-to-face might produce a totally different response from the same teacher reading the email. Given how difficult it can be to create strong, trusting bonds, a misinterpreted email can potentially damage the relationship between coach and teacher. Despite the potential pitfalls, we think it is better to provide written feedback to teachers when postconference time is limited. This feedback can be provided after the coach and teacher have established parameters for the feedback and after a brief face-to-face session if one is possible within twenty-four hours of the lesson.

Keeping the Focus on the Instructional Core

If one of the primary goals of the postconference is to highlight specific elements of teaching that affect student learning, then it is critical that coaches take the time to adequately prepare for their interactions with teachers. When coaches have not given sufficient thought to which aspect of the lesson might have the greatest leverage in improving teacher practice, they often miss opportunities to support teacher learning.

Even with all the skills in their coaching repertoire, it is easy for coaches to lose their focus. As coaches try to maintain a natural and relaxed conversation, they may shift the focus from teaching and learning (the instructional core) to more trivial kinds of talk. When confronted with conflicting ideas and emotional issues, coaches may back away from the source of stress, thereby letting the conversational thread unravel.

It is for these reasons that we strongly suggest that coaches take time to reflect on the lesson before talking to teachers about the lesson. Coaches can use this reflection time to think about how to structure the postconference, what the overall focus will be, how to initiate the conversation (what will my opening question be?) and what key points they want to make.

STRUCTURE

We think it is important for a coach to control the flow of the postconference. One way to do this is to sketch a plan of action for the conversation, which may be very difficult to do if the postconference follows right after the lesson. To create this map coaches might consider the following questions:

1. How do I to start the discussion? What do I say? What ideas do I bring up for discussion?
2. What are the potential difficulties or pitfalls?
3. What are the successes and how do I recognize these?
4. What evidence do I have to support what I am going to say (notes, student work)?
5. Are there artifacts of student learning I can bring in to highlight key points about teaching?

It is also helpful for coaches to consider creating a dialogue map (if I say this, then that might happen) to plan out tricky places in the postconference. These kinds of conversational maps are especially helpful with tricky coaching relationships or with important, but difficult conversations.

To adequately map the postconference takes time. Therefore, we highly recommend giving yourself 10 to 15 minutes to look at your notes to be able to pick the best way to start the conversation with a teacher. One way to focus the postlesson conversation is around one of your mutual goals and specific moments in the lesson that illustrate the implementation of these goals or where employing one of these goals might have been useful.

Preparing the Conversation

Because teaching is a highly personal act, highlighting aspects of a teacher's craft can backfire if coaches haven't done the necessary prep work. Such prep work might include thinking about the lesson in terms of the goals set for teacher development (this can include goals set by the teacher and coach or ones set by the coach), reflecting on what was outlined in the planning session (what ideas were discussed, how the lesson was structured), examining how the planned lesson was actually implemented in the classroom, and weighing which topic might be used to engage and maximize teacher learning. Coaches who are effective at facilitating postconferences link the planning and co-teaching in ways that help teachers think about their lessons in terms of what worked and what did not work as evidenced by student responses and learning. They also provide insights into how teachers might improve their craft, giving specific examples of what was said and done, and offering suggestions on ways to improve this.

"What Do I Say First?"

Coaches commonly begin the postconference by asking teachers to reflect on their lesson. Often coaches use the question, *so how did it go?* to begin. This seemingly simple question (what can be easier than asking teachers to think aloud about their lesson?) can have both positive and negative results. On the positive side, asking for teacher insights from the outset of the postconference sets the tone, signaling to teachers that the coach is interested in what they have to say. Asking teachers to reflect first is also a way for coaches to understand the lesson from the teachers' perspective. This gives coaches insights into how their views of the lesson are similar and dissimilar from the teachers'. This can sometimes be helpful to a coach as she thinks about a plan of action. (*The teacher mentioned student confusions. This might be a good starting place for a conversation about how to use students' misconceptions to open up discourse in the classroom.*)

There is, however, a downside to opening the postconference with a broad question like, *how did it go?* Coaches who open this door have to be ready, willing, and able to deal with the emotional roller coaster that may ensue. There are several possible scenarios here and each one has the potential to be difficult terrain for the coach to move through. If the teacher thinks the lesson was fabulous and the coach does not agree, the coach is in the position of not only disagreeing with the teacher's assessment, but of also being critical of something the teacher thought was good. If the lesson did not go well, a teacher might already be feeling bad. If the teacher begins the postconference by maligning herself or by becoming emotional, a coach may be in the awkward position of trying to soothe the teacher. Once caught in this consoling role, it may be very difficult for a coach to shift the conversation to a more analytical or critical one. It stands to reason that a teacher who has opened herself up and is in a vulnerable state might not be ready to hear anything about her practice, and a move in this direction on the part of the coach can feel intrusive, abrasive, or insensitive. Another possibility is that the teacher thinks her lesson was good, but is unwilling to say it publicly. She may begin by disparaging her lesson, but secretly believe otherwise. Coaches should also be aware that a teacher who disparages her own teaching is not necessarily inviting the coach to do so, too. It is not uncommon for coaches to find that when they echo the teacher's self-criticism their comments are not appreciated.

While there are many possible ways to begin a postsession, we feel it is often more helpful to start with something specific (e.g., *We said we were going to focus on our use of questions in our coaching session today. I've taken notes and I thought we could examine our questions.*) rather than something general (e.g., The question, *how did it go?*). The opening statement or question could be grounded in a teaching or learning behavior, in the goals for coaching, in successes that have happened, or in artifacts of student learning. In our experience, the more specific and carefully planned the opening of the postconference, the more control the coach has over the initial flow of conversation.

Coaches—no matter what the situation—need to remember that teaching is highly personal and their words, no matter how well intended or how beautifully phrased, carry the potential to alienate teachers should their comments be perceived as critical of *who I am and what I do*.

Possible Topics for Discussion

Part of the difficulty in structuring the postconference is that there is often a wide range of topics for coaches to consider as they plan their postlesson discussions. Possible topics for discussion include

> - use of pedagogy (e.g., What kind of instructional practices and strategies does this teacher use? How effectively are they implemented?)

> - use of content (e.g., How deeply does the teacher understand and implement the content? How does content implementation impact student learning?)

> - expectations for and evidence of student learning (e.g., Are teacher expectations high? What evidence is there in either student talk or written work that they are learning?)

> - ways the teacher assesses student learning in the classroom (e.g., How does the teacher deal with students' misconceptions and/or challenge their thinking?)

> - the nature of discourse in the classroom (e.g., What are the norms for talk and how do these impact learning?)

> - the role of the task or curriculum in supporting student learning (e.g., If the lesson was effective, what made it effective? If the lesson was flawed, what contributed to its ineffectiveness?).

In addition to the major topics listed above, there are other topics coaches may want to consider in planning their postconference discussions. These include

> ▸ pacing of the lesson and what might have affected the flow

> ▸ issues of control and student autonomy (e.g., Where is the power source in the classroom?)

> ▸ management issues (e.g., Did the lesson get derailed by too much correction of student behavior?).

Pick a High-Leverage Practice

Because of the wide range of topics coaches can pick from, we suggest keeping the following in mind when structuring the postlesson conversation. First, it is important to choose a high-leverage topic. This means that the topic will get at some essential aspect of practice, and that aspect is something a teacher needs to consider to improve his teaching. For example, focusing on the nature of talk allows a coach to explore the reasons why a teacher holds the reins so tightly in a lesson and doesn't slow down to explore either children's ideas or mistakes. The underlying root of this behavior might bring up other aspects of teaching. A teacher might be reluctant to let go of the reins because he is afraid of losing control of the students, or he might not explore student comments because he is unsure of the underlying content and how to facilitate a conversation around it.

It is also important in the postconference for a coach to weave in goals that have been set for teacher learning. For example, if a coach is working on helping a teacher develop clarity of questions, she might highlight the kinds of questions asked in the lesson in the debriefing session. In the act of restating teacher questions used during the lesson, a coach can then explore which ones worked, which ones did not, and why (How do we know when our questions are successful? What's our evidence?).

Use Scripted Notes from the Lesson

To structure a postconference, it is often helpful for coaches to use their notes from the classroom lesson. Having an accurate record of what transpired during the lesson can be used to help a coach reflect on what happened in the classroom. The more detailed and precise the notes, the more effective they can be to highlight specific aspects of teacher practice and how they affect student learning. By using their scripted notes, coaches can focus the postconference and help teachers think about what they would like to change or improve in their practice and brainstorm ways to do this.

The Role of Bookmarking

Bookmarking was discussed in Chapter 8 as an important tool to use in co-teaching to help the coach facilitate a postconference. A coach who has bookmarked specific segments of a lesson can bring these up as examples in the postconference discussion.

For example, a coach who has bookmarked a segment of a lesson might ask a teacher the following questions in the postconference: *What confusions came up for students when I asked _____? What ideas underlie these different misconceptions? How did I handle student confusions?* In this example, the coach is using mental notes, her bookmarking of a specific place in the lesson, to help a teacher understand how she facilitated student learning in a co-teaching moment. The coach might be doing this because one of the goals for teacher development is to learn how to deal with and explore student confusion as it arises in the lesson. The coach might also be doing this to help a teacher understand specific pedagogical choices that were employed to support student learning and/or discourse. Whatever the reasons underlying a coach's choice for bookmarking in a lesson, it is important for a coach to realize that this is a powerful coaching tool for structuring the postconference when one does not have detailed notes to work from.

SOCIAL AND DISCOURSE SKILLS

Coaches should be aware of some pitfalls in a debriefing session. They arise because as a teacher and coach reflect together on the lesson, explore beliefs, and examine aspects of teaching, there is great potential for emotions (both positive and negative) to come to the surface. For this reason, it is important for the coach to stay neutral when the conversation gets heated or when a teacher is asking for some kind of evaluation (e.g., *What did you think? Was it as bad as I thought?*) In the postconference then, it behooves a coach to be able to

COACH NOTE

In the postconference, a coach relies heavily on both communication skills and broader social skills. (For more in-depth analysis of these skills and how to develop them, see Chapter 5.)

> ➤ speak honestly, but in a way that does not offend

> ➤ clearly articulate her own thoughts, but be equally willing to listen to the ideas of others

> ➤ be able to let go of what she would like to say if a teacher is unable or unwilling to listen to that particular idea at that particular time

> ➤ know that there are boundaries to what can be said, but also recognize that to affect teacher practice sometimes those boundaries have to be crossed

> ➤ be open enough to listen to divergent ideas without losing sight of one's own

> ➤ have the courage to dig deep, but also know when to back off

> ➤ empathize with teacher emotions when they arise, but not let one's own emotions interfere with coaching (A key idea: *It ain't personal!*).

The art—and challenge—of the postconference is not only knowing what to say, but also knowing when and how to say it.

Listening Is Key

Sometimes the best way to generate conversation is to begin with the simple act of listening. But listening is also tricky because it is normal for most humans to hear what is said through their own filter. Even slight distortions can have ramifications for the effectiveness of the debriefing session. This transcript segment, which is from a different coaching session than the one illustrated in the case study, is an example of this kind of misinterpretation.

> **Teacher:** That was such a mess! The introduction went on way too long.
>
> **Coach:** Perhaps we can brainstorm ways to tighten up the introduction. Maybe if we look at the questions you used, we could find ways to make them more effective.
>
> **Teacher:** You thought my questions were ineffective? I didn't think it was my questions; I thought it went on too long because kids weren't behaving. I had to keep redirecting them. That's what made it messy.
>
> **Coach:** Oh. I agree; the students were fidgeting a lot.
>
> **Teacher:** I don't think there's anything wrong with my questions. It's not my questions; it's my students' inability to sit still and listen.

The teacher begins by commenting on her lesson. But the coach's interpretation of the word *mess*, used by the teacher, and her underlying assumption that her view matches the teacher's view, shifts the dynamic instantly. The teacher is surprised when the coach connects the word *mess* to her use of questions and becomes defensive because she believes that the messiness was a result of how students were behaving, not of what she was doing. A more skillful coach might realize that implying that "your lesson was messy because of your use of questions" has the potential to alienate a teacher who is unprepared for this comment (or who doesn't yet know that her questions or pacing may be the source of fidgety students). A coach with better social and communication skills might have followed the teacher's comment with a more exploratory question, perhaps re-voicing what the teacher said and then asking, "why do you think the lesson was so messy?" Slowing down to gather information here gives the coach a window into teacher thinking; this insight then offers her more options for responding. If the coach wants to explore questioning, she will have to figure out how to move in this direction and find ways to link what the teacher thinks is problematic with her own different perceptions.

Hearing the Subtexts in Conversations

Active listening, being able to hear and understand the subtext in conversations, is also key for coaching successfully. For example, a teacher says, "the kids are so confused when they speak." A possible subtext of the teacher's comment might be: *I am so confused when kids speak.* Underlying this might be an emotion (fear of not understanding what kids are saying), which might be directly tied to the teacher's understanding of content.

A coach who recognizes the subtext in a teacher's comment can understand and empathize with his fears. To bring these fears to the surface, a coach might select different students' statements she heard during the lesson and explore their possible meanings with the teacher. Once this door is opened, a coach might also address the emotions that arise in teaching and offer possible pedagogical solutions (e.g., *When I don't understand what a student is saying, I will pose a question to the class. Does anyone understand what _____ is saying?*). This kind of conversation also has the potential to bring up a teacher's belief system (*I feel that I have to know everything. When I don't know something, I feel like a failure.*), which can be a high-leverage moment for a coach because changing a teacher's practice often means shifting a teacher's beliefs.

Rehearsing for Crucial Conversations

One way for coaches to build their social skills is for them to rehearse before going into a postconference, mapping out what a teacher might say and how they might respond: *If I say this, she might say that. Then I could say* . . . . This kind of dialogue flow chart is especially helpful if the coach needs to explore difficult topics, if the lesson went poorly and the coach is unsure of how to begin the debrief, if the coach does not have a lot of experience coaching, or if she does have experience with a particular teacher, but they have a difficult or contentious relationship. In the latter case, the coach should bear in mind what might trigger negative reactions and try to avoid these in her planning of the postconference.

Whatever the nature of the relationship, it is important for the coach to develop the capacity to engage in the kind of dialogue that results in changes in teacher's practice. This sometimes means having *crucial conversations*. But how these conversations are structured can make the difference between deepening a teacher-coach bond and damaging it. Coaches have to internalize when and how to communicate their own ideas; when to speak and when to be silent. Coaches also must understand the difference between *responding* and *reacting*. Responding offers space and leaves room for controlling the process; reacting is unconscious and, as such, is emotionally charged and often uncontrollable. Because controlling emotions in a postconference is crucial, coaches need to be aware of their own triggers and biases (see Chapter 4 for a more in-depth discussion of self-awareness). Given how difficult it is to build and maintain deep trusting bonds, a coach should be wary of her language and recognize that the power of words is both positive and negative.

Case Study

Background on the Postconference with David

In their planning session, Toni talked with David about three key areas: (1) how to pace the minilesson to keep it within a 10 to 15-minute time frame, (2) how to model student strategies using the double number line, and (3) how to facilitate student talk and develop more precise ways of communicating. While she had addressed these three things in her co-teaching with David in the classroom, her primary focus (and this is evident in when and how she entered the lesson) was on helping David facilitate and refine student discourse.

In the short time she had to plan (10 minutes) for the postconference, Toni used the notes she took during the lesson. These helped her think about where to start the conversation with David and why to start there. Further, by focusing on when and why she entered the lesson (her role as co-teacher), Toni was able to pick a major focus for their postconference: discourse in David's classroom. This included children's use of language and how David facilitated classroom talk. Discourse is considered high leverage because it has the potential to help David improve his practice in all content areas and in ways critical to supporting and deepening student learning.

In the postconference, Toni focuses the conversation on a high-leverage practice: facilitating student discourse. Even though Toni is using a narrow lens to view the lesson, she still can address the other two topics, pacing and modeling, that they explored in their planning session.

Postconference Tool #1: Hit the Ground Running

Toni begins the debriefing session by naming what she'd like to focus on in the conversation. She says,

> Okay, Dave, so let's debrief the lesson. There were some really lovely things that happened and there are some things I'd like to really think about and one of the big ones is the development of precision in children's language. And maybe thinking about where in the lesson we were working on that and then what kinds of things we need to do as teachers to develop students' language.

Toni quickly frames what she thinks is important (the development of precision in students' language) and explicitly states that she would like for them to examine the lesson using this lens. She focuses on children's use of language because she knows that this is intertwined with David's pedagogy: how children speak is a reflection of how he is using *talk moves* in his classroom and what his expectations are for speaking and listening in his classroom community.

Toni's directness jump-starts the conversation from the get-go. It is important to note that she cushions what may be a difficult discussion in two ways. First, she offers a compliment right from the beginning. (Note also that she does not name all the "lovely things that happened" in the lesson because doing so might eat up time and shift the focus of the postconference.) Second, Toni makes the conversation inclusive by using the word, *we*. This is not about *your* lesson, but about *our* lesson. When Toni invites David to think "about where in the lesson *we* were working on that" [i.e., precision of language] and what kinds of things *we* could do as teachers to develop students' language," she opens the door for them both to reflect publicly and name specific things that happened in the lesson. In asking David to think about "what kinds of things we need to do" to develop language, Toni is also setting the stage for David to consider other options for facilitating discourse. Posing this question helps her gather information and gives her an opportunity—depending on what David says—to offer specific suggestions on ways he might improve his practice. It is also solution oriented and keeps the focus on student learning, not on the teacher. It assumes that the teacher is looking for ways to improve and is in no way critical of what he did or did not do.

Postconference Tool #2: Give the Teacher Thinking Space

Although Toni has named "precision in children's language" as something they might focus on during their postconference discussion, she is aware that David's interpretation of what this means is not necessarily hers. At this moment in the postconference she is gathering information about David's understanding and perceptions of the lesson. To facilitate the discussion, Toni uses the chart paper document created during the minilesson to ground their conversation.

COACH NOTE

How does a teacher interpret a coach's comments? In any given lesson, the mismatch between what two people see and understand has the potential to create problems in the postconference. This is one reason it is important to give a teacher time to reflect on a comment or question, and then, use what the teacher says to structure the discussion.

> **David:** I think in the string, in today's string, I should have probably paused after the second equation. So after 4×7, when they started noticing that something is being doubled.
>
> **Toni:** Let's go to it and look at it. [Pulls out the chart paper where student strategies were recorded during the lesson.]
>
> **David:** Sure.
>
> **Toni:** Okay.
>
> **David:** So before we actually got into the solving of 4×7 and they started noticing that the 2 doubles into 4 I think that's where I should have paused and started naming factors, product, and then working toward precision. But also, at the same time, having them think about what do we mean by describing something precisely.

Toni: Okay.

David: So that they give it a definition and they come to an understanding of what that is without me necessarily feeding them a definition that they might not understand or might not really make sense to them.

Toni: Part of it is not accepting what children say because I noticed a lot of your paraphrasing is exact paraphrasing of their language . . . which is good, but it also keeps them in the same place.

In this short time, Toni gains insight into David's interpretation of how (and where in the lesson) he might have pushed for precision of language. That this is not necessarily her view is evidenced in her statement, "Part of it is not accepting what children say because I noticed a lot of your paraphrasing is exact paraphrasing of their language." Here Toni names a big-picture problem—it is not that students aren't using precise words like factor and product, but that David is paraphrasing entire segments of students' unclear language, ironically reinforcing what is said (and how it is said). Because his paraphrasing is the root of classroom discourse norms, a key way to improve children's language is to change this teaching behavior. For example, David might voice the students' comments in ways that infuse correct terminology into the students' language. Although Toni recognizes that David's paraphrasing is a major problem that is affecting both the pacing of his lessons and student learning and communication, she moves away from this topic to explore *his* noticings! This is a key move because *teacher noticings* are the starting place for building insights into practice.

Toni: So if we even go back further to the introduction of the game . . . one of the things that took us so long—was me—because I wanted to actually think about what's the product? What are the factors?

David: Right.

Toni: Because they were describing the game in non-mathematical ways. So I think part of what we have to do is hold them accountable to the mathematical talk.

David: Yeah.

Toni: Right? And so look at how long it took for us to think about what are the factors . . .

David: Right.

Toni: . . . and you had children who didn't even know what the factors were.

David: Right. Right. And that's just something that in hindsight now, in my instruction I have not been very purposeful with naming factors, products, and being consistent with that language. And so it's something we did use, it was introduced, but it was inconsistently maintained and made into a routine in our daily work with math.

Following David's lead (it is after all the second time he's identified children's not knowing the words factor and product as being problematic), Toni uses her notes to find specific examples of children's language (the words *it* and *number*) and gives him suggestions as to how he might address their imprecision.

Toni: Right. Okay. And so that might be something to think about when you're listening to children . . . and they're using words like, "it" . . .

David: It, right.

Toni: Or "the number" . . . and that, within this context, this number [points to a factor in the equation on the chart paper] has a different meaning than this number . . . [points to the product in the equation on the chart paper]

David: Right.

Toni: . . . because we're talking about factors and products. All right. So, like any other things . . . how else do we support children's development of language?

By focusing on two specific examples that occurred in the classroom, the coach is developing David's ear for listening to children's speech patterns and helping him identify moments when he can challenge them to communicate more clearly (e.g., When children say "it," ask them, what's the "it?" When children use the word *number*, help them recognize that in a multiplication equation the numbers have different mathematical meanings.). Toni is also emphasizing visuals because she knows that these can be tools to ground the classroom talk and develop children's clarity of expression.

Postconference Tool #3: Gathering Information to Determine Next Steps

After naming specific things David might do to support language development, Toni returns to her goal for the postconference. Her question, "how else do we support children's development of language?" is used to re-focus the conversation on this important topic. Although Toni has specific things in mind that she would like to address, she is still gathering insights into David's perception of the lesson and what it means to develop

COACHING MOVES & TOOLS

1. *Gather information.*
2. *Give thinking space.*
3. *Offer the teacher opportunities to share his noticings.*
4. *Use teacher noticings to shape the conversation.*
5. *Use inclusive language (it's our lesson, not your lesson).*

children's language. When David shares his ideas, Toni gathers critical information that helps her think about how to proceed. David's response

> Giving them enough opportunities to build some . . . an understanding of what it is they're working with. And so when we were working with 2 groups of 7 in early multiplication and they're constructing meaning out of the different contexts that we had with these, with the problems, at those moments, I think, introducing the mathematical terms and connecting it to the work they were doing back then . . . it would have helped them develop the understanding of what factor means, what's the product, what's the difference between those two and why is it important to label them now that we're in this kind of work.

shows that he is still focused on helping children use specific words related to multiplication. Even though what he describes is important to developing children's understanding of the content he is teaching, it is not necessarily going to radically change the nature of talk in his classroom. Children in this instance may learn the words factor and product, but using these words will not, in and of itself, change the nature of discourse in his classroom. Changing the words does not change the learning behaviors. Based on David's response, Toni shifts gears to give him specific examples from the lesson that will help him understand her point of view about children's use of language, what is affecting their talk, and how it is affecting his teaching. (This is highlighted in transcripts in the next section.)

Postconference Tool #4: Celebrate a Teacher's Accomplishments

Although Toni recognizes that David does not always hold his children accountable for how they are speaking, she also knows the history of his class, that he has spent a good deal of time trying to develop the kind of classroom community where children were willing to risk sharing their ideas publicly. That he has succeeded in this goal is a major accomplishment to celebrate with him in the postconference. However, Toni wants to encourage David to consider the next place in his students' journey: children have to learn how to communicate their ideas with clarity and other children have to develop better listening skills. Toni also knows that changing the established speech and learning behaviors that have become the norms in David's classroom will not be easy to do.

Before continuing to explore what may be a difficult, but crucial topic, Toni compliments David on the children's confidence and recognizes all the work he must have done to develop their willingness to share their ideas publicly. She also highlights the positive change in children's communication—they are now able to speak with confidence. However, Toni also wants David to begin to develop boundaries for children's talk.

Toni: So that's one piece of the work. I guess I was thinking more about listening to children speak. It's wonderful how confident they are in their abilities to talk. So you've done a lot of work around that. And that's great, but this idea of editing what you're saying for your audience. I forget the little girl's name who was sitting here. She was going on and on and on. . . . And so maybe one of the things is giving them wait time, which is why I think the thumb signal is really good. Wait time—make sure, when you're getting ready to speak, you're going to speak with clarity. So this idea that I'm just going to keep talking until I say something . . . that somebody understands is, she was kind of going around in circles and saying a lot . . .

David: Yes.

Toni: . . . and so the refinement of language I think comes from making children stop, be ready to speak before they speak.

To help David develop more rigorous talk, Toni gives him an example of what happened and offers suggestions for how he might set norms for talk in his classroom. These suggestions include having children use a quiet thumb signal to indicate that they are ready to speak (this signal also gives thinking time to the other students and slows down the communication flow), using wait time to let children mentally prepare what they'd like to share with the group, and stopping children when they are not articulating their ideas with clarity and saying something like, "You don't seem ready yet; I'm going to give you a bit of time to get clear about what you'd like to say to the community. Remember, when you give a thumb signal, it means you're ready to share your ideas."

Postconference Tool #5: Be Prepared to Challenge Perceptions and Beliefs

When David states that he thinks the child in question was speaking as clearly as she could, Toni challenges this belief by pointing out that the child "was speaking to you."

> COACHING MOVES & TOOLS
>
> 6. *Celebrate success*
> 7. *Challenge teacher beliefs.*
> 8. *Use specific examples to support your point*

David: . . . but you're right, I do think that overall that modeling or that practice could be taking place a little more consistently.

Toni: So do you think we could actually work on that? So the idea of, who are you actually speaking to, because she was talking to you . . .

David: Right.

Toni: . . . and if she had looked at her peers, it's like . . .

David: They were . . .

Toni: . . . gone.

David: . . . checked out.

Toni: And so to bring more children into the conversation, and to even stop her and to say, how do you, what do you think people are making, what kind of sense are they making of what you're saying.

Toni names another behavior that is affecting the discourse in his classroom: the children are not necessarily concerned with their peers' understanding of their ideas. When they speak, their focus is on communicating with David. Evidence of this is that when they speak, they look directly at him and ignore what is happening around them (e.g., their classmates not listening, fidgeting, etc.). This behavior is then reinforced by David's paraphrasing of what is said. Children's ideas are flowing through him, making him the center of the discourse. This kind of classroom dynamic often prevents children from becoming accountable (*I don't have to listen because my teacher repeats whatever is said*), slows down the discussion (e.g., children often repeat the same ideas because they have not been listening to what has been said), and sustains confusion because confusion is not addressed as it is happening. Students who have ownership of their learning do not wait for a teacher to ask, "who understands?" but rather raise questions to help themselves understand an idea or strategy that is being shared. This slowing down of the talk around understanding is a shared move—a learner move as well as a teacher move.

To help David think about this discourse dynamic, Toni offers him a suggestion: when a child is speaking unclearly, have her look at her peers—at the looks on their faces, their behaviors—and consider, based on what you're seeing, do you think they are following your thinking? This slight change in a speaker's behavior has the potential to shift the power source in the classroom in profound ways.

Postconference Tool #6: Use Evidence to Build Understanding

To help David understand how she was viewing talk in his classroom, Toni gives specific examples (evidence) of what happened (from her point of view) and then offers specific solutions (how she would work to develop student talk). This coaching segment is highly guided; Toni is offering David a view through her lens, naming what she sees and how she would facilitate discourse.

Toni: So when children couldn't paraphrase what she was saying it was because it was really hard to hold on to, to the different ideas. She had a lot of ideas coming up.

David: She did, yeah.

Toni: And so then one of the moves is to say, do you remember one thing she said? And the first part was crystal clear.

David: Mhmm.

Toni: Right? 'Cause she said, "I noticed that one factor stayed the same." And then maybe to even say to her, you know when you, that first thing you said was so clear, I wonder if you could make the rest of it as clear as that?

David: As that.

Toni: And then to hold on to that. So like, highlight what she's doing that's clear . . .

David: Right.

Toni: . . . and then think about, so what other kinds of things could you do.

Toni is focusing on a co-teaching moment in the lesson where she slowed down the lesson to hold the children accountable for both speaking with clarity and for listening and recognizing what they did or did not understand from what was being said. (See the transcript that accompanies the co-teaching video segments.) In revisiting this moment, Toni demonstrates a way David might facilitate talk when a child is not speaking clearly.

One way to slow down the conversation is to encourage student paraphrasing. In these moments, a teacher might bring other learners into the discussion by asking, "Who understands what _____ said?" If children do not respond, a teacher might ask, "Do you remember one thing she said? Can you parrot any part of it back?" Doing this holds everyone accountable: it makes the listeners accountable for how they are listening, and makes the speaker accountable for the clarity of her expression. If the students are not following what is being said, then it is their job to slow the speaker down, to say something like, "I heard you say, 'one factor stayed the same,' but I didn't understand the rest of what you said." This kind of learning stance holds the community accountable to the ideas being shared. The speaker is challenged to be clearer; the listeners are challenged to think about how much they understood and what their questions are if they do not understand what is said.

This was not happening in David's minilesson. The speaker was talking to the teacher; the other students were not attending. When Toni slowed down the conversation at this point, there was a major shift in the dynamic in the classroom. She highlights this moment for David as an example of a place in the lesson where children's imprecise language needed facilitation. She offers him specific tools to help him think about how he might implement these talk moves into his teaching in the future.

COACH NOTE

It is important for coaches to break down what they are seeing into manageable chunks for a teacher to process. To say a child was too verbose does not help the teacher; to say here's what the child said (use exact words), here's where it was effective (use exact words), and here's where it broke down (use exact words), is one way to help a teacher develop an ear for what is happening in his classroom. Breaking communication down into manageable segments is one way to train both teachers and children to listen. It is also one way to help children listen to themselves as they speak and think about, Was I clear? How do I know I was clear? If I wasn't clear, what might I do to become clearer?

Although Toni knows she is challenging David to see through a different lens, she also knows that by naming specific talk moves she is setting the groundwork for their work together in the future.

Postconference Tool #7: Looping Back

In this segment of the postconference, Toni continues to explore talk moves that might have helped children communicate more clearly. She also loops back to an earlier statement (in the beginning of the postconference, she says, "I noticed a lot of your paraphrasing is exact paraphrasing of their language"). In the next transcript segment, Toni re-highlights talk moves because she knows they are high-leverage: if David shifts this one behavior (e.g., becomes more effective using talk moves), it will have major implications for both his teaching and student learning.

>**Toni:** Alright. So I'm, I'm actually thinking of specific talk moves. And we didn't use pair talk today at all. We didn't have the kids turn and talk and maybe there wasn't really an occasion, given what happened here.
>
>**David:** Yeah.
>
>**Toni:** But I don't know.
>
>**David:** Yeah.
>
>**Toni:** So we didn't really build that into our plan.
>
>**David:** Right.
>
>**Toni:** But that might be something to think about. The other thing is when are the opportunities for students to paraphrase what other students are saying . . .
>
>**David:** Right.
>
>**Toni:** . . . and how frequently are you as the teacher paraphrasing?

Here, Toni is trying to get David to be more aware of the frequency with which he is paraphrasing. But note that he is not thinking about *his* paraphrasing of student ideas, but of how frequently he uses student paraphrasing in his practice.

>**David:** Right. And that's something that I do . . . I do use pretty consistently. I'm not, I mean in this string, I'm not sure that I did use it enough times.
>
>**Toni:** Para—students paraphrasing each other?
>
>**David:** Right. And so we'll either say parrot or paraphrase just so that they know they're being held accountable for listening to each other.
>
>**Toni:** Okay.

Because the teacher may not be aware of the frequency with which he is paraphrasing, Toni asks for clarity. When he says, "I'm not sure that I did use it enough times," is he thinking about his own paraphrasing or student paraphrasing? That he is unaware of the frequency of his own paraphrasing is something Toni wants to explore; she also wants to examine one effect of his actions. Because David is not consistently holding students accountable to listening to each other's strategies (they know he will paraphrase whatever is said), they do not have to listen to each other. The result is student inattentiveness. This is a teaching behavior David needs to change if he hopes to have students engage in more rigorous discourse in his classroom.

Postconference Tool #8: Keep a Long-Term Perspective for Teacher Development

In the next transcript segment, Toni offers evidence of how students are speaking and not listening to each other. She also pinpoints specific aspects of practice that he needs to develop. Because she does not want to overwhelm him, Toni puts things in perspective by letting him know that what she is talking about is a long-term goal; they will continue to work on this in the future.

> **David:** And making sense out of it in their own—in their own words, connecting their own understanding to what, what's being said or what's being explained. And so I, I did use it a few times, I'm not sure I did it enough. I think that would have . . . gotten a few more scholars to really connect to the work that we were doing. I think they each had an idea of what was going on, but then connecting those ideas could have gone a little bit better.
>
> **Toni:** And I think that probably describes it really well. They each had an idea, but those ideas . . .
>
> **David:** Right.
>
> **Toni:** . . . weren't being synthesized because, at one point, didn't we have kids saying the same thing over and over again?
>
> **David:** Pretty much, yes.
>
> **Toni:** And so not really listening to each other . . .
>
> **David:** Right.
>
> **Toni:** And I'm going to say what I want to say no matter what you say.
>
> **David:** With the—right.
>
> **Toni:** But that would be something to work—'cause you're going to be teaching fourth grade . . .

David: Mhmm.

Toni: You could work on them . . .

David: Definitely.

Toni: . . . next year.

Toni uses the teacher's description of what was happening in the classroom to say that children were not listening and one piece of evidence was that the children kept repeating the same ideas over and over without any realization that what they were saying had just been said by another student.

Because she is setting long-term goals for teacher development, Toni names other things they might work on in their future collaborations. In the next transcript segment, Toni names specific tools they might work on next year: videotaping their lessons, creating transcripts of the lessons, and analyzing these transcripts for specific moments where talk moves were used or might have been used to develop student thinking.

Toni: The pacing was interesting because it felt slow and fast at the same time. So maybe next year, one of the things we could work on as a team is filming the lessons, doing the transcripts, and then analyzing the transcripts for . . . where are the places where I'm not going to speak? Where are the places where I'm going to use something like a quiet thumb signal? Where are the places where I use pair talk? Because you can't use it all the time and it's not that we weren't using it . . .

David: Right.

Toni: We weren't using it effectively.

David: Right. Or, or recognizing those moments where one of those tools . . .

Toni: Right.

David: . . . would really push the conversation . . . further ahead.

Toni: Right. Yeah.

David: Yeah. 'Cause I felt that same tension of, there were moments where I thought, this is kind of dragging and there were moments where I felt like I was going a little too fast. So I needed to slow down. But then in looking at the kids, there were some kids who were way ahead and then there were others who were completely puzzled. And so, yeah, that, that was a tricky . . . tricky moment.

Postconference Tool #9: Explore How Specific Teacher Choices Affected Pacing

When Toni states that the lesson "felt slow and fast at the same time," David's response shows that he thinks some children were lost because the ideas were too difficult. But Toni has a different view, so she continues to name specific things he did that affected the pacing of his lesson.

> **Toni:** I think it was a good grouping, like the students you put together in that group, they were more or less in the same place, in the kind, in the ways they were thinking and then the . . . the string was in the right place for them too. But I think it was too slow. Maybe one of the things where we're starting, remember where we said we're going to put this up [indicates the first problem, 2×7] and we know that everyone knows it and we just get the answer like that.

> **David:** Right. And then just keep going.

To do this, Toni revisits their plan for the lesson: they had planned to put up the first problem (2×7) and, because children would easily know the product, they would not spend any time discussing how children got their answers. David forgot this and explored the first problem with the question, *How did you get your answer?* (To revisit this part of the lesson, go to Chapter 8, pages 142–143). This slowed down the pace of his minilesson.

Postconference Tool #10: Use Written Artifacts from the Lesson to Ground Discussion

It is important to have artifacts to use in a postconference because what has been recorded in the lesson can support teacher learning. In this transcript segment, Toni uses what was written on chart paper during the lesson to help David reflect further on his practice:

> **Toni:** Any other thoughts about the lesson?

> **David:** More of what you just highlighted. That precise sentence right there that describes what's going on with the equations [indicates the generalization written on the chart paper]. I feel like that should have taken place more—earlier and throughout the unit, just so that they know they can describe it precisely in some way and then that further explains the work that you'll be doing later on.

> **Toni:** Okay, and then one other thing for the generalization is we started to have them think about a strategy . . . but the question is, will this strategy always work?

David: Exactly.

Toni: And then, how do you know it? Once they've generalized it, we don't have to keep working with them on this. We could actually give them problems where they could try to apply different strategies.

Toni builds on David's noticing that having written this generalization on chart paper is a powerful tool for developing student reasoning. She then names a question, "will this strategy always work?" that David could use as a tool in his minilessons to promote deeper thinking and help students generalize the big ideas that are coming up for discussion.

Toni also uses the written document to look at David's modeling of children's thinking and gives him suggestions on ways he might improve his representations.

Toni: The other thing, I know it was really difficult writing here . . .

David: Yes.

Toni: . . . but I think our modeling needs work.

David: Yes. I agree, completely.

Toni draws David's attention to the visual because their writing on chart paper was not very effective. This is partly because they did not have enough space to highlight important ideas. It was also because they did not map out how they would use board space in their planning of the lesson. Although they do not go into depth here, Toni brings this up because she knows that one way to help children express their ideas is to have mathematical representations of their thinking that they can then speak from.

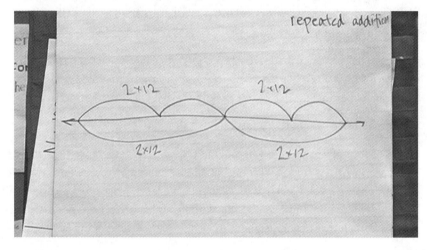

David: On the top. So the orange line was just that 2×12 is one group and then we're doubling it, so that, to show I guess the doubling relationship one more time.

Toni: So then this is your 4×12.

David: That red line. Right.

Toni: Right. I should color code it. 'Cause I guess the way I was thinking about it was . . . the strategy they used, which was the 2×12 . . . being a known fact, right? And this is our 24 . . . and then thinking about the relationship and modeling that . . .

David: Yup.

Toni: . . . on the bottom. And there's your double number line.

David: Okay.

Toni: And so what you're saying is that we're now going to have four jumps . . .

David: Right, right.

Toni: . . . and then where, how is that related to 2 jumps of 12?

David: Mhmm.

Toni: Right.

David: So putting the known on top and then doing the work on the bottom?

Toni: What, what I, the fact I'm using and then, here's . . . right? Is that right?

David: Yes, 'cause the known, what they're naming goes on top and then we're using that known on the bottom to extend, to show what they're describing.

Toni: So that you have two groups of 2×12.

David: Right.

Toni also emphasizes David's use of the model because she knows he is uncomfortable representing student thinking on the double number line and that using this mathematical model will continue to challenge him in the future. By exploring how he used the model in his minilesson, Toni highlights other possible ways to model (e.g., how she might have modeled the connection between 2×12 and 4×12). Even though she knows that modeling with the double number line is not easy, she also knows that the only way to become more comfortable with it is to actually use it consistently. By helping David think about the importance of the model, how it helps children develop mathematical connections, she offers evidence to support its use in his future minilesson work with students. To keep all this information in perspective, she continues to emphasize that this is a long-term goal for them to work on.

Toni: So that's another thing we could practice in the fall together, like really getting fluent with the models.

David: Mhmm. Yes.

Toni: 'Cause I think the mathematical models are tricky to use . . .

David: Mhmm.

Toni: . . . and yet, if you can use them really well, they really help students understand some of the mathematical relationships.

Postconference Tool #11: Reiterating Key Points as a Summary

Toni revisits all the ideas they have touched on: modeling, pacing, language development, and how to facilitate dialogue when children are not clear in their explanations. She invites David to think about what he would like to work on in the fall when they continue to collaborate. David names what he would like to work on and Toni renames several key ideas as well.

David: I mean, based on my past work with strings, I know I need to work more on using these models. So the ratio table, number lines, just having that easily connect to the, to the number work that we're doing.

Toni: And . . .

David: So the kids make the connections between the two.

Toni: And representing student strategies.

David: Yes.

Toni: That's the trickiest part. So maybe three things to work on if we think about next year, which seems a long way off, but it's really not—'cause you'll probably be starting with multiplication?

David: Yes.

Toni: All right, so working on, I think we need to develop the array as a model too.

David: Yes.

COACHING MOVES & TOOLS

9. *Loop back to connect planning and co-teaching.*

10. *Be willing to challenge teacher beliefs.*

11. *Keep a big-picture, long-term perspective.*

In the next transcript segment, Toni reiterates several ways to use talk moves to develop precision of language. In the process of doing this she names something that will affect the pacing of David's minilesson.

Toni: So that they have that in their toolbox. Doing mental math and developing really efficient strategies . . . and then thinking about precision of language and helping kids get, get more clear with their explanations.

David: Yup.

Toni: And actually even stopping them. And I know that that's an emotional thing . . .

David: Yeah.

Toni: . . . but saying, I'm going to come back to you.

David: Yeah.

Toni: . . . because I think you need more time to think about what it is you want to say.

David: To think about that, yeah.

Toni: Because we wasted a lot of time with kids just sort of . . .

David: Figuring it out.

Toni: Okay, let's come back to you. And if we can do that, that's one way of cutting some of the time too.

David: Yeah, that makes sense.

Toni knows that when David tries to change his expectations for discourse in his classroom this behavior change will be difficult for him *and* his students. For this reason, she lets David know that they will work on these goals (modeling, pacing, and discourse) in the future.

In Conclusion

In this postconference, Toni supported and challenged David's learning. She posed questions to see what he understood and gave him sufficient time to express his thinking about the lesson. While she was respectful of David's ideas, she also did not hesitate to challenge them. Toni did this by offering opinions and ideas that conflicted with his. In the postconference, Toni picked a high-level practice to focus on (how to facilitate rigorous classroom discourse) and wove in other issues of practice (pacing and modeling) and connected these to David's facilitation of talk. Toni ended the postconference by naming specific things they could work on in the future.

To facilitate a productive postconference, a coach has to be willing to speak truthfully. She has to be able to identify moments where she can challenge teacher thinking, but she also has to find moments to celebrate teacher accomplishments.

The teacher's journey is the coach's journey as well. Although the coach may see the road ahead from a different perspective, that perspective cannot be just given to the teacher. The art of coaching is about finding pathways that help a teacher navigate a course of action for himself. This is done by illuminating where he is on the journey and naming pitfalls in the road ahead and possible ways to avoid or overcome them. The next step is up to the teacher. This means the coach must be willing to let go and trust in the process. Faith in the teacher's ability to make the journey empowers him to take the needed steps and move in new directions.

Conclusion

Coaching is a vehicle that can be used to upgrade teaching into a full-fledged profession designed to meet the changing demands of the twenty-first century. We can no longer operate in the same ways we have for the past 100 years and hope to meet the more demanding goals of our time. We need to educate every student, no matter their circumstances, in ways that prepare them for an uncertain future in a complex global community. How can we possibly accomplish this seemingly impossible goal in a factory-model system that was designed to educate students along a bell curve?

Educators have a right and a responsibility to change education in ways that we are not yet fully prepared to do. We have an obligation as educators to continue to learn more about the dynamics of teaching and learning throughout our careers and to do so with the best interests of our students and our democracy in mind. Our founding fathers created the public school system to ensure that we would graduate citizens capable of contributing to society and capable of intelligently assessing and responding to the issues of the times. In order to do so, we must acknowledge the complex nature of the work of educators and support each other in developing the beliefs, attitudes, dispositions, knowledge base, and skill set that will enable us to meet the learning needs of every student in our care. This is no easy feat. Coaching is one process that can help us take steps in this direction.

Content coaching is a sophisticated process that attempts to understand the big picture of education and how the process of coaching can improve schooling at every level of the system. We realize that the big picture is impacted by the everyday practice of teachers in real classrooms across this country. We have seen how policymakers have relied on heavy-handed policies during this past decade (e.g., No Child Left Behind and Race to the Top). These policies equate standardized testing with evidence of effective teaching and learning. They have attempted to use standardized tests in ways that have resulted in an unprecedented level of fear and anxiety on the part of educators. While their stated intent has been to ensure that all students are receiving an effective education, they have resulted in teachers resorting to teaching to the test and an eroding sense of autonomy. Rather than ensuring that all students are learning to high standards, we are ensuring that all students are learning to become better test takers. Doing the wrong thing well has taken us further from doing the right thing better. Principals put pressure on teachers to raise test scores because they have been under the gun from their supervisors to do so, and they in turn have been under the gun from state and federal governments to do so. Unfortunately, this has exacerbated the historically adversarial relationship between teachers and administrators. We can no longer allow ourselves to comply with policies that inhibit teaching in favor of testing. How can coaching help?

Through infusing rich learning conversations into the professional discourse via coaching, study lessons, and regular meeting times for professionals to work collaboratively, we have an opportunity to examine what it takes on a day-to-day basis to reach every student in our classrooms. We can work together to prepare more rigorous lessons and keep refining our craft to ensure that all students have access to important relevant content. We know from our experience in the field that it is this kind of approach that actually increases test scores. Ironically, by not focusing on the tests and focusing instead on excellent teaching and evidence of learning, test scores go up.

Coaching conversations focused on evidence of student learning in real time in relation to actual students can and should happen at every level of the system and become a norm in all of our schools and districts. Administrators and teachers need to reach across historically adversarial positions to invent new policies and practices to meet the new goals of educating every student to high standards and in ways that bring out, rather than inhibit, teacher development. When we invest in teacher development, teachers can in turn better develop the capacity of students to grow into well-rounded, self-aware, caring, and self-managing human beings who have the life-skills and knowledge base to contribute to our society.

Thinking deeply about our lesson design, spending much more time planning lessons thoughtfully and collaboratively, designing engaging lessons through our choice of tasks and projects, and creating opportunities for students to discuss and write their way into learning, is done best collaboratively--not in isolation. Giving one another permission to experiment and engaging one another in conversations about the outcome of those experiments is the work. Tweaking what we do based on the results we get, the information we glean from informal assessments, and being open to the suggestions of colleagues and coaches is a good starting place.

In essence we are describing a cultural transformation in which schools operate as true learning organizations at every level. This book has offered many examples of ways to move toward this type of cultural transformation. We imagine everyone in a district coaching and being coached: from the superintendent, to the principal, to the teachers, to the students. Taking the stance that everyone has something to learn and something to contribute and practicing the habits of lifelong learners is a powerful way to capitalize on the capacity in a system. If education is to be the learning profession, then we must walk the walk of learners. We must share our failures and use them as learning opportunities. How might we allow them to inspire us to try something different, rather than respond to them with shame, blame, and punitive sanctions? The bottom line is not perfection, constant success, high test scores. The bottom line is creating a culture in which learning, innovation, and collaboration are the norms—a learning culture. When adults in schools create such environments, children will thrive. Student capacity to think critically, reflectively, creatively, and analytically will develop because the adults around them model these behaviors and emphasize their development during lessons. Test scores will naturally rise.

We hope that our book is seen as an invitation to educators and policymakers to realize how complex and daunting the work of classroom teachers is. We hope the ideas and practices we have described will ignite conversations among teachers, administrators, and policymakers as we shape education in this new century. We believe that it is time to rethink our present ways of working and time to design new systems for learning. Isn't it time that we stop expecting teachers to be able to perform, perform, perform, with little or no time to plan? What other profession expects people to perform all day, every day, with little time to reflect, refine, learn, and develop? We can't think of one—not athletes, actors, engineers, architects, lawyers, doctors, or scientists. Somehow, we must carve out substantial periods of time for educators at every level to learn from and with one another (and from outsiders). We believe developing a coaching culture is one possible way to do this.

If you remember nothing else, remember that we are all interdependent players in a dynamic, living system. Each of us influences the system through our actions and we are influenced by the system particularly through our interactions with others. We have an opportunity to utilize coaching as a process to leapfrog out of our present comfort zones and into uncharted territory where the ground is fertile for innovation. Should coaches, as agents of change, choose to look beyond *What is?* and ask instead, *What is possible here and who else cares?*, we are likely to find colleagues, supervisors, and policymakers who are ready to dive more deeply into exploring the dynamics of teaching and learning. If we remember that we are partners on a never-ending journey, that none of us knows all the answers, has all the information, or can see into the future, if we remain humble and open to possibility, we can productively challenge what is not working for our profession or our students, build on what is working, and reinvent schooling for the twenty-first century.

APPENDIX A: GUIDE TO CORE ISSUES

LESSON DESIGN

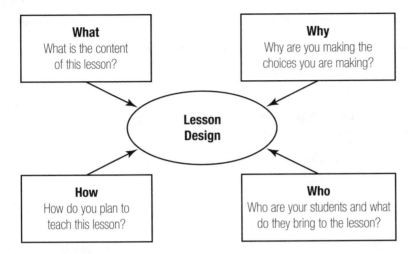

What

1. What is the specific content of this lesson and how do you know the activity matches the goal for student learning?

2. What are the big ideas and/or essential questions we want students to grapple with?

3. What specific strategies, skills, or applications are being developed?

4. What standards does the lesson address?

5. What tools, materials, documents will students need and how will they support student learning?

Why

1. Why is this specific content to be taught (e.g., learning theory)?

2. Why teach this content in this particular way?

3. Why are you choosing this lesson at this time (e.g., How does this lesson connect to prior and upcoming lessons?)?

4. Why are you using the particular lesson format you've chosen?

5. Why are you using the grouping structure you've chosen?

Revised version adapted from West, L., and F. C. Staub. 2003. *Content-Focused Coaching*SM: *Transforming Mathematics Lessons*. Portsmouth, NH: Heinemann. Originally created by the Learning Research and Development Center, University of Pittsburgh.

How

1. How will you introduce the lesson (e.g., What opening question do you have in mind? What will get written on the board?)?

2. How will you use a model, manipulative, or visual to support student learning?

3. What lesson format will you use (e.g., workshop model, small-group instruction)?

4. How will you group the students?

5. How will you differentiate your lesson to address the needs of the wide range of students in your class (e.g., How will you assist students who have difficulties and challenge those who need it?)?

6. How does this lesson engage students in thinking and activities that move them toward the stated goals?

7. How will you ensure that the ideas that are being grappled with will be highlighted and clarified?

8. How will you ensure that students are talking to each other about important content in an atmosphere of mutual respect?

9. How will students make their thinking and understanding public (e.g., What opportunities will students have to communicate, revise, and refine their thinking both orally and in writing?)?

10. What are the different ways you will assess student learning and use it to adjust your teaching (e.g., conferring, turn and talk, stop and jot, exit tickets)?

11. How much time do you predict will be needed for each part of the lesson?

Who

1. What relevant, related ideas have already been explored with this class and how does this lesson build upon them?

2. What can you identify or predict students may find difficult or confusing or have misconceptions about?

3. What relevant context (cultural background of students, for example) could you draw upon in relation to the essential understandings or big ideas to be explored in this lesson?

4. Given the content in this lesson, what do you expect students will say or do to demonstrate confusion or learning?

5. What ideas might students begin to express and what language might they use?

APPENDIX B: SAMPLE COACH SCHEDULES

The sample schedule below is based on an elementary example, but is easily adapted for middle school. It is based on real schedules used by full-time coaches in schools. In this example, Teachers A, B, and C are the lead teachers who are the focus of the coach's work. They meet with the coach on their prep time, during lunch, or during an additional prep period provided by the principal. Teachers D, E, and F are teachers who are not leads, who can be offered or can request a particular coaching cycle with a negotiated duration (e.g., one cycle, one month, one semester of weekly cycles, etc.). The coach also meets with each grade level once per week, usually to plan a lesson in great detail, sometimes with follow-up in the classes of all or specific teachers at the grade level.

MONTHLY

Period	Monday	Tuesday	Wednesday	Thursday	Friday
Before School	Prepare for Planning Sessions.	Debrief with Teacher B using yesterday's student work to inform lesson.	Prepare for grade-level meeting.	Analyze work from second-grade lesson to share at grade-level meeting.	Prep for grade-level meeting, leadership meeting, coach training session.
1	Preconference Lead Teacher A: fifth grade (with or without partner teacher(s) observing).	Debrief yesterday's fifth-grade lesson with Lead Teacher A on her prep and use the student work to inform today's lesson.	Grade-Level Meeting: fifth grade. (Teacher A's grade level) Share student work and learning from lesson tried in Lead Teacher's class—invite others on team to try the lesson in their classes. (Get schedule and arrange to co-teach with one or more of these teachers.)	Grade-Level Meeting: second grade. Share work from Teacher D's class—develop lens for analyzing student work and providing timely, relevant, actionable, feedback.	Preconference with Teacher F. Study student work samples together and outline sequence for summary discussion.

Period	Monday	Tuesday	Wednesday	Thursday	Friday
2	Preconference Lead Teacher B: fourth-grade inclusion class—both special ed. and general ed. or content specialist teacher present.	Co-teach with Lead Teacher C: third grade.	Grade-Level Meeting: fourth grade.	Observe two or three classes teaching collaboratively planned lesson with principal (and maybe lead teacher/s).	Grade-Level Meeting: kindergarten
3	Co-Teach lesson in Lead Teacher A's fifth grade class.	Grade-Level Meeting: first grade—Co-plan one lesson in detail.	Meet with Leadership Team.	Meet with principal to share perspectives on observed lessons and continue to work toward mutual agreement on evidence of student learning and effective instruction.	Co-teach with Teacher F.
4	Co-teach in Lead Teacher B's fourth-grade class.	Plan upcoming grade-level meeting and debrief.	Lunch	Lunch	Debrief during Teacher F's lunch period.

Period	Monday	Tuesday	Wednesday	Thursday	Friday
5	Lunch	Debrief over lunch with Lead Teacher C on her lunch break.	Co-teach with Teacher D: second grade.	Prep Period: Study school data, or talk with colleague who requested support, or gather materials for upcoming district-wide institutes, or analyze student work from collaboratively planned lessons, etc.	Lunch OR leave for Coach training at District Office (Bi-weekly, half-day training).
6	Preconference with Lead Teacher C: third grade.	Grade Level-Meeting: third grade (Teacher C's team) Share student work and what was learned.	Co-teach with teacher on fifth grade who is trying out lesson shared in grade-level meeting.	Preconference with Teacher E: kindergarten (not lead teacher).	Coach training cont. OR Meeting with Principal and/or Leadership Team (Twice monthly meetings occurring on weeks when there is no outside coach training).
7	Prep for After-school Book Study Group.	Preconference with Teacher D (not lead): second grade.	Debrief with Teacher D from second grade.	Co-teach with Teacher E.	Coach training OR Follow-up paperwork, planning, emails.

Period	Monday	Tuesday	Wednesday	Thursday	Friday
After School	Facilitate Book Study Group.	Analyze student work from co-taught lesson in preparation for next grade-level meeting.	Debrief with fifth grade teacher.	Debrief with Teacher E.	Yoga and Meditation.

WEEKLY

If a school has a thirty to thirty-five period week, coaches might allot their time in the following ways:

> Three to six periods for grade-level, department, or PLC meetings.

> Three to six periods for meetings with principal, coach colleagues, and/or the leadership team at the school level focused on assessing progress, addressing issues, and determining next steps; and attending coach training sessions provided by the district or outside consultants.

> Nine to fifteen periods—three per teacher (or teacher team)—per week to develop lab-site classrooms and cultivate teacher leaders (in year one). In later years these periods can be spent with a healthy mix of new teachers, potential lead teachers, and teachers in need of improvement. The duration of time spent with each teacher can be cyclical and include an entire school year, a semester, a term, or be based on the duration of a unit, etc.

> Five periods for lunch.

> Five periods for planning.

Number of Periods Per Week	Coach Works With:
1–3	Principal Meeting alternates with Coach Meeting at District Level
3–6	Grade Levels or Departments (K–5) (6–8) (9–12)
3	Lead Teacher (plan, co-teach, debrief)
3	Lead Teacher (plan, co-teach, debrief)
3	Lead Teacher (plan, co-teach, debrief)
3–6	Teacher or Teacher Teams on Rotational Basis (plan, co-teach, debrief) (Possibilities: one unit of study, one month on, one month off, six weeks twice a year)
5	Lunch periods
5	Planning periods
30–35	Total Periods
36*	*Thirty-six weeks out of a forty-week school year (Four weeks flexible time: beginning, end, and mid-year may require different schedule due to paperwork, set-up time, testing, training for coaches, etc.)

APPENDIX C: ACTIVITIES

ACTIVITIES FOR CHAPTER 4, *"Know Thyself"*

MIRROR, MIRROR

WHEN TO DO THIS ACTIVITY: Anytime.

TIME FRAME: 15–30 minutes.

PURPOSE: To develop a more accurate picture of our own tendencies in interactions with others. To observe how we tend to respond to individuals we find difficult to coach and contemplate ways to respond differently in situations that trigger defensive patterns.

COMMENTARY: Children with spatial difficulties often walk into other children or furniture. Their perceptions of themselves operating in space are sometimes directly contradicted by what happens as they interact with the world. We can use this analogy for what happens in relationships when things go awry; we can think of ourselves as walking into the wall of another person. Often our own lack of self-awareness, our ignorance of the interspace of human interactions, and our blindness to our habitual defense mechanisms cause social clumsiness.

Most people tend to think that their emotional reaction to a situation is the same as everyone else's. We often don't realize that individuals respond differently to the same circumstances or events. Our emotional responses are learned behaviors and generally are so habitual that we think we do not have any choice in how we feel about a person, situation, or event. However, as we entertain the belief that we can manage our own emotions, even choose what we want to feel, and come to know ourselves more deeply, we become much more successful in our interactions with others. We can learn to frame situations in more productive ways, interact more skillfully, and create learning cultures in which we thrive.

Questions for Exploration:

- How well do you manage your own emotions?

- How easily are your defenses triggered? Do you tend to take offense easily?

- When others say or do something that you dislike, what is your tendency (e.g., to shut down, to stew, to use sarcasm, to avoid, to judge, to tell others about how rude or awful the perpetrator was)?

ACTIVITY

Think of a teacher you find difficult to coach and a coaching situation with her that triggered your emotions. Think about what happened in that situation; what was said, the surrounding circumstances. Remember as many details as possible. Name the feelings you have in relation to the person involved.

Use prompts like the following to assist you:

1. I don't enjoy coaching _____ because she/he. . . .

2. When _____ said/did, I felt _____.

Consider the conclusions you may have come to or the judgments you may have made about that person:

Examples:

3. I think she is rude and I don't think she likes me.

4. I think she is uncaring and I doubt she'll ever be a good teacher!

Now what?

There is a maxim that states: *You spot it, you got it.* This means that when something in another person is a trigger for you, it is very likely that they are triggering something you don't like about yourself! This is often hard to believe, because we prefer to think of ourselves as good, wonderful, loving, caring people who are never rude. However, what if your conclusions or judgments are just part of your defense system that got triggered because you felt unsafe, hurt, or upset? What if you are expected to continue to work with this person? Maybe there's a way to clean the slate and begin anew.

Ask yourself:

1. If I were willing to take a risk and clear the air, what is in it for me?

2. What do I want for myself?

3. What do I want for the other person?

4. What do I want for our relationship?

Assuming you want to repair the relationship and move toward some mutual goal or purpose, consider making an appointment to meet with that person. Things you can say that would help clear the air are listed below. To give yourself a chance to rehearse before meeting with the person who pressed your buttons, try on these statements with a partner.

- I would like to meet with you to clear the air about something that is bothering me. I want us to be able to work well together and I don't want there to be any hard feelings between us. (Establish safety.)

- When you said/did (state the facts) I felt _____, and what I want from you is _____. (Clear the air by stating the facts, expressing your feelings, and asking for what you want.)

- Ask the other person if they have anything they want to clear with you. (Find out what the other person's experience/feelings are in relation to you.)

- Can we agree to _____. (Make a new agreement.)

SELF-MANAGEMENT OF LEARNING

WHEN TO DO THIS ACTIVITY: Anytime. Note: It is especially useful to do this activity right after the obstacles to learning activity because it provides specific strategies for overcoming some of our obstacles.

TIME FRAME: 15–20 minutes

PURPOSE: This activity is designed to provide us with specific strategies for managing our own learning with increasing spontaneity and sophistication.

COMMENTARY: Metacognition is the term used by psychologists and educators to express the idea that we can know what we know; it includes self-awareness, self-monitoring, self-management, and self-reflection. By observing how we think, operate, interact, and how the world responds to us, we come to navigate our way through life more successfully. Metacognitive strategies develop our capacity to learn and succeed, and they can be taught and practiced like any other strategy. We offer a list of strategies for improving our capacity to learn in this activity.

Questions for Exploration:

- What does it mean to manage your own learning?

- Why might the ability to self-manage one's behavior and learning be critical to successful coaching?

ACTIVITY: *Part 1 (10 minutes)*

Think of a time when you learned something. Jot down how you managed to learn what you set out to learn. What tools or strategies did you use (e.g., I asked questions. I sought advice from knowledgeable others. I practiced a lot.)? You can read the list entitled "Self–Management of Learning" to assist you in naming strategies. If you are working in a group, share your reflections. What are the commonalities and differences in your strategies?

Self-Management of Learning (Resnick and Hall 2000)

1. Pacing yourself.

2. Having an idea of what constitutes mastery and where one is in the process.

3. Reflecting on what is being learned—considering, evaluating, and improving on your own work.

4. Having a repertoire of ways to memorize.

5. Having a repertoire of ways to use resources.

6. Having a repertoire of smart things to do in reasoning, problem-solving, and decision-making.

7. Checking new insights against prior understanding.

8. Connecting new information to existing stores of background knowledge.

9. Holding yourself accountable to high standards of understanding.

10. Using strategies of paraphrasing, self-explanation.

11. Reaching for deep understanding.

12. Knowing how and when to ask questions.

13. Knowing when it is appropriate to struggle through.

14. Seeking extra help or more information when needed.

15. Knowing when and what kind of help is needed.

16. Figuring out what you are having trouble with.

17. Controlling the conditions of your learning.

18. Working productively without distraction.

19. Working independently in a variety of settings.

20. Participating actively.

21. Advocating for your own understanding.

22. Helping others to understand—giving thoughtful feedback without doing the work for them.

23. Giving thoughtful and responsible feedback.

24. Engaging in discussions respectfully, constructively, inclusively, using evidence and reasoning.

25. Receiving, evaluating, and adapting to feedback and guidance.

26. Carefully considering feedback from others.

27. Analyzing and synthesizing ideas.

ACTIVITY: *Part 2 (10 minutes)*

Now that you have identified the strategies you presently use, select a new strategy that you'd like to add to your repertoire. If you realized that one of the things that prevents you from learning is, for example, *I don't have time* then your new self-management strategy might be *pacing myself*. What is one small step you can take in the direction of pacing yourself that would allow you to have the time to learn? One example might be making a to-do list that prioritizes the most important things. Another might be putting a time limit on doing email each day.

FACT OR FICTION

WHEN TO DO THIS ACTIVITY: Anytime.

TIME FRAME: 1 hour.

PURPOSE: To learn to sort fact from fiction. To realize when we are telling ourselves stories and acting upon assumptions. To provide a way to inquire into assumptions in order to develop productive working relationships.

COMMENTARY: Learning to sort fact from fiction is a critical, learnable skill that requires self-awareness, a bit of humor, and self-discipline. It requires us to develop new interpersonal skills that make it safe for both parties to inquire into the *evidence* and question its meaning objectively. It means we must take nothing personally and refrain from acting on assumptions—challenging to say the least. This is especially difficult in coaching because making inferences, and having conjectures about people and their professional needs, is part of the work of a coach. Moreover, should the coach act on those inferences or conjectures without checking them out, she may damage a relationship before trust can be built and/or go charging down the wrong road, and, therefore, never end up at the destination of improved student learning. Part of good coaching practice is to gather lots of evidence, inquire into the meaning of the evidence, and work from mutually shared conjectures that invite the best from others.

ACTIVITY

In this activity the reader is asked to write about a teacher she works with, preferably a teacher she finds challenging or puzzling in some way. It is important that the coach understands that no one will read what is written, and the document will not be shared if the writer does not wish to share it. In addition, if the participants are concerned about teacher privacy, they can use a different name or initials or just say, "fourth-grade teacher." The purpose of this activity is to examine the coach's present perceptions about a teacher and then consider new possibilities. The activity is done in steps as listed below. It is important that readers do *not* read ahead to the next step until they have completed the previous step. No peeking ahead or you will spoil the possibility of useful insight.

1. Take out a blank sheet of paper and write the name of the teacher (pseudonym is allowed) at the top. Write down as many specific facts as you can think of. To help get started, consider answering the following questions:

   - Approximately how many years has this teacher been teaching?

   - What grade level(s) has she taught, and what grade is she presently teaching?

   - How many students are in her class?

   - Whose idea was it for you to work together?

   - How many coaching sessions have you had so far?

2. Now just free write. Write down everything you can think of in relation to the teacher, your interactions with her, and the things that trouble you. You can write about feelings, opinions, and anecdotes. Include things others have said, describe her teaching style and her relationships with students, etc. The idea is to paint a portrait of this teacher as presently perceived by the coach. Set a timer and allow at least 5 minutes for this exercise. When the time is up, you can decide to continue for an additional 2 minutes or stop. *Please do not read the rest of this activity until you have completed this step.*

3. Next, take a highlighter or a different color pen and underline just the *facts* in your writing. (This should take 1–2 minutes.) If you are working with a partner, read one of your facts without naming the person or giving any other details. Ask your partner to listen to the fact and decide whether it is a pure fact or whether there is an assumption coupled with the fact. Here is an example from an actual exchange:

   > A participant read her fact to her partner as follows: "The teacher refused to mark students late during the first week of summer school because she wanted students to like her."

   Is this a fact? Is there an assumption embedded in the fact?

   - "The teacher did not mark students late during the first week of summer school." (This is a fact. The coach had direct evidence of this and the teacher told her so.)

- "Because she wanted students to like her," is a story the coach made up. It is an assumption. The teacher never told the coach why she did not mark students late.

   The participant went on to give us another fact: "If the students were late twice during summer school the policy was that they could not get a passing grade."

- With this new fact, we can speculate on several reasons why the teacher did not mark her students late during the first week. We would not know if any of our speculations were accurate until we actually asked the teacher what her motive was for not marking students late.

4. Once you are clear about how to untangle fact from fiction or fact from assumption, then reread your document and notice the places that you have created a story about a fact that is based on an assumption that may or may not be accurate.

5. One way to work with your facts in a way that might help you reframe your work with the teacher in question is to take out a new sheet of paper and create a four-column journal like the one below. Use this tool to help you unpack your facts from fiction. Using the example shared in step 3 above, here's what the journal entries might be:

Facts	Speculations/ Conjectures	My Thoughts About This	Possible Actions (Whatever the case, the first step is to find out the other person's point of view.)
Teacher did not mark students late during first week of summer school.	Wants students to like her.	She needs to learn that she can't be friends with kids. That's a bit harsh—there is a need for a friendly atmosphere, but there is also a need to maintain authority. Someone's got to be in charge, don't they?	I could ask her directly why she chose not to mark students late in week one. We could engage in conversation about the teacher/student relation-ship. Consider the pros and cons of being liked and how that may impact the capacity to manage a class.

Facts	Speculations/ Conjectures	My Thoughts About This	Possible Actions (Whatever the case, the first step is to find out the other person's point of view.)
			Engage in conversation about her thoughts on motivating kids to succeed.
	Thinks the policy is too punitive and believes kids need a second chance.	Whether or not she likes the policy, she has to carry it out. Or does she? Now that I think about it, making it hard for failing kids to pass may not be the best policy. On the other hand, we can't all just do whatever we want.	Discuss with her the tension between following policy and following conscience and the risks involved with the latter. Maybe make new recommendations to the district about this policy if we come up with anything that could work better?
	Is really unorganized and didn't think it mattered if kids were late or maybe too hard to keep attendance.	I remember how difficult it can be to coordinate everything going on until there is some kind of routine in place. I'm wondering what routines might help her and if there is a reliable student who could take attendance?	Ask her about her organizational goals and management strategies to find out what her desired outcomes are. Discuss organizational systems that can help her get a handle on management. The attendance detail is a necessary nuisance.

6. After completing the chart, reflect either with a partner or on your own. Consider the value in noticing when we are acting on assumptions and the stories we tell ourselves, and the value of inquiring into whether our assumptions are accurate. Also consider the value of considering several different assumptions/scenarios prior to acting on any of them. This practice is not as easy as it sounds, but it is an extremely

helpful practice in shifting from blaming and judging to opening a space for new possibilities.

7. Make a commitment to inquire into at least one of the assumptions that you made. This can be done simply in a couple of steps:

    *   One way to do this is the next time you meet with the teacher just say something like, "There's something I want to ask you and I'm really interested in your response because I realized I made an assumption about something you did that may be erroneous. Is it okay for me to share with you an observation I made this summer?"

    In this way you create an atmosphere of safety. You put your motives on the table. You also ask permission, which gives the other person a sense of control and indicates your respect.

    *   Then share the fact: "I noticed that during the summer, you did not mark students late during the first week of summer school."

    *   Next ask for information, "I'm really curious about your reasoning for that choice." (This needs to be said with neutral language and with a light tone.) Depending on her response, ask the teacher if she would be willing to discuss this further or ask if she is open to considering a few questions from you about the choice. Reassure her that the questions are offered as an opening to conversation and not a judgment of her. (See the book, *Crucial Confrontations* for more information on techniques for having difficult conversations.)

8. Be specific about which assumption you intend to act on. Stating your intention to a partner gives the commitment a bit of weight and makes it more likely that you will follow through.

9. Finally, determine a time frame in which to take this step and check-in with your partner after you have executed your action step. This sets clear and high expectations that you will do what you say you are committed to doing.

NOTE: We have used this activity with coaches around the country and have found that many sincere, eager coaches are often surprised to find that the way they think about others is based on stories they are telling themselves and that these stories are affecting the way they treat others, which, in turn, may be causing others to resist their offers of support. Coaches are also surprised to learn that this is a common occurrence whenever human beings interact around things that connect to their identity and beliefs, and that with awareness and practice, checking out our assumptions can have a very positive impact on relationships with colleagues.

Recommended Readings:

Patterson, K., J. Grenny, A.Switzler, and R. McMillan. 2002. *Crucial Conversations*. New York: McGraw-Hill.

Stone, D., B. Patton, and S. Heen. 1999. *Difficult Conversations: How to Discuss What Matters Most*. New York, NY: Viking.

WHAT ARE YOUR HABITS OF MIND?

WHEN TO DO THIS ACTIVITY: Anytime.

PURPOSE: This activity is designed to reveal how specific habits of mind are critical for effective learning and coaching.

TIME FRAME: 30 minutes.

COMMENTARY: "Habits of Mind are dispositions displayed by intelligent people in response to problems, dilemmas, and enigmas, the resolution of which are not immediately apparent" (Costa and Kallick 2009). They are another way of developing metacognitive strategies. Every successful learner utilizes habits of mind that help them confront their learning obstacles; these behaviors are nameable and learnable. One example of a habit of mind that successful learners use is persistence; they keep on trying even when they are challenged or frustrated.

For coaches, it is important to develop habits of mind that help them interact successfully with other people. First, we need to become aware of the habits we currently practice (not what we think we do, but what we actually do!), and then reflect on whether or not these habits are getting us the results we desire. Recognizing and understanding your own habits of mind is the first step in improving or changing them.

Questions for Exploration:

1. What habits of mind do you already have as a learner?

2. What new habit might you like to develop?

3. How do these habits of mind support and influence you as a coach?

ACTIVITY

1. Read the *Habits of Mind* handout and identify the ones you think you already have a good handle on and notice the ones you may not yet have mastered.

2. If you are working in a group, share your reflections with your group. What are the commonalities and differences in your lists? How do your specific habits of mind support your coaching? Which new habits might enhance your coaching?

3. Select a new habit of mind that you think would best enhance your coaching and consider what that habit would specifically look, feel, and sound like in a coaching session. Consider one small step you might take to try on this new habit and build it over time. For example, having a questioning attitude might get you to slow down and inquire into the coachee's ideas before offering one of your ideas. Thinking flexibly might mean that you try out different lesson scenarios before selecting one. Imagine yourself trying on this new habit with one particular teacher, in one specific setting, in as much detail as possible. By using your imagination to visualize yourself practicing this new habit, you will preset your unconscious mind to actually try on the habit when the time comes.

Habits of Mind Handout (Costa and Kallick 2009)

1. **Persisting:** *Stick to it!* Persevering in a task through to completion, remaining focused.

2. **Managing Impulsivity:** *Take your time!* Thinking before acting; remaining calm, thoughtful, and deliberative.

3. **Listening with Understanding and Empathy:** *Understand others!* Devoting mental energy to another person's thoughts and ideas; holding in abeyance one's own thoughts in order to perceive another's point of view and emotions.

4. **Thinking Flexibly:** *Look at it another way!* Being able to change perspectives, generate alternatives, consider options.

5. **Thinking About Your Thinking (Metacognition):** *Know your knowing!* Being aware of one's own thoughts, strategies, feelings, and actions and their effects on others.

6. **Striving for Accuracy and Precision:** *Check it again!* A desire for exactness, fidelity, and craftsmanship.

7. **Questioning and Problem Posing:** How do you know? Having a questioning attitude, knowing what data are needed, and developing questioning strategies to produce those data. Finding problems to solve.

8. **Applying Past Knowledge to New and Novel Situations.** *Use what you learn!* Accessing prior knowledge; transferring knowledge beyond the situation in which it was learned.

9. **Thinking and Communicating with Clarity.** *Be clear!* Striving for accurate communication in both written and oral form; avoiding overgeneralizations, distortions, and deletions.

10. **Gathering Data Through All Senses:** *Use your natural pathways!* Gathering data through all the sensory pathways—gustatory, olfactory, tactile, kinesthetic, auditory, and visual.

11. **Creating, Imagining, and Innovating:** *Try a different way!* Generating new and novel ideas, fluency, originality.

12. **Responding with Wonderment and Awe:** *Have fun figuring it out!* Finding the world awesome, mysterious, and being intrigued with phenomena and beauty.

13. **Taking Responsible Risks:** *Venture out!* Being adventuresome; living on the edge of one's competence.

14. **Finding Humor:** *Laugh a lot!* Finding the whimsical in incongruous and unexpected places. Being able to laugh at one's self.

15. **Thinking Interdependently:** *Work together!* Being able to work with and learn from others in reciprocal situations.

16. **Remaining Open to Continuous Learning:** *Learn from experiences!* Having humility and pride when admitting we don't know; resisting complacency.

ACTIVITIES FOR CHAPTER 5, *"Communication Is Key"*

WHY NOT LISTEN AND LEARN?

WHEN TO DO THIS ACTIVITY: Early in the work to develop the awareness of how to listen or anywhere along the way to revisit important listening skills.

TIME FRAME: 30–45 minutes for entire activity. This activity has two parts and is best done with a partner or in small groups.

PURPOSE: To develop the capacity of coaches to inspire and engage others through hearing what others care about, are passionate about, and eager to invest in. Then tapping into that energy to get the job done.

COMMENTARY: "There are many benefits to this process of listening. The first is that good listeners are created as people feel listened to. Listening is a reciprocal process—we become more attentive to others if they have attended to us" (Wheatley and Crinean 2004).

One of the hardest things for most of us to do is to communicate with one another in ways that are compassionate, caring, and empowering—especially when our circumstances are demanding, isolating, and driven by external pressures that alienate and divide.

Learning to listen deeply to and without judging other people is a powerful practice that brings compassion and creativity into our world—the kind of creativity that generates real solutions to vexing issues that seem insurmountable.

Listening well sounds easy. It's not. It requires us to wake up to the fact that we tend to listen through filters, often do not hear the intended meaning of what was said, and sometimes take things personally that are not personal at all. As a result we are unable to relate in ways necessary for us to succeed. Learning to listen in active, compassionate ways increases the likelihood of getting what we are seeking and contributes to the well being of others. It also reconnects people—teachers, administrators, and coaches—who have been isolated from one another due to the historical hierarchy in most schools. In addition, it helps us to refocus our attention and efforts on what really matters to us so we can give and receive the assistance we need to transform our schools into true learning centers that enrich rather than demoralize.

In our experience, the better we listen to others, the more likely we can find the just-right method for creating an alliance in which we work together toward a mutual purpose. We continue to learn to listen in ways that bring out the genius in others, and we want our readers to be able to do likewise. Learning to listen well has not been an easy journey—and we continue to work at it. We have to be prepared to lift ourselves up and dust ourselves off when we fail to remember to tune in to the desires of others and instead impatiently try to get them to do what we think is right. Whenever we find ourselves more concerned with being right than with learning and growing, we should know something is off. We want you to be able to tap the passion and imagination of the people you work with so that all of us can create new possibilities and shed outdated modes of working that aren't feeding us or serving students. It all starts with learning to listen.

Questions for Exploration:

- What does listening have to do with the responses we get from other people?

- What is the role of listening in coaching?

- What might you be doing that prevents you from listening in ways that inform, empower, and inspire?

ACTIVITY: *Part 1 (10 minutes)*

Read the document "Listening Stumbling Blocks" and consider which of these you have fallen into. Circle at least three and share them with a partner. Share examples of when you have a tendency to get tripped up by these stumbling blocks.

ACTIVITY: *Part 2 (10 minutes)*

Consider ways you can help yourself be a better listener. For example, if you're inclined to interrupt others when they are speaking, perhaps writing notes to remind yourself of what you want to say will help you remember to wait until the speaker is finished. In our experience, it requires self-awareness to notice when you are getting distracted, judging, interrupting, etc. Using internal self-talk to remind yourself to refocus can be very helpful.

Think with your partner about ways you can use this tool in coaching sessions, professional development sessions, with students, etc. to launch conversations about listening well to one another and to partner with others in building a true learning community in which all participants listen respectfully, compassionately, and with an open mind to the ideas and concerns of others.

Listening Stumbling Blocks

Which of the following stumbling blocks have tripped up your capacity to listen well to others?

ME TOO: Having the tendency to identify with what the speaker is saying, sometimes injecting an anecdote, turning the spotlight on oneself, and maybe not hearing what is actually being said.

DISTRACTER: Having the tendency to change the subject or put down an idea before it is even fully expressed.

JUDGER: Having the tendency to listen with a critical ear and prejudge the merit of an idea, perhaps dismissing it prematurely.

PREPARER: The tendency to rehearse what you want to say in response before the speaker has completed their thought and losing sight of the speaker's full message.

NITPICKER: Having the tendency to look for something to disagree with, pushback at, challenge, or argue about, often coming from the need to be precise and/or right.

FORTUNE TELLER: Having the tendency to think you know what someone is going to say before they say it and responding from that assumption.

SIFTER: Having the tendency to hear just what you want to hear and disregarding the other parts of the message.

PEACEKEEPER: Having the tendency to pretend to agree with others just to placate them or avoid confrontation.

DRIFTER: Having the tendency to get distracted when others are speaking by checking cell phone, email, looking at a passerby, daydreaming, looking away from the speaker, and so forth.

CONCLUDER: Having the tendency to complete a person's point for them, rather than allowing them to finish their thought.

ARISTOCRAT: The tendency to assess another's speech, accent, costume while they are talking rather than listen to what they are saying.

OBLIVIOUS: The tendency to ignore signals like body language, emotions, stress levels, and just attend to the surface level of the message; missing the underlying meaning or nuance in the message.

THE DRAMA OF IT ALL: ROLE-PLAYS

WHEN TO DO THIS ACTIVITY: Anytime. Especially when people are experiencing frustration and/or resistance. You will need a partner for this activity.

PURPOSE: To develop the capacity of coaches to have direct, honest, frank, productive conversations with peers and supervisors that lead to positive actions toward mutual purpose.

COMMENTARY: While most people feel a bit awkward when it comes to role-playing, it is nonetheless one of the most powerful methods for developing communication and facilitation skills. When done well, role-plays will dramatically improve the level of competence and confidence coaches have in relation to their capacity to influence their environment and the people in it. Role-plays incorporate many of the characteristics of effective learning strategies: they are

- Relevant—when done well, role-plays address immediate, perceived needs or concerns. They are important because they are simulations of the actual work—rather than a discussion of the work.

- Active—role-plays require active participation in trying on new skills.

- Opportunities for feedback—immediate, specific feedback is one of the surest ways to improve a skill. Role-plays provide the opportunity to receive this type of feedback on the spot.

- Collaborative/social—they tap into the social network and build community, camaraderie, and a supportive atmosphere.

- Safe—they allow people to take risks in low-stake conditions and practice behaviors until they feel skillful enough to try them in high-stake conditions.

While content coaching is about ensuring that all lessons result in student learning important content, it is unlikely that teachers and coaches will be able to focus on content if interpersonal dynamics are troublesome. This is why role-plays can be so important—they are designed to assist you in naming and practicing specific communication techniques that will strengthen your ability to address real issues while simultaneously building professional communities.

Teachers are often very invested in their jobs. They tend to love their students and/or their subject and sincerely want to make a difference. These tendencies often mean that people become identified with their roles and any feeling of inadequacy or incompetence in the role is often experienced as a sense of failure as a person. Savvy coaches understand that when someone's identity is on the line, they may react in negative or emotional ways. For this reason, it is crucial to make sure that the ground is tilled so that people can separate their egos from the work at hand and learn to be objective as they experiment with ways to be more effective. Like any other practice (note that teaching is called a "practice") that is complex and nuanced, it takes lots of attempts at it before one gets it right. The complexity of teaching is often underestimated, which is reflected in the fact that the demands on teachers are constantly increasing without any recognition that the expectations for them are already demanding. This lack of respect for the craft of teaching often results in teachers feeling more and more anxious about meeting new expectations. When we feel anxious we usually resort to primitive responses—flight or fight for example—instead of intelligent inquiry and emotional maturity. Role-plays can help coaches become more sensitive to the various defense patterns people have (including their own).

Before you begin role-playing, it helps to have some specific moves or behaviors that you will try on in the role-play. Below is a list of such moves. This work is based almost entirely on the work of Kerry Patterson and his team who wrote two excellent books, *Crucial Conversations* (2002) and *Crucial Confrontations* (2004) which can be used to further support your work.

ACTIVITY

Choose a real situation from your own practice or one of the scenarios below to practice communication skills for having challenging conversations with colleagues or supervisors. If you choose a situation you are presently grappling with, play the person in the situation that you are having difficulty with and allow your partner to play you (e.g., the coach). This will give you new insight and perhaps new strategies for handling the situation in real life when the time comes.

Here are some possible scenarios:

SCENARIO 1: You arrive at your scheduled coaching session and the teacher shows you a lesson plan that consists of students filling out a worksheet. You are a bit taken aback and are trying to decide how to respond when the teacher defends the plan by stating, "The kids don't know their facts and they need to practice them. This worksheet gives them plenty of practice."

SCENARIO 2: The principal does a walk through and notices that the teacher you are coaching is not on the correct lesson according to the pacing calendar. The principal says: "I am in charge around here and I want everyone to follow the pacing calendar. I have to ensure that the kids get good test scores. I knew that teacher couldn't handle the science. She's behind everyone else on the grade. You need to fix this." You have been trying to get the teacher to slow down and pay more attention to student needs. You know you need to buffer the teacher from the principal's disapproval.

SCENARIO 3: You arrive for your scheduled coaching session with a veteran teacher. She meets you at the door and tells you she is angry that the principal insisted upon her having a coach. You had a feeling this was going to happen, and dreaded the meeting. She then says,

"Never mind. Come in and do your thing. I'll take care of my paper work." You are not about to use this precious coaching period for her to do her paperwork and you are determined to find a way to at least get your foot in the door for the purpose of coaching.

SCENARIO 4: Joe, one of the people the principal has asked you to coach, is 20 minutes late for a 40-minute coaching session once again. He comes running into the room explaining that he had to make a phone call to a parent. This is the third session out of the four you have had where he is late. He has told you that he wants to work with you, but you notice that he is not only late, but when he finally does show up he is not prepared for the conference. He has his textbook with him and has run off the worksheets provided. He tells you he just hasn't had time to think about the lesson more deeply. He does have to teach four different math classes after all.

SCENARIO 5: You have recently been assigned to be a coach by your principal. The principal and you have agreed that your job is to improve student achievement through improved instruction. You are eager to work with teachers individually and in groups and have laid out a pretty ambitious schedule to at least touch base with every teacher during grade-level/department meetings. You have thought about the teachers you think will work well as leaders and those who need some support and realize you can't fit them all in your schedule. Then your principal tells you that she wants you to work with small groups of students who are struggling and also to prepare and distribute all of the test prep materials.

Here are some communication skills to try on during your role-play. They are in no particular order:

1. **Establishing safety.** Saying or doing something to make the other person feel safe. (E.g., I'm really eager to work with you and to find out what you care about and how I might be able to partner with you.)

2. **Finding mutual purpose.** (E.g., I wonder what matters to you. I wonder what you find challenging in relation to. . . . What are you passionate about when it comes to teaching and learning?)

3. **Both/And.** Stating what you want and what you don't want. Be sure to establish that you respect the other person and have no hidden agenda. (E.g., I really want us to be able to work together well and I don't want to waste my time waiting for you.)

4. **Win/Win.** Speaking tentatively about possible ways for both parties to get what they want. (E.g., I'm wondering how we can make sure you have time to contact parents, or deal with students who are misbehaving, and meet on time when we schedule coaching sessions?)

5. **Paraphrasing.** Rephrasing what was said to let the other party know they were heard and to ensure you heard the intended message. Remember to use a neutral and calm tone. (E.g., What I hear you saying is that you are too busy to work with a coach and you resent the principal's insistence that you work with me. Is that correct?)

6. **Tune In.** Notice body language, verbal cues, or the unwillingness to talk. Take a guess at what is going on. (E.g., It seems like you are frustrated and maybe feeling a bit angry? I'd really like to understand what you are experiencing.)

7. **Tease out facts from story.** When there is a specific behavior or incident that is interfering with the work, sift out the facts from the stories you are telling yourself and invite the other person to do so as well. (E.g., We have met four times. Three of those four times you were significantly late for a relatively short meeting. I am beginning to tell myself stories about this behavior and would like to clear the air so we can work well together going forward. The stories I'm telling myself are that you don't want to work with me and that you don't think coaching is useful.)

8. **ASK.** Assume nothing. Ask the other person what is really going on. (E.g., Continuing the example from 7: Please tell me what is really going on. What are the facts as you see them and what stories might you be telling yourself about our work together?)

9. **Make new agreements.** When you clear the air and resolve any differences, test out possible solutions. (E.g., Continuing the example from 8: Okay, so I'm hearing this time slot really doesn't work for you. You are finding it difficult to juggle all your responsibilities during this one prep period you get. You also said that you do want to work with me and you see the benefits of coaching. How would you feel about meeting after or before the scheduled school day?)

Recommended Readings:

Patterson, K., J. Grenny, R. McMillan, and A. Switzler. 2002. *Crucial Conversations: Tools for Talking When Stakes Are High*. New York: McGraw-Hill.

Stone, D., B. Patton, and S. Heen. 1999. *Difficult Conversations: How to Discuss What Matters Most*. New York, NY: Viking.

ACTIVITY FOR CHAPTER 6, *"Assessing Teacher Development: The Starting Place for Coaching Teachers"*

PAINTING A TEACHER PORTRAIT

WHEN TO DO THIS ACTIVITY: Anytime.

TIME FRAME: 1 hour.

PURPOSE: To hone a coach's ability to *teacher watch*. This includes:

- developing an eye for analysis (What does this teacher know? What's my evidence? What are this teacher's beliefs about teaching and learning? What's my evidence? What ways will we work together and why am I making these choices for our work?);

- learning how to gather evidence; and

- devising specific ways to use the collected information to determine the starting place for working with a teacher.

COMMENTARY: There are a great many facets to teaching and learning. Various people in education and educational research have devised frameworks for categorizing teachers, their styles, and how they respond to change in useful ways. In our experience working with coaches, many have found it helpful to consider some of these frameworks in their work with individual teachers (Danielson 2007). But because descriptions taken from a rubric can be interpreted in different ways, we must come to a common understanding of what the descriptor actually means. A key part of this work then is to take time to reflect with our colleagues on our observations of the interactions within the classroom. These reflections can then be used to give us insights into ourselves as coaches and into the teachers with whom we work.

ACTIVITY #1: *Developing a Lens for Analyzing Teaching*

1. Think about what would be helpful to know about a teacher you work with in order to specifically pinpoint the focus of your work together. Brainstorm (alone or in small

groups) a list of questions, characteristics, or dimensions of teaching[1] and learning that would be valuable to gather information about (e.g., planning and preparation, classroom environment, instructional practices). *Where would you place this teacher on that continuum?*

2. The purpose of this exercise is strictly to help get a clearer picture so you can be more effective; it is not to evaluate and/or judge teachers. There are a variety of ways to gather important information (e.g., looking at the teacher's classroom, talking with her, using a survey, noticing her social contacts within the school, etc.). Think about which information would be most useful to you, and how you might use this information. If you are facilitating a large group, create a collective list gleaned from the lists generated in small-group discussions.

3. Compare and contrast your list with the list in Activity #2. Create a list that serves your context. Choose a few questions, qualities, etc., to focus on for the rest of the activity; you can come back to the other questions when you have time.

4. Select a teacher you work with on a regular basis (this could be the same person you reflected on in the "Fact or Fiction" activity on page 190).

ACTIVITY #2: *Reflecting on Teacher Attributes*

Reflect in writing on the following questions:

1. Focus on the selected teacher. What is her/his teaching assignment, number of years teaching, years in their district, years at this school, career stage, reason for selection?

2. How many sessions have you had with this teacher? How often do you meet?

3. What can you say about this teacher's relationship with her peers? What do you know about how she is perceived by her peers, e.g., Is she considered a leader by her peers?

4. What is the principal's view of this teacher? Does the principal see her as a leader? How does the principal plan to support her professional growth?

5. What was the teacher's initial response to your coaching? Describe your early work with the teacher and your impressions, observations, etc.

---

[1] "5 Dimensions of Teaching and Learning." Center for Educational Leadership, University of Washington. http://www.asdk12.org/CulturalResp/PDF/5Dimensions_TeachingLearning.pdf

6. What are your goals for this teacher and how were the goals established? What are the teacher's goals for her practice? Do you have explicitly stated mutual goals? How has this teacher grown in relation to these goals? How have your goals evolved over time? What do you hope to accomplish between now and the end of this school year with this teacher?

7. What do you see as this teacher's strengths? Use supporting evidence and give specific examples.

8. Are there challenges in working with this teacher? If so, what are they and what ways have you found to work with these challenges?

9. What would you like to be able to discuss with this teacher that you have not yet broached? What is preventing you from discussing the issue? What would assist you?

Compare and contrast:

1. Compare and contrast your beliefs about learning with what you know about this teacher's beliefs. Think of student learning as mirroring a teacher's beliefs about teaching. Consider the students in this teacher's class. What can you say about them? What problem/issue is the teacher most concerned about in relation to her students and their learning? How close does her concern match your concerns? Have you discussed this with the teacher? If not, why not? If so, what was her reaction?

2. Compare and contrast what you think this teacher is passionate about, values and cares about, with your own? Cite evidence to support your statements or opinions. How might you use this information to find common ground in your work together?

APPENDIX D: COLLABORATIVE GOAL SETTING

Teaching is a complex act. The standards movement has changed the goals of teaching to include the idea that every child can learn to high levels (international benchmarks) if given effective support from knowledgeable teachers. The NCLB policy has brought to the surface glaring discrepancies in achievement levels of different groups of students. Research by Linda Darling-Hammond (2000), and many others, makes a strong case that the skill level of the teacher is a primary and determining factor in student success, with some teachers able to improve student learning (value added) by two years in one given school year. Elmore and colleagues observe, "most educators are working, for better or worse, at, or very near, the limit of their existing knowledge and skills" (City 2009, 8). These and other findings and pressures have given rise to the notion that educators need to engage in professional learning throughout their careers.

Coaches have been assigned by many districts to assist in the professional learning process. Therefore, coaches need to be able to set clear, measurable (qualitative and quantitative) professional learning goals with teachers that result in improved student learning. Teachers then need the support of the coach, the building administration, and colleagues as they practice approximating new behaviors and instructional strategies in order to improve student learning.

FOCUS ON THE INSTRUCTIONAL CORE

There are three ways to improve student learning at scale:

1. Increase the level of knowledge and skill the teacher brings to the instructional process.
2. Increase the level and complexity of the content that students are asked to learn. This includes providing cognitively demanding tasks. The qualities of cognitively demanding tasks:
   a. Are standards-based.
   b. Are of high interest to the students.
   c. Actively engage (hands-on) whenever possible.
   d. Develop and challenge student thinking in some new way.
   e. Demand that students apply their knowledge in new situations.
3. Ensure that students are actively developing their habits of learning and capacity to communicate both orally and in writing (City 2009).

One could argue that focusing deeply on any one of the above facets, over time, and with colleagues, will impact the other two because they are intricately interwoven. For example, the teacher's choice of a task is intertwined with teacher beliefs about students, their capacity to learn, and her comfort level with disequilibrium and productive struggle.

Content coaches use teacher beliefs and choices to expand their pedagogical and content knowledge. They use preconferences to help teachers plan to incorrporate the following into their lessons:

Possible High-Leverage Learning Goals:

▸ Developing a toolbox for lesson design starting with the *Guide to Core Issues*.

▸ Designing and enacting lessons that are centered on *tasks* with high cognitive demand yet give access to all students (differentiation), as evidenced in student work and discourse.

▸ Enacting lessons in which the content is explicit, transparent, and centers around big ideas or essential questions that students can articulate and discuss both orally and in writing.

▸ Developing the capacity of students to talk, listen, and reason in the content area as evidenced by their organic exchange, critique, and questioning of each other's ideas and work.

▸ Developing the capacity of teachers to hear what students are attempting to articulate and working with their emerging understanding.

▸ Learning how to skillfully facilitate whole-group student discourse around an essential idea or network of ideas.

▸ Creating a collaborative learning environment in which students move beyond working mostly independently to working with others to collaboratively solve problems, create and complete projects, and give and receive relevant feedback aimed toward improvement.

▸ Moving from ability-based practices of grading to effort-based practices designed to develop self-management of learning and habits of mind for lifelong success.

▸ Developing the capacity to confer with students individually, in small groups, and in whole groups to informally assess student understanding and use it in real time to improve student learning.

‣ To strengthen adult content knowledge and develop a larger repertoire of pedagogical strategies in order to give more students (including English Language Learners and Special Education students) access to rigorous content.

‣ Improve the quality of student writing in the content areas and use that writing as opportunities for informal assessment.

‣ Increase and refine student use of academic language.

References

Ackoff, R. 1994. Presentation given as part of "W. Edwards Deming: His Learning and Legacy." Retrieved April 10, 2013, from www.youtube.com/watch?v=OqEeIG8aPPk.

Askew, M. 2008. "Mathematical Discipline Knowledge Requirements for Prospective Primary Teachers, and the Structure and Teaching Approaches of Programs Designed to Develop that Knowledge." In *The International Handbook of Mathematics Teacher Education, Volume 1: Knowledge and Beliefs in Mathematics Teaching and Teaching Development* 1, eds. P. Sullivan and T. Wood. Rotterdam: Sense Publishers.

Ball, D., and F. Forzani. 2009. "The Work of Teaching and the Challenge for Teacher Education." *Journal of Teacher Education* 60 (5): 497–511.

Berliner, D. C. 2004. "Describing the Behavior and Documenting the Accomplishments of Expert Teachers." *Bulletin of Science, Technology & Society* 24 (3): 200–212.

Campbell, P. F., and N. N. Malkus. 2011. "The Impact of Elementary Mathematics Coaches on Student Achievement." *The Elementary School Journal* 111 (3): 430–454.

Chapin, S. H., S. O'Connor, and N. C. Anderson. 2009. *Classroom Discussions: Using Math to Help Students Learn*. Sausalito, CA: Math Solutions.

Charles, R. 2005. "Big Ideas and Understandings as the Foundation for Elementary and Middle School Mathematics." *NCSM Journal of Mathematics Education Leadership* 8 (1).

City, E. A., R. F. Elmore, S. E. Fiarman, and L. Teitel. 2009. *Instructional Rounds in Education: A Network Approach to Improving Teaching and Learning*. Cambridge, MA: Harvard University Press.

Costa, A. L., and B. Kallick. 2009. *Habits of Mind Across the Curriculum: Practical and Creative Strategies for Teachers*. Alexandria, VA: Association for Supervision and Curriculum Development.

Danielson, C. 2007. Retrieved April 10, 2013, from www.danielsongroup.org.

———. 2007. *Enhancing Professional Practice: A Framework for Teaching*, 2d ed. Alexandria, VA: ASCD.

Darling-Hammond, L. 2000. "Teacher Quality and Student Achievement." *Education policy analysis archives*, 8. Retrieved February 16, 2013, from http://epaa.asu.edu/ojs/article/view/392.

Davis, B., and E. Simmt. 2003. "Understanding Learning Systems: Mathematics Education and Complexity Science." *Journal for Research in Mathematics Education* 34 (2): 137–167.

Dewey, J. 1933. *How We Think: A Restatement of the Relation of Reflective Thinking to the Educative Process*. Boston: D.C. Heath and Company.

Dweck, C. S., and E. S. Elliott. 1983. "Achievement Motivation." In *Handbook of Child Psychology, Vol 4: Social and Personality Development*, ed. E. M. Hetherington. New York: John Wiley.

Einstein, A. 1955. Statement to William Miller, *Life Magazine*, May 2, 1955, as cited at http://en.wikiquote.org/wiki/Albert_Einstein.

Fernandez, C., and M. Yoshida. 2004. *Lesson Study: A Japanese Approach to Improving Mathematics Teaching and Learning*. Mahwah, NJ: Lawrence Erlbaum Associates.

Fosnot, C.T., and M. Dolk. 2001. *Young Mathematicians at Work Constructing Multiplication and Division*. Portsmouth, NH: Heinemann.

Freire, P. 2000. *Pedagogy of the Oppressed*. New York: Continuum.

Fullan, M. 2011. *The Six Secrets of Change: What the Best Leaders Do to Help Their Organizations Survive and Thrive*. San Francisco, CA: Jossey-Bass.

Goleman, D. 2003. "What Makes a Leader." In *Organizational Influence Processes*, 2d ed., eds. L. W. Porter, H. L. Angle, and R. W. Allen. Armonk, NY: M. E. Sharpe.

———. 2005. *Emotional Intelligence: Why It Can Matter More Than IQ*. New York: Bantam Books.

Hattie, J., and H. Timperley. 2007. "The Power of Feedback." *Review of Educational Research* 77.1: 81–112.

Horton, M. 1998. *The Long Haul, An Autobiography*. New York: Teachers College Press.

Institute for Learning. 2000. "Principles of Learning." Retrieved May 13, 2013, from http://ifl.lrdc.pitt.edu/ifl/index.php/resources.

Jacobs, V. R., L. C. Lamb, R. A. Philipp, and B. P. Schappelle. 2010. "Deciding How to Respond on the Basis of Children's Understandings." In *Mathematics Teacher Noticing: Seeing Through Teachers' Eyes*, eds. M. G. Sherin, V. R. Jacobs, and R. A. Philipp. New York, NY: Routledge.

James, W. 1890. "The principles of psychology," New York: H. Holt.

Johnson, S., and M. Donaldson. 2007. "Overcoming the Obstacles to Leadership." *Educational Leadership* 65 (1): 8–13.

Kegan, R. 1982. *The Evolving Self: Problem and Process in Human Development*. Cambridge, MA: Harvard University Press.

Marzano, R. "Dr. Marzano's Teacher Evaluation Model." Retrieved April 10, 2013, from www.marzanoevaluation.com.

Neufeld, B., and D. Roper. 2003. "Coaching: A Strategy for Developing Instructional Capacity: Promises and Practicalities." *The Aspen Institute Program on Education: The Annenberg Institute for School Reform*. Cambridge, MA: Education Matters, Inc. Retrieved April 10, 2013, from www.edmatters.org/webreports/CoachingPaperfinal.pdf.

Noyce Foundation. 2007. "Silicon Valley Mathematics Initiative Pedagogical Content Coaching." Retrieved April 10, 2013, from www.noycefdn.org/documents/math/pedagogicalcontentcoaching.pdf.

Patterson, K., J. Grenny, R. McMillan, and A. Switzler. 2002. *Crucial Conversations: Tools for Talking When Stakes Are High*. New York: McGraw-Hill.

———. 2004. *Crucial Confrontations*. New York: McGraw-Hill.

Ravitch, D. "No Bad Idea Left Behind." *The American Interest*: May 2010.

Resnick, L., and M. Hall. 2000. "Principles of Learning For Effort-Based Education." Retrieved April 10, 2013, from www.instruction.aurorak12.org/ar/files/2011/06/Resnick-Principles-of-Learning-for-Effort.pdf.

Rogers, C. 1961. *On Becoming a Person: A Therapist's View of Psychotherapy*. Boston, MA: Houghton Mifflin Harcourt.

Rosenberg, M. B. 2003. *Nonviolent Communication: A Language of Life*. 2d ed. Encinitas, CA: PuddleDancer.

Salovey, P., and J. D. Mayer. 1990. "Emotional Intelligence" *Imagination, Cognition, and Personality* 9 (3): 185–211.

Schon, D. A. 1984. *The Reflective Practitioner: How Professionals Think in Action*. New York, NY: Basic Books. 8–9

Sherin, B., and J. R. Star. 2010. "Reflections on the Study of Teacher Noticing." In *Mathematics Teacher Noticing: Seeing Through Teachers' Eyes*, eds. M. G. Sherin, V. R. Jacobs, and R. A. Philipp. New York, NY: Routledge.

Shulman, L. 1986. "Those Who Understand: Knowledge Growth in Teaching." *Educational Researcher* 15 (2): 4–14.

Senge, P. 1990. *Fifth Discipline The Art and Practice of the Learning Organization*. London: Random House.

Steiner, L., and J. Kowal. 2007. "Principal as Instructional Leader: Designing a Coaching Program that Fits." Issue Brief. Washington, DC: The Center for Comprehensive School Reform and Improvement.

Stone, D., B. Patton, and S. Heen. 1999. *Difficult Conversations: How to Discuss What Matters Most*. New York, NY: Viking.

Taylor, R. T., D. E. Moxley, C. Chanter, and D. Boulware. 2007. "Three Techniques for Successful Literacy Coaching." *Principal Leadership* 7 (6): 22–25. Retrieved April 10, 2013, from www.nassp.org/portals/0/content/55194.pdf.

Tell, C. 2001. "Appreciating Good Teaching: A Conversation with Lee Shulman." *Educational Leadership* 58 (5): 6–11.

Tobert, B. and Associates. 2004. *Action Inquiry: The Secret of Timely and Transforming Leadership*. San Francisco, CA: Berrett-Koehler.

U.S. Department of Education. "No Child Left Behind." Retrieved April 30, 2013, from www2.ed.gov/nclb/landing.jhtml.

Vella, J. 2002. *Learning to Listen, Learning to Teach*. San Francisco, CA: Jossey-Bass.

Vygotsky, L. S., and M. Cole. 1978. *Mind in Society: The Development of Higher Psychological Processes*. Cambridge: Harvard University Press.

West, L., and F. C. Staub. 2003. *Content-Focused Coaching: Transforming Mathematics Lessons*. Portsmouth, NH: Heinemann.

Wheatley, M. 2002. "Listening as Healing." *Shambhala Sun*. January.

Wheatley, M. J., and G. Crinean. 2004. "Solving, Not Attacking, Complex Problems." Retrieved February 19, 2013, from http://www.margaretwheatley.com/articles/solvingnotattacking.html.

Wren, S., and D. Vallejo. 2009. "Effective Collaboration Between Instructional Coaches and Principals." *Balanced Reading*. Retrieved April 10, 2013, from www.balancedreading.com/Wren_&_Vallejo_Coach_Principal_Relatinships.pdf.